AT YOUR FINGERTIPS

AT YOUR FINGERTIPS

A HISTORY OF THE ROMAN CATHOLIC CHURCH
UNTIL THE COUNCIL OF TRENT

REV. LAURENCE J. SPITERI, JCD, PhD

ST PAULS

Library of Congress Cataloging-in-Publication Data

Spiteri, Laurence J.
  At your fingertips: A history of the Roman Catholic Church until the Council of Trent
/ Laurence J. Spiteri.
        p. cm.
  ISBN 13: 978-0-8189-1273-3
  ISBN 10: 0-8189-1273-1
  1. Papacy—History. 2. Church history.   I. Title
  BX965.S65   2008
  282.09—dc22

                                        2008031107

Nihil Obstat:
Karen Wilhelmy, C.S.J.
Censor Deputatus
February 6, 2008
Imprimatur:
His Eminence
✠ Cardinal Roger M. Mahony
Archbishop of Los Angeles
February 6, 2008

The Nihil Obstat and Imprimatur are official declarations that the work contains nothing
contrary to Faith and Morals. It is not implied thereby that those granting the Nihil Obstat
and Imprimatur agree with the contents, statements or opinions expressed.

Produced and designed in the United States of America by the
Fathers and Brothers of the Society of St. Paul,
2187 Victory Boulevard, Staten Island, New York 10314-6603
as part of their communications apostolate.

ISBN 10: 0-8189-1273-1
ISBN 13: 978-0-8189-1273-3

Printing Information:

Current Printing - first digit   1   2   3   4   5   6   7   8   9   10

Year of Current Printing - first year shown

2008   2009   2010   2011   2012   2013   2014   2015   2016   2017

*An understanding of the past gives us an insight
into the present and
helps us procure for the future.*

This book is being dedicated to
His Eminence Cardinal Raffaele Farina, SDB
- a first class Church historian -
as we celebrate his creation as Cardinal
by His Holiness, Pope Benedict XVI
on 24th November 2007
and his Golden Jubilee of Priesthood Ordination
(1958 - July 1st - 2008)

Table of Contents

Preface

The history of the Catholic Church is a most fascinating subject. It speaks about spiritual and temporal realities. This very short introduction covers the centuries from the inception of the Catholic Church to the eve of the Council of Trent. It aims at providing a quick overview of the first fifteen hundred years of the history of the Catholic Church and invites the reader to do further research.

The history of the Catholic Church is a narrative which speaks about saints and sinners, authentic doctrine and heresies, commitment and rejection, upheaval on the spiritual and the temporal levels, successes and failures of Popes and secular rulers, compromises and clashes, humility and personal ambitions, peace and war, reconciliation and rebellion. The history of the Catholic Church shows the spice of life, the ups and downs of a spiritual journey that is delicate, needs constant balance and evaluation and renewal, exhibits human frailty, and indicates that the finger of God guides His People amidst worldly travail.

You and I, along with over a billion other Roman Catholics today, form part of the contemporary pages of such an extraordinary history. May our lives write them with love, faith, humility, fidelity and gratitude. May our chapter in the history of the Catholic Church be guided by Peter, and vitalized and sustained by the Lord of history.

Monsignor Laurence J. Spiteri, JCD, PhD
21st January 2008

Introduction

To each his own story!

There are diverse ways to present the history of the Church and similarly the history of Christianity and/or Christendom and, more precisely, the history of the Catholic Church. The author of this book presents to its intended reader, "The History of the Roman Catholic Church." It can be stated that the book is directed toward a reader without bias, though fully aware of the fact that through the passage of time — even in areas confined and uniform in beliefs which are likewise bombarded by the media and ideologies — the "tampering with the evidence" has now become almost commonplace. Consequently, the author writes with the conviction to supply an instrument for knowledge, neutrality and useful evaluation which I believe are necessary. The book's orientation and objective are carried out professionally in such a way that, assisted by an unpretentious, fluid and practical style, render its reading attractive and persuasive.

The author states his objectives in the Preface and makes his own, so to speak, the motto of the famous French historian, Jean Chelini, who stated that, "the Church does not need an apology but truth" (*L'Eglise sous Pie XII,* Paris: Fayard, 1983, cited as an epigraph). I sincerely wish that this little volume, which is thick in its contents, be read by many, especially the young, so that they will come to know what has happened over fifteen centuries (down to the Council of Trent) in the history of the Church to which institution they belong. I wish that the readers will approach this history with the same objectivity with which this historian presents his writing, and with the same excitement and curiosity of one who reads one's own family history and surprisingly discovers one's own identity therein.

We are waiting for the author's second volume that will cover the time span from the Council of Trent down to our own. This phase of more recent history supplies the understanding of the way the Church thinks and acts in our time and how many may come to recognize themselves in her.

> *Cardinal Raffaele Farina*
> Cardinal Librarian of the Roman Church
> Archivist of the Vatican Secret Archives
> 1st March 2008
> Vatican City

From Humble Beginnings to Constantine

1. The Roots of Christianity

A fundamental premise of the Catholic Church is that she has been divinely instituted by the Lord Jesus Christ. She began in Jerusalem with a very small group of disciples, most of whom were terrified by His recent execution as a criminal. Upon the descent of the Holy Spirit on Pentecost,[1] however, the timid disciples were transformed into a group of very courageous, adventurous and well traveled bearers of the *Good News*. The Good News consisted in the fact that Jesus of Nazareth was the true Son of God and the Messiah who, through His sufferings and death, offered salvation to all the world. He had risen from the dead and, before returning to heaven, He entrusted His followers with a mission. The newly anointed disciples[2] began fulfilling the mandate the Lord: "*Go into the world and teach all nations, baptizing them in the Name of the Father, and of the Son, and of the Holy Spirit.*"[3]

There is an ancient and true saying: all roads lead to Rome. The city was founded in obscurity during the eighth century before the Christian era. It was destined to become the seat of a vast empire that spread from Spain in the west, to the center of the Middle East,

---

[1] Acts of the Apostles 2:1-4.

[2] The descent of the Holy Spirit upon the disciples signified their anointing.

[3] Matthew 28:19; Mark 16:15-16; and Luke 24:47.

and from England in the north, to the nations in North Africa[4] in the south, including the double kingdom of Egypt.

The Roman political and civil leaders had realized the importance of establishing fast, reliable and excellent means of communication by land and sea between the city of Rome and all of its vast lands.[5] Consequently, Rome built many excellent roads and established a very powerful navy. Information traveled fast. These means of transportation and communication became very effective vehicles to help the first Christian disciples spread the Good News rapidly throughout the countless cities and towns within the Roman Empire, and even beyond. St. Paul used land and sea[6] transportation to bring the Good News to many places. On the other hand, St. Peter and the rest of the other Apostles and their disciples seem to have done so by traveling mainly on foot.

Initially, the imperial authorities in Rome and elsewhere ignored what they perceived as an obscure, insignificant and localized Jewish sect of Christians. But soon, due to the conversion of some of the Roman nobility as well as for political reasons and the fact that Christianity believed only in One Lord who was King of kings, the Roman emperors and local imperial representatives began to feel threatened. They started taking note of the new religion. They concluded that the Christian message of universal salvation was diametrically opposed to the Greco-Roman culture, its social system, its morals and its beliefs. Such was the case with some emperors, like Nero (54-68) and Diocletian (284-305), who felt compelled to eradicate completely Christianity through vicious persecutions.

The first and second generations of Christians had concluded that the end of the world, that is the Second Coming of the Lord, would take place during their lifetime. Their expectation was based principally on a misunderstanding of the Lord's statement

---

[4]   This part of Africa was called Roman Africa.
[5]   Some of these roads can be still traced today such as, for example, the Via Appia Antica in Rome and the Via Ignatia from Rome to the eastern part of Greece.
[6]   St. Paul relates in 2 Corinthians 11:25 that he had suffered three shipwrecks.

to the beloved disciple[7] and of a clause in the writing of St. James.[8] Hence it was of paramount importance for Christians to spread the Good News as fast as possible. There was no time to waste for the Lord's return was at hand. The urgency of rapidly spreading the Good News, however, lacked a set program for Christianizing beyond sticking to the essentials of baptism, the celebration of the Eucharist, and instruction of how to lead a good moral lifestyle. In time, Christians began to realize that the Lord's return was not to take place in the very near future. Accordingly, the local Christian communities became subject to a sociological process that remains necessary, to this day, for any kind of group of people to survive and flourish. Thus, the local Christian believers began the rudimentary process of organization. Written documents which went beyond the fluid Gospels[9] and Apostolic Letters began to emerge. The era of the Apostolic Fathers was initiated.

---

2. The Apostolic Fathers of the Church

The title *Apostolic Father* is bestowed upon important Christian writers who lived during the time immediately following the Apostolic Age.[10] Their works have survived in whole or in part. The better known writings of this era are those of St. Clement of Rome (88-97), St. Ignatius of Antioch (martyred 107), and the unknown author of the ancient Christian text called the *Didache.*

---

[7] See John 18:32.

[8] See James 5:7-8.

[9] The Gospels, as in the case of most of the Old Testament, were originally proclaimed by word of mouth (oral tradition) which, as expected, was very fluid in proclamation though not in substance. Eventually, the Gospels began to be written down and some parts of them, especially the Gospel of St. John, underwent several revisions before they reached their final and definitive version that is recognized by the Catholic Church as inspired Scripture.

[10] Biblical scholars use the term Apostolic Age to refer to the historical period in the Church which concluded with the death of the last Apostle, who is traditionally held to be St. John.

(a) St. Clement, the third Bishop of Rome, wrote the *First Letter of Clement to the Corinthians* in the name of the Church of Rome to deal with internal struggles of the Corinthian Church resulting from the deposition of some of its bishop-presbyters.[11] St. Clement called for repentance, the reinstatement of the bishop-presbyters, and obedience to the legitimate superiors in the Church. He stated that the Apostles had appointed the bishop-presbyters in every place, and that such men were responsible to direct the ministry for they were the spiritual leaders of the local Churches. He also affirmed the celebration of the Eucharist as the proper function of the bishop-presbyters. The so-called *Second Letter of Clement to the Corinthians*, which has been proven not to be of his authorship, spoke of the character of Christian living and the obligation for repentance.

(b) St. Ignatius was the immediate successor to the Apostle St. Peter as Bishop of Antioch. While on his journey from Antioch to Rome, where he was destined to be martyred, he wrote letters of encouragement to the Churches of Ephesus, Magnesia and Tralles, and another letter to the Church of Rome in which he begged its members to not deprive him from his approaching martyrdom. While in Troas, he also wrote to the Churches of Philadelphia and Smyrna, and a letter to St. Polycarp of Smyrna (martyred in 155). These letters form a tapestry of a man passionately devoted to the Lord. In his writings, Ignatius warned of the Judaizing heresy with Docetic elements; insisted that Jesus Christ is truly God and truly man; affirmed that Christ continues to live in the Eucharist; and described bishop-presbyters as the authentic protectors of the true Faith and the ones who gave permission for Christian couples to marry. St. Ignatius stated that the Church of Rome was to be given special reverence because it was founded by the Princes of the Apostles, St. Peter and St. Paul.

(c) The *Didache* is a Christian Greek text written in the early second century. It was also called the *Teachings of the Twelve Apostles*.

---

[11] At the time there was no clear-cut distinction between bishops and presbyters.

The Fathers of the Church put great value on it. The document was divided into two sections. The first section dealt with Christian morality, while the second section dealt with the liturgy and Church discipline. The text included a hierarchy of apostles, bishops and deacons. It also contained teachings on baptism, reconciliation and the Eucharist.

(d) The other Apostolic writings are those of Hermas (second century), of St. Polycarp of Smyrna, of Papias of Hierapolis (c. 60-130), the authors of the Epistles attributed to Barnabas (end of first century), and addressed to Diognetus (late second century).

---

3. The Christian Classical Age of Martyrs

The classical persecution of Christians did not begin with the Romans, but erupted when some Jewish leaders in Jerusalem stoned to death the deacon Stephen around the year 35. The persecution soon took root due to the execution of St. James the Greater by King Herod Agrippa I (37-44) in his efforts to please some Jewish leaders around the year 42.[12]

The persecution of Christians under the Roman civil authorities lasted from around 64[13] to 312.[14] It was not an ongoing event, though Christians were often persecuted. Christians, from the earliest times, considered martyrdom, *the baptism of blood*, as an equivalent to baptism by water when one had not received it before martyrdom. A feast with a liturgical celebration at the martyr's tomb on the anniversary of his or her death[15] has been observed since the end of the second century. Later on, churches were erected

---

[12] Acts of the Apostles 7 (Stephen) and 12 (James the Greater).

[13] This was during the time of the Emperor Nero (54-68).

[14] This was the date of the Emperor Constantine's Edict of Milan legalizing Christian worship.

[15] The day on which a martyr was executed was considered his or her birthday into heaven.

over the tombs of well known martyrs.[16] On the other hand, the Catholic Church, from ancient times, consistently has ranked martyrs before all other saints, except Our Lady, who is addressed as the Queen of Martyrs. All of the Apostles traditionally have been considered martyrs, even though, for example, St. John does not seem to have met a martyr's death.

---

4. Institutional Development

(a) The institutional development in the Catholic Church already had germinal evidence by the end of the second century. It was defined in a system of governance by a hierarchy of bishop-presbyters and deacons, based mainly on Sacred Scripture. Christians were profoundly conscious of the fact that the Resurrection of Jesus Christ created the Church and that this was not the concoction of some human invention. They saw their fellowship as a gift of the Holy Spirit and the Church as having been erected by the Apostles on the foundation of Jesus Christ. The unique Christ-centered self-image of the early Church was revealed clearly in its two most important rituals. The first ritual practiced by the early Christians was that of Baptism by water. The ritual was regarded as an essential part of conversion to Christ and admission into the Christian community. The second ritual was the Eucharist that was celebrated in obedience to the Lord's command,[17] and in the firm conviction that Jesus was present in it as the Risen Lord. The celebration was accompanied by the *Agape*, a communal religious and sacred meal. The celebration of the *Agape* before the Eucharist was condemned by St. Paul,[18] though the one following the Eucharist was acceptable. The distinction between the two celebrations had

---

[16] For example, the church-basilicas of the Vatican (St. Peter's), St. Paul-Outside-the-Walls, and St. Laurence-Outside-the-Walls.

[17] See Matthew 26:26-28; Mark 14:22-24; and Luke 22:17-20.

[18] See 1 Corinthians 22:17-34.

been maintained since apostolic times. In due course, Christians had an early morning assembly for the Eucharist that was followed by a later celebration of the *Agape*.[19]

(b) As the Apostolic Age ended, the early Christians began to realize that the end of the world was definitely not within sight. Thus, the Church became faced with the problem of how to stay in touch with its origins and preserve its unity and continuity with the original apostolic witness. This involved both a sociological and an ecclesial process. A threefold solution was gradually devised: a specially commissioned ministry was established, an authoritative list of apostolic writings was issued, and a rule of faith or creed was drawn up.

The system of commissioned ministry was based on a system of governance by elders and deacons that had prevailed in some Churches from the beginning, as was the case with the Church in Jerusalem.[20] In this system the minister was ordained to his office by the laying on of hands.[21] On the other hand, the First Epistle of St. Peter[22] speaks of a system already in operation, with a definitely fixed circle of presbyters[23] engaged in an orderly ministry. Around the year 96, the apostolic origin of this presbyteral system was asserted in the *First Letter of Clement to the Corinthians*. The letter was written to the Church in Corinth in an effort to heal a schism that resulted when a group of presbyters was deposed. Clement urged their restoration to authority by arguing that the deposed presbyters were the successors to the Apostles.

The term *bishop* was originally a secular Greek term which meant *supervisor* or *overseer*. It gradually came into Church usage and was almost synonymous with the title *elder*. At first presbyters

---

[19] The *Agape* is mentioned by Augustine in the fourth century, though by his time it had become a charitable meal.

[20] The "Jerusalem Model," however, was superseded quickly by the Roman imperial model of administration.

[21] See 1 Timothy 4:14; and 2 Timothy 1:6-7.

[22] The Letter was written around the year 65.

[23] They were called the *episkopoi-presbyteroi*, bishop-presbyters. See 1 Peter 5:1; 1 Timothy 5:17-18, Titus1:5, 7-8; and James 5:14.

governed the local churches collectively.[24] Gradually, one presbyter took control and concentrated the various ministries in his hands. He was now called *bishop* so as to distinguish him from his presbyter collaborators. The system, set up according to the model of Roman imperial administration, was established everywhere by 150 and, henceforth, Church governance became operative on a hierarchical model. There was the need only for one bishop for each local church.[25] He was to preside over the Eucharist, to ordain, to correspond with the other local churches, to represent the local church at a general gathering (*council* or *synod*), to stand as the focus of unity, and to serve as the authoritative person in doctrinal matters.[26] The authority of the bishop rested on the fact that he stood in legitimate succession in a line reaching back to the Apostles themselves. St. Irenaeus, bishop of Lyons (130-202), writing in 185, stated in his *Against Heresies* that it was very clear that Rome was the pre-eminent example of apostolic succession for its bishops were the direct successors to St. Peter and St. Paul and, thus, faithful to the original deposit of faith.

The second measure, which the early Church took to guarantee the integrity of its tradition and safeguard its identity with the Church of the Apostles, was to recognize a specific number of writings as *Sacred Scripture*. Writings were recognized as part of Sacred Scripture if they met two criteria: the consensus of the Church that the writings listed[27] were associated with an Apostle in some way, and that such writings contained solely orthodox teachings.[28]

---

[24] The model for Church governance at this time was collegial.

[25] The bishop came to be considered as the head or leader of the college of presbyters.

[26] The bishop was perceived as the local authority who was empowered to counteract through his teaching the heresy of Gnosticism which the then Church had to confront.

[27] This was called the Canon of Scripture.

[28] Some writings that have been attributed to an Apostle, such as the *Gospel of Thomas* and the *Apocalypse of St. Paul*, were rejected because they did not meet the second criterion of orthodoxy. Such writings contained some false teachings.

Finally, the third measure to uphold the Church's authority and to protect orthodoxy was the formulation of a creed, the *rule of faith*, which was a compendium of the main teachings of bishops. This *rule of faith* was already included in the writings of St. Irenaeus in the late second century. The unity in faith among the Churches was preserved by frequent correspondence and visits among the different Church communities and through area synods.

Church leadership of the first three centuries had decided that the governance structure of the Church should develop according to the model of the Roman imperial administration. Thus, dioceses located in provincial capitals gradually assumed some authority over other cluster dioceses in a specific geographical area, and the bishop of that Church became the metropolitan. Over time the metropolitan bishops also became clustered and formed a somewhat loose union under a suprametropolitan or primatial Church. These Churches, in turn, clustered together to form patriarchates. The civil Roman administrative model allowed for different levels of autonomy based on collegiality among the bishops.

At first, there were three patriarchates: Rome, because of the local Church's foundation by St. Peter and St. Paul; Alexandria in Egypt, because it was founded by St. Mark the Evangelist; and Antioch, because it was the first See of the Apostle St. Peter before he journeyed to Rome to establish the Church there with St. Paul. In time, Jerusalem, being the birthplace of the Church, and Constantinople, being the new imperial capital, also became recognized as patriarchates. But Rome, the See of St. Peter, enjoyed certain unique attributes that elevated it beyond all other Churches, including patriarchates, and became destined as the center of Church unity.

5. Apologists

The title *Apologist* was given to Christian writers between 120 and 220 for meeting specific qualifications. They addressed themselves to the task of making a reasoned defense and recommendation of the Christian Faith to non Christians, especially to the Roman imperial authorities. Their object was to gain a fair hearing for Christianity and to dispel popular slanders and antagonistic rumors against the Church by providing some account of Christian beliefs and practices. Apologists taught that Christianity was politically harmless and morally and culturally superior to paganism. Among these writers were St. Justin Martyr (c. 100-c. 185), Tatian (middle of second century) and Tertullian (c. 160-225). It was during this period that some of the educated classes in the Roman Empire became Christians.

St. Justin Martyr is the most outstanding of the Apologists. He converted from paganism to Christianity around 130. In his *First Apologia*, addressed to Emperor Antoninus (138-161) and his two adopted sons, St. Justin became the first Christian thinker who attempted to reconcile faith and reason. He advocated that although traces of the Truth could be found in pagan philosophies, Christianity alone was the rational creed. St. Justin wrote that the Word of God, or *Logos* (Λογος) had become incarnate in order to teach the truth and to bring salvation to all humanity. He also defended Christians against charges of immorality. The later chapters in his writing spoke about the Church's baptism ceremonies and the Eucharistic belief and celebration. St. Justin's *Second Apologia* dealt mainly with refuting charges made against Christians.

6. Heresies and Division Show Their Heads

(a) *Docetism* was a teaching during the early Church, dating back to the apostolic times. Docetism was not a clear-cut or well formulated heresy, but a tendency to consider the humanity and sufferings of Jesus Christ as apparent rather than real. The heresy, for all purposes, denied the Incarnation and Redemption.

(b) The first major heresy that the Church had to confront was *Gnosticism,* in the second century. Gnosticism was not a uniform religion. It had many brands, depending on which teacher was followed. In essence, it taught that there was a fundamental opposition between the world of matter and the world of spirit. While matter was completely evil, spirit alone was good. It was impossible for God to come into contact with matter because God was pure spirit. Consequently, Gnosticism denied the Incarnation and Redemption. A lower god, the Demiurge, created the world. The true Gnostic considered himself as a chosen person who was given a very special and superior knowledge, due to his possession of a Divine spark that rescued him from the evil material world. The principal opponents of Gnosticism were St. Irenaeus, Tertullian and St. Hippolytus (c. 170-236).

(c) *Manichaeism* was a heresy formulated by the Persian Manes (c. 216-276). His heresy was a higher developed brand of Gnosticism. For a period of nine years St. Augustine, before his conversion to Christianity, followed this heresy. Manichaeans rejected the Old Testament and had a dualistic interpretation of the problem of evil that was caused by a supreme principle. They believed in a hierarchy of grades in a person's spiritual life that aimed at unveiling the certainty of universal truths by undergoing bodily purification and asceticism that released the soul of all evil matter. The sect rapidly grew in Egypt, Rome and Roman Africa. The chief opponents of Manichaeism were the deacon St. Ephraem of Syria (c. 306-373) and St. Augustine. Manichaeism reappeared later in the form of the Cathari and Albigensian heresies in the 12th and 13th centuries. Both were condemned by a number of Church Councils, particularly at the Lateran Council IV in 1215.

(d) The Church in Roman Africa has somewhat obscure origins. The earliest evidence of its existence appeared in 180. By the year 200, Tertullian spoke of a Church that was widespread and well organized. While the Roman Christians still spoke Greek, the Church in Roman Africa already used a Latin Bible and liturgy. By the time of St. Cyprian (210-258), Bishop of Carthage (248-258), there were already one hundred bishops under the primacy of Carthage. These numbers indicate a quick and phenomenal growth. The persecution of the Roman Emperor Decius (249-251), in 250, weakened the Roman African Church and led to the controversy of the re-admission into the Church of the *lapsi* through re-baptism. Rome withstood this heresy and affirmed that baptism was to be administered only once. But, the heresy became the background for the Donatist schism that appeared in the following century.

(e) The schism of *Donatism* followed the persecution of Emperor Diocletian. It began in 311 at Carthage when some Christians refused to accept Caecilian as their new bishop on the grounds that he had been ordained by Archbishop Felix of Aptunga, whom they accused of betraying the Church during the Diocletian persecution.[29] Donatus, the rival bishop of Carthage, was the leader of the schism. It claimed that there was a pure Church, a Church of the elect, of the holy and martyrs, unspoiled by and fiercely opposed to the world, and an ark of refuge from evil society. The Donatists re-baptized Christians who had lapsed into paganism due to the persecution. They also upheld the heretical teaching that the validity of a sacrament depended on the holiness of its minister. St. Augustine led other Catholic theologians of his time in opposing this schism. The Catholic group acknowledged that the Church was comprised of saints and sinners for it was intended to embrace all of humanity, that it could not be sharply demarcated from the world, that the ultimate separation would take place at the Final

---

[29] Upon a thorough investigation it was discovered that the archbishop was falsely accused.

Judgment, and that baptism could be received only once and re-entrance into the Church was carried out through reconciliation and penance. They also affirmed that the Church's purpose was to be a sociological sign of God's presence in the world and that its sacraments were holy, even though sometimes the ministers were not. Emperor Honorius (395-423), a devout Catholic, sided with the Catholic Church and published the *Edict of Unity* in June 405 that officially suppressed the Donatist Church.

7. The Sprouting of Monasticism

(a) As Roman society became more and more decadent and corrupt in both East and West, Christians in the Eastern Empire began to flee the cities and to seek Christ "outside" society. These Christian refugees found solace in solitary living in the Egyptian desert. Such was the case with St. Anthony of Egypt (250-356), who is considered the Father of Monasticism. St. Anthony became a hermit in the Egyptian desert around 285. Soon Christians were flocking to the Egyptian desert and imitating his lifestyle. St. Anthony came out of his solitude around 305 to organize these people into a community of hermits. He gave them a rule of life. Each hermit was to follow the rule of life as best suited to his particular situation. There was very little common life. The hermits came together on Sundays for Mass, to receive Holy Communion, and to listen to some spiritual instruction. The number of these hermits grew considerably by the end of St. Anthony's life, by which time he exercised considerable influence over them.

(b) St. Pachomius (c. 290-346) took monasticism a step further around 320 by organizing his followers into colonies with a common way of living. They were expected to follow the same rule and schedule. They also lived under strict obedience to a superior. This rule of life eventually would influence the monastic genius of St. Basil the Great in the East and St. Benedict in the West.

8. Church Gains Freedom

The dying Eastern Roman Emperor Galerius (305-311) issued an edict of toleration of Christians in 311. His counterpart, Emperor Maximinus Daia (305-313), was forced to issue a similar edict in 312.[30] But, it was the Emperor Constantine the Great (306-337) who emancipated the Church in the same year and attached the Christian emblem — the monogram of Christ — to the banners of his troops. From that point onwards, the history of the Catholic Church became intimately joined with the fortunes of the state, as Roman emperor after Roman emperor in both West and East[31] showered the Church with honors and privileges... and interference.

The Church gained its freedom through Emperor Constantine the Great, whose mother, St. Helen, was a very fervent Catholic. He defeated his rival Maxentius (306-312) in 312 and attributed his victory to the Christian God. This victory made Constantine the Great the uncontested Western Emperor in Rome. Although he was not baptized until he was on his deathbed, he was very protective of the Church throughout his reign. He met with the Eastern Roman Emperor Licinius in 313 and the two reached an agreement on a policy of complete religious tolerance within the entire empire and that confiscated Christian property was to be returned to the rightful owners. He moved the imperial capital to Byzantium[32] on the Bosphorus Sea in 324, when he became the sole Emperor for both West and East.

Constantine the Great increasingly identified the interests of the empire with those of the Church, but never hesitated to interfere

---

[30] At the time, the Roman Empire had a number of men who declared themselves or were acclaimed by their armies as emperors.

[31] The exceptions were emperors Licinius (311-324) and Julian the Apostate (361-363).

[32] He named it after himself, calling the city Constantinople and the New Rome. Nowadays the city is called Istanbul.

in Church affairs so as to secure unity in both the empire and the Church. It was for this purpose that he called, at his own expense, the Council of Nicaea in 325. It was the first universal Council in the Church[33] and the one that gave it the Nicene Creed. Constantine the Great charged the Council with settling the question of *Arianism*. Down the centuries, other emperors, both in the West and in the East, would call Councils. Nevertheless, throughout the history of the Church, the majority of General Councils assembled at the beckoning of a Pope. The Council of Nicaea was the first of a number of Councils that were called to counteract heresy and define Church teachings.

Constantine the Great showed great generosity to the Church by lavishing donations on it and by erecting magnificent basilicas. He erected the first Vatican Basilica[34] over the tomb of St. Peter in Rome, a basilica over the Tomb of Jesus in Jerusalem, and gave the Lateran Palace as the place of residence for the Popes.[35] Furthermore, he invested the judicial decisions of bishops with civil authority. Constantine the Great also modified Roman law in the direction of Christian values, and made Sunday a day of rest. This alliance between the Church and the State profoundly influenced every aspect of the Church's thought and life and laid the foundation of the relationship between Church and State in the Middle Ages with the Pope emerging also as a powerful monarch. The Church-State relationship, known as Caesaro-Papism, would carry many advantages and many disadvantages for the Church.

---

[33] There was a prior and major Council in the Church. The Council of Jerusalem, mentioned in Acts of the Apostles 15, took place around the year 50.

[34] The present Basilica of St. Peter's is the second basilica. It was built between the years 1506 to 1626.

[35] The Lateran Palace remained the papal residence until 1309 when the Popes took up permanent residence in Avignon (until 1378).

Ecumenical Councils Battle Heresies

9. The Classical Doctors of the Church

The Catholic Church in both West and East has been blessed with outstanding men known for their extraordinary theological insights and personal holiness. Some of them were acknowledged as outstanding and singular theologians in the Catholic Faith. They distinguished themselves in their very unique defense, exposition and preservation of the orthodox teachings of the Church. Their major contributions cannot be fully appreciated until one examines the historical setting they lived in and the doctrinal issues they had to confront.

The list of the classical Doctors of the Church is limited to four for the Latin Church and four for the Greek Church. The Western Doctors of the Church were St. Ambrose (340-397), bishop of Milan (374-397); St. Augustine (354-430), bishop of Hippo (395-430); the priest St. Jerome (347-420); and Pope St. Gregory the Great (c. 350-604, Pope 590-604). All four were declared "Doctors of the Church" by Pope Boniface VIII on 20th September 1295.

(a) St. Ambrose, a very effective Roman lawyer, was the civil Roman governor of Aemilia-Liguria, with its seat in Milan, when the Catholic laity of Milan demanded that, although yet a catechumen, he be appointed their bishop in 374. He reluctantly accepted and was baptized before he was ordained bishop. St. Ambrose was a strong defender of the Church against Arianism and paganism. He maintained that the Church was above civil authority. His many writings include treatises on Christian ethics, with a special reference to the clergy; the theology of the sacraments; and many homilies and instructions on Faith and Sacraments for catechumens. He also wrote on ascetical subjects and promoted monasticism in Italy.

St. Augustine led a spiritually and intellectually restless life until he was converted and baptized as a Catholic in Milan by St. Ambrose in 387. His theological and philosophical contributions are vast. His understanding and explanation of Christian truths are uniquely outstanding. He confronted two heresies and a schism when he was still a layman and, then, as bishop.[1] His teaching on grace would shape the theology of grace for the Catholic mind down the centuries. He contributed greatly to the Church's teachings on salvation, original sin, sacramentology, the Trinity, and the interpretation of Sacred Scripture. He actively promoted asceticism and monasticism in Roman Africa.

St. Jerome was another convert to the Catholic Faith. He is the only classical Doctor of the Church who remained a priest. His genius rested in his translation of Sacred Scripture from its original languages into Latin. His translation became known as the *Vulgate*, and remained the only recognized translation in the Catholic Church for many centuries. His scholarship was unsurpassed in the early Church. St. Jerome also wrote commentaries on Sacred Scripture, many theological and historical treatises, and treatises against Pelagianism and Arianism. Additionally, his writings had a great influence on the development of Catholic theology on Mary and spirituality. He promoted asceticism and monasticism in both East and West.

---

[1] These were the heresies of Manichaeism and Pelagianism, and the Donatist schism. It should be noted that St. Irenaeus, in his *Against Heresies* (IV, xxiii, 7) was the first to use the technical term *schism*. Schism is distinguished from *heresy*. While schism entails a separation from the Catholic Church based on a disunity in charity, heresy involves the formal denial or doubt of any defined doctrine of the Catholic Faith.

St. Gregory the Great was only a deacon when he was elected Pope on 3rd September 590. He is the only classical Doctor of the Church who was a Pope. He was a very versatile writer. He wrote about the practical life of bishops, hagiographies, biblical exegesis, the doctrine on Purgatory, veneration of authentic relics, and homilies on the Gospels. He composed the Gregorian Sacramentary. He also sent countless letters to diverse Catholic churches with instructive, moral, and theological statements.

(b) The classical Eastern Doctors of the Church are: St. Athanasius (293-373), bishop of Alexandria (328-373); St. Basil the Great (330-379), bishop of Caesarea (370-379); St. Gregory of Nazianzus (330-390), ordained bishop of Sasima in 372 and patriarch of Constantinople for a very short time (381); and St. John Chrysostom (c. 347-407), patriarch of Constantinople (398-407). All four were declared "Doctors of the Church" by Pope St. Pius V in 1568.

St. Athanasius, who suffered three exiles for his fidelity to the Catholic Faith, wrote theological treatises on the Incarnation, the Divine nature of Jesus Christ, soteriology, the divinity of the Holy Spirit, and just war. He was a consistent and prolific theologian against Arianism and Apollinarism. In addition, he was the chief defender of the Catholic Faith at the Council of Nicaea. It is to him that the Catholic Church owes the expression of the true nature of Jesus Christ in the phrase *consubstantial with the Father.*

St. Basil the Great was a very strong opponent to Arianism, against which his many writings defended the teachings of the Council of Nicaea. He also wrote treatises on the Holy Spirit and against Apollinarism. His monastic rule continues to maintain its great influence to this very day on monastic life in both Eastern Catholic and Orthodox Churches.

St. Gregory of Nazianzus remains, perhaps, the most eloquent preacher of theology in the history of the Church. His more famous writings include treatises on the Holy Spirit, his refutations of Apollinarism, and a very impressive collection of theological poems. A very sizable amount of his homilies are still in existence and prove the genius of his deep theology expressed in understand-able terminology.

St. John Chrysostom was very well known for his oratory at preaching at the time of his election as Patriarch of Constantinople in 397. His teachings and famous homilies explained clearly the tenets of the Catholic Faith. His writings on the responsibilities of the priest have perennial value. To this day, no one has been able to match the depth and his mastery of the interpretation of Sacred Scripture, particularly on the writings of St. Paul. He was also a great moral reformer of clergy and laity alike. His fidelity to the Catholic Faith cost him much personal suffering and two exiles, while Patriarch of Constantinople.

---

10. Major Early Heresies and Schisms

Heresies and schisms bring division within a believing community. They also carry a very serious threat to the social order. Thus, both civil and ecclesiastical authorities in the Roman Empire reacted and took measures to deal with these events.

(a) The heresy of *Arianism* was introduced by Arius of Alex-andria (c. 250-336), a priest who was excommunicated a number of times during his lifetime. This heresy occasioned the direct interference in matters of faith by civil authorities. The heresy de-nied the divinity of Jesus Christ. Arius taught that Jesus Christ was the Son of God, but he was not eternal because he was a creation of God the Father. He taught that although Jesus Christ was not God by nature, he was a very unique human being. Ultimately, this doctrine, as in the case of the Docetist heresy, denied, in essence, the Incarnation and Redemption.

The heretical teaching was condemned first by Arius' local bishop, St. Alexander of Alexandria (313-328), at the Synod of Alexandria in 320. Arius refused to renounce his heresy and was thereby excommunicated. Since Arius was a very gifted preacher, his heresy continued to spread and agitate people, clergy and laity alike, to the point that there was great unrest in the recently re-unified Roman Empire. Constantine the Great, seeking peace and unity in both empire and Church, called the Council of Nicaea in 325 to settle the matter.

Arius had many bishops on his side, but St. Athanasius rose to defend the Catholic Church's authentic teaching: Christ is truly God and truly man, co-eternal and co-equal with God the Father. The Nicene Creed was formulated at this Council. Arius and the heretical bishops were excommunicated again by the said Council and banished by the civil authorities. It should be noted for the very first time the highest civil authority, Emperor Constantine the Great, did not only convene a Council but also inflicted a civil punishment on religious heretics. Ironically, Constantine the Great was baptized on his deathbed by an Arian bishop, because Arianism continued to flourish in the empire.

One of Constantine the Great's sons and successors, Emperor Constantius (337-361), sided with the Arians. He attempted to impose Arianism as the empire's religion (355-60) and began a short-lived persecution of Catholics in 350. He forced into exile Pope Liberius (352-366), St. Athanasius, bishop of Alexandria, and St. Hilary (c. 304-367), bishop of Poitiers. Imperial interference in matters of faith became commonplace. Some churchmen attempted to resist such interference. For example, St. Ambrose, as the bishop of Milan,[2] had to deal with Emperors Gratian (375-383), Valentinian II (383-392), and Theodosius the Great (379-395). St. Ambrose insisted, against the imperial wishes, that the emperor was within the Church and not above it. None of the emperors dared punish him because the learned and saintly bishop had the active support of the people.

(b) *Apollinarism* was a heresy established by Apollinaris the Younger (c. 310-c. 390), bishop of Laodicea. His teaching was condemned first by the Council of Alexandria in 362, then by a

---

[2] Milan was the imperial residence for the Western Roman Emperor at this time.

series of Synods of Rome which took place between 374 and 380, and finally by the Council of Constantinople I in 381. Apollinaris had already gone into official schism by 375. In essence, Apollinaris taught that while Christ possessed complete Divinity, he lacked complete humanity and that Christ did not redeem human nature but only what is spiritual in humanity. The teaching denied the Incarnation and Redemption.

(c) The heresy of *Pelagianism* was established by the theologian and monk Pelagius[3] at the beginning of the fifth century. St. Jerome and St. Augustine strenuously opposed the heresy. Pelagius taught that no matter how deeply wounded man was in his physical and spiritual condition by Adam's fall, he never lost his freedom; that God's help (*grace*) was limited to externals, such as the Ten Commandments and the teachings and example of Christ; and that man did not need divine help since he could reach salvation without the assistance of grace. St. Augustine, like St. Jerome, was profoundly impressed by human moral weakness and its deeply rooted tendencies toward evil. He was convinced that man shared Adam's guilt[4] and, as a result, was deprived of the gifts originally bestowed to complete his faculties. Through Adam's sin, all humanity lost the gifts of immortality, immunity from physical decay, and the strong inclination toward virtue. Instead, man became subject to death and sickness, darkened in mind, and inclined toward evil. Man could not avoid sin without God's grace, which is God's own way of moving man's will to choose the good. This grace works in the very interior of man's will. On the other hand, grace does not take away man's freedom for it needs man's consent to work. Only those who receive this grace are saved, while those who do not are damned. Why some receive it and some do not is a mystery hidden in the inscrutable justice of God, the mystery of predestination. The *Council of Orange,* held in 529, upheld St. Augustine's teaching to

---

[3] The origins and death of Pelagius are very obscure. He was born in the British Isles in the late fourth century and died around the middle of the fifth century.

[4] This is the teaching on Original Sin.

a certain point, but rejected his notion of predestination. The said Council affirmed that, as a result of Adam's sin, both death and sin were transmitted to all of his descendants; that man's will has been so vitiated by original sin that he can only love God if prompted and assisted by grace; that baptismal grace enables all Christians with the help of Christ to do what is necessary for salvation; that in every good action, even the first impulse comes from God.

(d) The heresy of *Nestorianism* was named after its founder, Nestorius, Patriarch of Constantinople (428-451). Nestorius taught that Jesus Christ had two separate personalities and natures, one divine and one human; and that Mary was the mother of the human nature and not of the divine. Therefore, Nestorius declared Mary was not the Mother of God for she was only the mother of Jesus the man. The Councils of Ephesus and of Chalcedon condemned this heresy.

---

11. More Upheaval in Roman Africa

Many dramatic events took place in Roman Africa in what is today called Tunis. The great persecution of Christians, from 303 to 312, had the terrible sequel of the Donatist Schism. The Donatists set up their own rival bishops wherever there was a Catholic one. Constantine the Great lost no time in efforts to confront the schism. Emperor Honorius (395-423) officially suppressed the schism in 405, but soon after his death there was a civil war in the empire. The hold of imperial Rome was rapidly weakening. The Vandals conquered Roman Africa in 429. They remained in charge for the next hundred and twenty years.

The Roman African Church produced great theologians such as Tertullian, St. Cyprian, and St. Augustine. Notable features in the fourth century were the war against paganism, Manichaeism, Donatism, the growth of monasticism, African resistance to papal claims,[5] and a series of African Councils[6] whose canons were eventually incorporated in both Greek and Roman canon law. Such brilliant achievements were ended in 429 by the conquering Arian Vandals. The army of Emperor Justinian the Great re-conquered Roman Africa in 534, and restored the Catholic Church and monasticism. Church Councils became very active again. Pope St. Gregory the Great regularly corresponded with the Roman African bishops. The Berbers, the region's latest conquerors, were gradually converted by 640. Meanwhile, the heresy of Monothelitism, which taught Christ had only one will,[7] challenged the Roman Africa Church.

The conversion of the new Berber leaders was short-lived. Alexandria fell to the Arabs and to their Moslem faith in 642. The next major city to do so was Carthage, in 698. Christianity in Roman Africa was almost eradicated when many Christians were either massacred or sold into slavery. Many centuries later, around the middle of the nineteenth century, Catholic and Protestant missionaries began making some headway in that continent. Today, there is a young but vibrant Catholic Church in Africa, though not so much in North Africa, which has remained mainly Moslem.

---

12. The First Four Ecumenical (General) Councils

Great, extraordinary, learned, and saintly men rose to defend the true Catholic Faith. They did so not only through their writings, but also at Ecumenical Councils.

(a) The *Council of Nicaea* was the first Ecumenical Council in the history of the Church. It was not convoked by a Pope but by

---

[5] Eventually the Church in Roman Africa accepted Roman Primacy.

[6] The most renowned Councils of the Church in Roman Africa were the Councils of Carthage of 251, 252, 254, 255, 256, 348, and a series of Councils from 393 to 424, 525, and 534.

[7] The Catholic Church declares that Christ has a divine will and a human will.

Emperor Constantine the Great, at his own expense. The Council met in 325 in the city of Nicaea in Asia Minor. The reigning Pope, St. Sylvester I (314-335), sent two Roman priests to it as his legates. Three hundred bishops participated. The Council had a very specific task, namely, to answer a basic doctrinal question regarding the relationship between God the Father and Jesus Christ. This issue had divided the Christian community into Catholics and Arians.[8] The major consequence of the Council was the formulation of the Nicene Creed which declared that Jesus Christ is truly the Son of God, "God from God... true God from true God, begotten not made, one in being (*consubstantial*) with the Father." The Council affirmed that Jesus Christ, the Second Person of the Trinity, is truly God.

(b) Another emperor, Theodosius the Great (379-395), convoked the second General Council, *Constantinople I*, in 381. There were no papal representatives this time for it was originally considered to be a Synod for the Eastern Churches. The Council dealt with the still vibrant Arian heresy and Apollinarism. The Council proclaimed anew the Catholic doctrine of the full divinity and the full humanity of Christ, and affirmed the opposition to and condemnation of Arianism and Apollinarism by the Catholic Eastern Churches. The Council became recognized as an Ecumenical Council when it was acknowledged as such at the Council of Chalcedon in 451.

(c) The *Council of Ephesus,* assembled in 431, was summoned by yet another emperor, Theodosius II (408-450), at the request of Nestorius, Patriarch of Constantinople (428-431). Pope St. Celestine I (422-432) sent three papal legates to represent Rome's view and to present to the Council Fathers a papal letter which refuted the heresy of Nestorius. The Council declared that Christ is truly God and truly man and that Mary is the *Theotokos* (Θεοτοκος), that is, the Mother of God.

(d) Despite the proclamations and condemnations of the

---

[8] Arians were followers of Arius, a priest from Alexandria, Egypt.

Council of Ephesus, the Nestorian heresy continued to prosper under imperial protection. Consequently, Pope St. Leo the Great made several requests to Emperor Theodosius II (408-450) to call a Council to counteract the heretical teachings of Nestorius and the Monophysite heresy which taught that Jesus Christ at the Incarnation did not have two Natures (Divine and human) but one single Divine Nature. The *Council of Chalcedon* finally assembled in 451.[9] Over five hundred bishops participated. The Pope had been asked to personally preside over the Council, but since he could not do so, he sent five legates with a personal document that spelled out clearly the authentic Catholic doctrine. The Council declared that the Catholic Faith follows the contents of Pope St. Leo's *Tome*, namely that, "two natures are united without change, and without division, and without confusion in Christ.... This is the faith of the Fathers and of the Apostles. This we all believe. Peter has spoken through Leo."[10]

The adherents to both heresies rejected the formula of Chalcedon. The Nestorians rejected Chalcedon because they felt it confused the relationships of the Divine Persons in the Trinity. On the other hand, the Monophysites denied that Christ's humanity is consubstantial with ours.

The Council of Chalcedon was more complicated than prior ones because it attended to Church issues that went beyond doctrine. The Council Fathers protested against imperial interference in Church affairs and re-organized Church jurisdiction, elevating Jerusalem and Constantinople to the level of patriarchates. It reaffirmed the primacy of honor of Constantinople and made it the Court of Appeals for all the Eastern Churches. Once the acts of the Council were sent to Rome, Pope St. Leo refused to grant the patriarch of Constantinople the primacy of honor. Patriarch

---

[9] By this time, Emperor Theodosius II had been succeeded by Emperor Marcion (450-457).

[10] *The Seven Ecumenical Councils of the Undivided Church*, trans H. R. Percival, in *Nicene and Post-Nicene Fathers*, 2nd Series, ed. P. Schaff and H. Wace (Grand Rapids, MI: Wm. B. Eerdmans, 1955), 245.

Acacius of Constantinople (471-489) responded, in 474, by leading the Eastern Churches into schism and severed unity with Rome. This resulted in his excommunication by Rome. The schism proved to be crucial for future Rome-Constantinople relations. It taught the East how to be Catholic without a Pope and set the pattern for much of its later behavior, climaxing in the Great Schism of 1054. The Acacian schism lasted thirty-five years, that is, until the death of Acacius in 489. For the first time in Church history, the East was entirely lost to the Universal Church because half of it adhered to the Monophysite heresy, while the other half was in the Acacian schism.

The reunification within the Catholic Church began under Emperor Justin I (518-527), a devout Latin Catholic. The papal legate arrived in Constantinople in 518, with a document containing the Profession of the Catholic Faith that every bishop had to sign. Severus, the Monophysite Patriarch of Antioch (512-518), refused to sign the Profession of Faith. After his official deposition and excommunication, he fled to Egypt from where he led his own church in secret and ordained hundreds of priests to counteract the Catholic Faith.

---

13. Justinian the Great

Emperor Justin I was succeeded by Emperor Justinian the Great (483-565) in 527. At the time that Justinian was declared emperor, the barbarians had already conquered most of Western Europe. Consequently, the emperor began a military campaign to regain Rome's lost lands. He re-conquered Italy from the Goths, and Roman Africa from the Vandals. He was one of the greatest Roman emperors who established a very sound juridical system for the empire through his *Justinian Code*. His long reign and influence over the Church within his dominions was to increase the power of the state over the Church and to undermine, inadvertently,

Papal Primacy. Nonetheless, Justinian the Great was personally Catholic in faith and genuinely interested in making the Church flourish. He built basilicas throughout the empire, the most famous of which were the *Hagia Sophia*[11] in Constantinople and the basilica in Ravenna, Italy,[12] which was the resident imperial city for the West.

Justinian the Great persecuted heretics and forced pagans to be baptized. Ten centuries later there was another (Holy) Roman Emperor, Charles V (1500-1558), who, like Justinian the Great, saw himself as the protector of religion to the point of attempting to act as the Church's chief executive along with succeeding Popes and bishops!

Justinian the Great intertwined the temporal and the spiritual powers as the norm for imperial politics. Consequently, he never hesitated to interfere in Church policy. For example, when Pope Vigilius (537-555) resisted the imperial plans, the emperor did not hesitate to have the Pope humiliated and imprisoned until he acquiesced to the imperial wishes.

As in the case with Constantine the Great before him and with Charlemagne as emperor in the West after him, Justinian the Great was most resolute to restore doctrinal unity among all his subjects. Thus, he called the *Council Constantinople II* in 553 with the intention that the Council would not only issue another formal condemnation of Nestorianism, but also eradicate the heresy once and for all. The Council followed the imperial wishes and condemned Nestorianism as well as Monophysitism. But this Council, due to imperial interference, proved to be very controversial in many respects. It was Justinian the Great and not the Pope who called the Council on his own initiative. In fact, Pope Vigilius resisted the emperor who, in turn, had the Pope kidnaped in 545 and made him a virtual prisoner for the next eight years. The kidnaping of

---

[11] The basilica was constructed between 532 and 537. It was in fact the third church to occupy the site since the previous two had both been destroyed by riots.

[12] The construction of the basilica began under the Ostrogoths in 527 and finished in 548, under Justinian the Great.

a Pope by an emperor was repeated some thirteen hundred years later when Emperor Napoleon I (1799-1814) kidnaped Pope Pius VII (1800-1823) on 5ᵗʰ July 1809.

Though Justinian the Great had already extracted a public condemnation of Nestorianism from Pope Vigilius in 548, the imperial appetite was not fully satisfied. After Council Constantinople II, the emperor wanted his imperial papal prisoner to issue a condemnation of all past promoters of Nestorianism. The Pope objected to the inclusion in the condemnation of two bishops, Ibas and Mans, because they had refuted the heresy, had made their public Profession of the Catholic Faith, and had been re-instated by the Council of Chalcedon. The Pope argued that a condemnation of the two bishops could be misunderstood as a papal condemnation of Chalcedon. But the emperor was adamant. He bullied, cajoled, maligned, and threatened the very frail eighty-year old Pope until the emperor procured a second papal condemnation. Only after this had happened, was Pope Vigilius allowed to return to Rome in 555, though he died en route. This event happened three years after Justinian the Great had retaken Rome from the Ostrogoths in 552.

Justinian the Great had found the Ostrogoths to be much more fierce fighters than the Vandals in Roman Africa. The Ostrogoths, under their leader Totila (541-552), had fought the Roman armies for many years. Totila had put an end to the Byzantine rule in Italy in 540. He conquered Rome first in 546, left the City in 547, and went back to re-conquer it in 550. Totila was killed at the Battle of Taginae in 552, fighting the Byzantines. By the time the Ostrogoths were subdued in 553, pillage, rape, destruction and famine had devastated Italy. It was the subtle beginning of the *Dark Ages* in Europe.

---

14. Further Doctrinal Discord and Councils

(a) The death of Justinian the Great in 565 commenced another decline of the empire. Since his successors were weak emperors, the Persians, perennial adversaries of the empire, took the opportunity to expand their own empire by capturing the entire Middle Eastern provinces. Syria and Egypt, being mostly of Monophysite faith, fell easily due to their determination to be independent of anyone and anything Catholic. The tide turned briefly for the Catholic Church during the reign of Emperor Heraclius (610-641), a fine soldier and a great administrator. He reorganized the empire, and managed to recover the provinces lost to Persia during the first fifteen years of his reign. But, he was faced with the old problem of the Monophysite heresy when he tried to reorganize the recovered provinces in Syria and Egypt. By 641, both Syria and Egypt had been conquered by the Moslems. The two countries have remained principally Moslem ever since.

(b) Emperor Heraclius tried his best to patch up the differences between his Catholic and Monophysite subjects. Patriarch Sergius of Constantinople (610-638), the trusted adviser of the emperor, came up with a formula that was acceptable to the emperor. The new formula was heretical because it stated that although Christ had *two* Natures there was only one source of activity (*energy*) in the Lord because He was but *one* Person. A more popular version of this heresy was the claim that the Lord had only one will.[13] Sergius wrote to the new Pope, Honorius I (625-638), and requested ratification of the new formula. The new Pope did not realize all the intricacies in the issue and was misled into accepting Sergius' doctrinal formula. But Patriarch Sophronius of Jerusalem (634-638) saw Sergius' trap and denounced the formula as heretical. At the time, the heresy was being supported also by Patriarch Cyrus of Alexandria (631-643). Over the next eight years, there were a

---

[13] The heresy was called *Monothelitism*. It was condemned by the General Council of Constantinople III in 680.

series of Roman acts that explained what Pope Honorius I had accepted and what he had condemned. They also explained that Pope Honorius I had rejected Monothelitism. Patriarch Sergius' doctrinal formula was condemned and he was ordered to withdraw his consent from it. When he refused to do so, the Pope excommunicated him. The same fate awaited Patriarch Cyrus.

The new Emperor Constans II (642-668) issued an edict prohibiting either party to discuss the doctrinal matter. The new Pope, St. Martin I (649-655), having lived in Constantinople as papal legate for many years and having personally understood what the imperial edict entailed, publicly rejected it. This took place in October 649 during a local Lateran Synod over which the Pope personally presided. Constans II was beside himself. He resorted to a number of means through which he attempted to enforce the imperial edict. At first he tried to win over Pope St. Martin I, then he tried to assassinate him, and finally had him captured and brought to Constantinople as an imperial prisoner where he was much abused. The emperor then had the Pope tried and condemned to death in 654. The death sentence was commuted to permanent exile in the Crimea, where the Pope died the following year.

(c) Constans II was succeeded by his son, Emperor Constantine IV (668-685). The new emperor did not impose his father's imperial edict, and instead reestablished a peaceful cooperation between himself and all of the Popes during his reign.[14] This relationship led to the *Council Constantinople III* in 680. The reigning Pope, St. Agatho (678-681), had already held a synod in Rome earlier that year where the doctrine of the Two Wills in Christ was reaffirmed. The Pope sent a letter to the emperor declaring and explaining the true Catholic dogma. The emperor called the Council Constantinople III soon thereafter. The Council[15] condemned Monothelitism and the bishops unanimously professed the

---

[14] The Popes at the time of the peaceful cooperation with Constantine IV were Pope St. Vitalian (657-672), Pope Deusdedit II (672-676), Pope Donus I (676-678) and Pope St. Agatho (678-681).

[15] Council Constantinople III met from November 680 to September 681.

Catholic Faith. The Council essentially restated the Profession of Faith declared at the Council of Chalcedon, affirming the doctrine of the Two Natures and adding, as a necessary consequence, the statement of the reality of the Two Wills and the Two Operations in Christ.

By now, over three hundred and fifty years had passed since the conversion of Constantine the Great. During that time, a great imperial culture had emerged, with Constantinople as its center. The West had undergone radical changes due to the numerous and unrelenting barbarian invasions. The Eastern Empire had a different story to tell. Indeed, it had become a great Greek-Byzantine state. The Byzantines came to consider themselves as the true Romans instead of those living in Italy. The Byzantines viewed the contemporary inhabitants of Rome and the rest of Italy as being mainly the descendants of barbaric tribes who had occupied the Italian Peninsula for the previous three centuries. Notwithstanding, the Greek language was no longer the spoken language of the imperial family. For the first time in history, Latin became the language at the imperial Greek court. By the eighth century, however, the peoples living within the Eastern Empire had slowly become anti-Roman in sentiment, resentful of Papal leadership, and contemptuous of Western customs and culture that they viewed as utterly corrupted and barbarous. The combination of the occasional rebellions against the Popes led by some of the Patriarchs of Constantinople, the resistance and interference by emperors, the Acacian heresy, and finally, the Council Constantinople IV of 692 were the preludes for the Photian Schism and the subsequent historic Great Schism of 1054 led by Michael Cerularius, Patriarch of Constantinople (1043-1058). The majority of the Eastern Churches have led a spiritual life independent of the Bishop of Rome ever since.

(d) Soon after Council Constantinople III, the need for another Council became evident. The two prior General Councils[16]

---

[16] The Councils were those of Constantinople II (553) and III (680).

had not provided any Church disciplinary laws, but by this time such laws were needed. The new Council assembled in 692 in the domed hall of the imperial palace of Justinian II (685-695, 706-711) in Constantinople, thereby acquiring its more popular name of the Council *in Trullo*. The Council Fathers were exclusively from the East. They claimed authority to pass laws for the entire empire, including Rome. The Council, for the major part, did nothing but codify the laws of previous Councils. It added, however, a new set of laws that were clearly anti-Roman. It stated that the Roman law of clerical celibacy went against Apostolic tradition. The Council forbade fasting, even in Rome, on Saturdays during Lent, and went on to legislate new fast days. Pope St. Sergius I (687-701) refused to confirm the laws of *in Trullo* and only a revolution against the emperor in 695 saved him from the fate of Pope St. Martin I. The respite lasted for ten years, that is, until Justinian II was restored to the imperial throne. He resumed the issue with a new Pope, John VII (705-707), who sent the emperor a very ambiguous reply. The emperor ordered the Pope to Constantinople but John VII was dead by the time the orders reached Rome. Meanwhile, the papal legate, a Roman deacon who was to become Pope St. Gregory II (715-731), diplomatically convinced Justinian II that an accommodation could be arranged without having the Pope confirm the laws of *in Trullo*.

The Reshaping of Western Europe

After the death of Constantine the Great in 337, the Roman Empire was, for another time, officially divided into two: the West, with Rome as its nominal capital, and the East, with Byzantium (Constantinople) as its fixed capital. There were two co-emperors. In time the barbarians brought havoc to the Western Roman Empire while the Eastern (Byzantine) Empire continued to survive and thrive. In the heels of the gradual downfall of the Western Roman Empire, the Popes embarked on a new evangelization program: the conversion of the barbarian peoples. During this era there were many famous missionaries such as St. Martin of Tours (c. 316-c. 397), St. Patrick (c. 389-c. 461 or 493), and many adventurous and saintly Irish monks. Slowly but surely, Western Europe was becoming Christianized. There were the conversions of the Franks, the Spanish Visigoths, the Angles, the Irish and the Germanic tribes. Meanwhile, great Popes led the Church, such as St. Leo the Great and St. Gregory the Great. Popes were not to remain solely as religious leaders but, due to the social and historical forces of the times, they also emerged as civil leaders.

15. The Invasion of Southern Europe

(a) The Western Roman Empire had a gradual disintegration due to multi-faceted internal corruption on the political, social, and moral levels, and to the frequent invasions by barbarians. The Church was faced with the same reality but survived the great turmoil. Indeed, the Popes of the time were solid anchors that provided a sense of stability throughout the political, social, and moral upheaval in the Western world. St. Ambrose, St. Augustine and St. Jerome had formed the human foundation of all that was Christian in the culture of the approaching Dark and High Middle Ages. The three Saints had lived in the last generation that saw Roman rule as a real power in the West. Within a few years of St. Ambrose's death in 397, and during the lifetime of St. Augustine and St. Jerome, the catastrophe that had been looming to take grip of the Western Empire took place. Western Europe was violently overtaken by the breakdown in the hold of the centralized Roman government, and by the chaos resulting from the invasions of the barbaric Franks, Vandals and Huns. The Western Roman Empire eventually collapsed under such extraordinary pressure, but the Church survived.

(b) The barbarians who invaded the Western Roman Empire were peoples of different races. They were Saxons, Goths, Visigoths, Huns, Ostrogoths, Vandals, Franks and others. The things common among them were their easy mobility, their pagan or Arian beliefs, a pastoral lifestyle, and ownership of lots of herds of cattle. The empire attracted them because they saw in it a sense of security. Thus, it was not unusual for barbarian families or entire tribes to seek and procure admission into the empire. In fact, since the middle of the second century, barbarians began to be admitted into the empire for military purposes. Initially, they were organized as auxiliary forces, but gradually the barbarians grew to form the majority of the Roman army. In an empire where the ruler was usually a military man, who had the backing of many Roman legions, the influx of barbarians into the Roman army came to have a great impact and slowly transformed the empire itself. It was just a matter of time before Rome had emperors who were either barbarian or had barbarian roots.

When the West began to produce weak Romans as emperors, especially during the fifth century, hordes of barbarians attacked the frontiers of the empire and took away land from it. These peoples refused to deal with the Romans, succeeded in crossing the Rhine in 406, and occupied Gaul with their establishment of the Burgundian kingdom of Worms. The Ostrogoth chief Alaric (c. 370-410), of Arian faith, having been completely dissatisfied and disillusioned with his nation's service to the Roman army, invaded Italy in 409.[1] Rome was sacked on 24th August 410. The pillaging lasted three days. Alaric died a few months later on his way to capture southern Italy. At the time, the imperial residence was Ravenna and no emperor had lived in Rome for the previous one hundred and forty years or so. But, Rome had remained the symbol of the empire. The sacking of the city was calamitous.

Around the time of Alaric's death, the Franks, Burgundians, Alemanni, Huns, Visigoths and Vandals invaded Gaul, while the Suevi, Vandals and Visigoths invaded and occupied Spain. Many of the leaders of these tribes had already set themselves up as independent rulers, although they were nominally in the service of Rome. Britain, the most northern imperial frontier, also fell to barbarians. The Roman legions stationed there had been recalled to the continent in 410 to address the crisis in Italy. The Saxons, Jutes, Angles, Picts and Scots simply overran Britain. Fortunately, the barbarian tribes who had invaded the Western Roman Europe, at the time, did not bring great havoc to their newly conquered lands.

16. Social Changes

Roman Africa was not spared invasions. The invading Vandals of 425 turned public life upside down by destroying city after city. Their conquest, completed by 429, brought about the establishment of the first barbaric state which was openly hostile to Rome. The Vandals, who like the Goths had been converted to Arian-

---

[1] Alaric had invaded Greece and plundered Athens in 396, and then plundered the Balkans in 398.

ism, began an avid systematic persecution of the Catholic Church in Roman Africa. While Arianism had been dead in the Eastern Empire for fifty years, it became the established state religion in the Vandal kingdom.

When St. Leo the Great was elected Pope in 440, the Western Roman Emperor Valentinian III (425-455) was already confined to being master of Italy only. Once the emperor, who was the last descendant of Theodosius the Great, died, the barbarian generals in the Roman armies fought for control, crowned successive puppet emperors and were, in effect, the real rulers. The last puppet Roman emperor was Romulus Augustulus (475-476), who was forced to resign in 476. He was then sent to his counterpart in Constantinople[2] with the message that the West did not need another Roman emperor. The Ostrogoth chief Theodoric (489-526), of Arian faith, began to rule the West in 493, after twenty-two years of fighting other barbarian chiefs, particularly Odoacer (433-493). These events produced gradual adverse political effects. Centralization as had been known under the Western Roman Empire disappeared as local political and powerful leaders became rulers of their particular area. As history has proven many times, events that happened centuries before have effects centuries later.

Communication, under the new barbaric rulers, went seldom beyond the local level. The famous Roman roads were neglected, thereby rendering localities more isolated. Next came the flight from the city to the countryside, thereby making isolation more intense. These sociological and demographic events affected even the practice of the Catholic faith. Christian communities had been concentrated in the city in the past and, due to the new urban exodus, the practice of the Christian faith took on a rustic character. The Europe of the Middle Ages with its tiny kingdoms and principalities began to form roots.

---

[2] Emperor Zeno (474-491).

17. Monasticism Expands

People in both East and West, confronted with the chaos of their cities, searched for solace outside their respective societies.

(a) St. Basil the Great was born at Caesarea in Cappadocia in 330. A very learned and holy man, he withdrew from Byzantine civilization to become a hermit. It was during this time that he drew up the first ever complete code for monastic life.[3] At the time of its composition, there were two things peculiar to this Rule: a novitiate and that each community should be limited to forty monks. St. Basil had to abandon his eremitical life when he became bishop of Caesarea in 370, where he died nine years later. Within fifty years of his death, his brand of monasticism expanded rapidly and went beyond solitary places and deserts. It was found in towns and cities, even in the imperial capital of Byzantium. Furthermore, Irish monks were able to carry this form of monasticism to many parts of Western Europe.

(b) The first monks in the West, in Gaul and Italy, generally followed the rules of St. Pachomius and St. Basil, until the establishment of a new brand of monasticism by St. Benedict (480-547). His *Holy Rule* reflected the Latin genius for organization and is still followed by thousands of monks, nuns, and sisters to this very day. Although St. Benedict began as a solitary man at Subiaco, he ended up being a social and Church reformer and a founder, establishing a monastic community on Monte Cassino around 520. The chief characteristics of his *Holy Rule* are its practicality and common-sense approach. St. Benedict provided a full monastic rule of life for the common man who sought perfection and God. The *Holy Rule* supplied the monk with an atmosphere of stability, a sense of belonging, and a superior, the abbot, who was also bound to follow the Rule. Christ occupied the invisible central place in the community. The Benedictines spread quickly throughout Western

---

[3] The Basilian Rule is still followed by many monks today.

Europe. Their appearance was a ray of hope to a Western Europe that was in the throes of social and political chaos. No single person, except for the Benedictine Pope St. Gregory the Great, did more than Benedict to stabilize the barbarian peoples and plant the Catholic Faith solidly in their midst.

(c) Two other saints in the West, along with Benedict, stand out for the adaptation of the Catholic Faith to the new social and political climate. The first one was the Hungarian-born St. Martin of Tours, who pioneered missionaries to convert the country people. A convert to Christianity when a soldier in his late teens, he led an exemplary lifestyle as a Catholic, a hermit around whom other hermits had started gathering, as the bishop of Tours (361-c. 397), as a missionary, as the founder of a religious community, and a defender of the poor and the downtrodden.

St. Patrick was the first monk to become a missionary to the new rural Christianity. St. Patrick had fled Ireland, where he had been a slave, and had gone to Gaul, where he had become a monk. He subsequently was ordained bishop and sent back to convert the Irish. His tireless missionary efforts not only paid off by converting Ireland but also by turning it into a land full of monasteries that were renowned for their sanctity, learning, and missionary activities. The Irish missionaries met with many difficulties in lands where the name of Rome had never been heard. They had to adapt to very harsh climates, strange barbaric cultures and foreign languages. Irish monasticism, however, remained based on the harsh Egyptian model until the seventh century when it met the more benign brand of Benedictine monasticism.

18. New Secular Rulers and the Church

(a) The importance of the Catholic baptism of Clovis (c. 466-511), King of the Salian Franks (481-511), in 496, can never be overestimated. The Franks were the most barbarous of all the people who took land away from the Roman Empire. However, they had the distinct characteristic of allowing freedom of worship to all of their subjects. Thus, many Catholic bishops supported the Frankish kings from the very beginning, even when the kings were still pagan. The Frankish kingdom was the only one of all the barbaric kingdoms to survive and to have a permanent dominating influence in Europe for centuries to come.

The Franks of the sixth century conquered all of Gaul and freed it of all its Arian kings. But the Franks, once converted to Catholicism, abandoned freedom of worship and became very brutal in procuring the forced baptism of conquered peoples. In time, the descendants of King Clovis fought civil wars and brought about the total destruction of the little that had been left of the Roman order. The Church suffered greatly in this new version of anarchy. On the other hand, the Frankish kings offered it protection as well as patronage, but they were bestowed at a costly price. Henceforth, the Frankish king played a key role in the nomination of bishops and other important Church offices. He made sure that he had the loyalty of each appointee. Churchmen became not only spiritual leaders but also political rulers. These men would in time opt to uphold the will of their ruler even when it fell contrary to Church matters. Eventually, they would become prince-bishops and the like.

(b) Sixth century Spain was still ruled by Arian kings. St. Leander, Archbishop of Seville (579-601), however, won the conversion of King Recared (586-601) and his nobility in 589. Current Spanish Catholicism had its unique organization centered on the single primatial see of Toledo. At the time, Spain existed and lived in isolation from the rest of Europe. The imposing Pyrenees evoked a psychological stumbling block to communication.

The nomination of bishops was a right claimed by the Spanish kings. In this regard, Spain behaved like the rest of Europe, namely the abuses that went hand in hand with such a nomination procedure infiltrated the life of the Spanish Church until the fall of Spain to the Moors in 711. One bright star who appeared during this time was St. Isidore, Archbishop of Seville (600-630), a younger brother and episcopal successor to St. Leander. Originally a monk, he wrote a rule for monks, and in his many writings he stood as the link between the Church Fathers and the schoolmen of the later centuries. St. Isidore is considered to be the last of the ancient Christian Philosophers and the great Latin Fathers. He was the most learned man of his age and exercised a far-reaching and immeasurable influence on the educational life of the Middle Ages. Due to his many profound and far reaching writings, Pope Innocent XIII (1721-1724) proclaimed him, "Doctor of the Church" on 25th April 1722.

---

19. Emergence of Papal Monarchy

One of the greatest Popes to ever occupy the Chair of Peter was St. Gregory the Great. The invasion of the barbaric Lombards, when he was in his mid-twenties, had left a deep impression for the rest of his life. St. Gregory was the Prefect of Rome when he decided to leave everything behind him and become a Benedictine monk. Pope Pelagius II (579-590) sent him as papal legate to Constantinople in 580. He stayed there for about six years. He was elected Pope at age fifty, succeeding the same Pelagius II in 590. St. Gregory left a very rich doctrinal legacy to the Church that remained popular for more than a thousand years after his death. His clear, simple and practical writings popularized the faith for the layman. He was a chronic invalid, yet full of energy and determined to spiritually nourish the members of the Church entrusted to his care. His correspondence shows that he actively contacted all parts of the Church.

When St. Gregory was already Pope, the barbaric Lombards moved south, with the intention of conquering Rome. The Romans turned to him for help instead of turning to the imperial exarch. St. Gregory ransomed captives and organized great relief services for widows and orphans. Finally, in 598, he secured a thirty-year truce. The people of Rome considered him the true ruler of the City.

St. Gregory is considered as the founder of the Papal Monarchy in a very real sense. He was also a great Church reformist. He began with a general reform of the Church in Italy. He tried to do the same in Gaul, but was unsuccessful to stop laymen from being appointed bishops by the Frankish kings. He sent a new wave of missionaries to England, under St. Augustine of Canterbury (596-604), who met with great success.

---

20. Islamic Invasions

Mohammed (c. 570- 632) was born of a noble family of the Kareish tribe in the city of Mecca in Arabia around the year 570. He is the founder of Islam, a system of religious beliefs influenced by Judaism, Christianity, and Hellenism. The basic teachings of Islam rest upon the Qur'an, which was influenced by both the Old and New Testaments.[4] The Qur'an is the sacred book of Islam, containing the revelations, commands, and messages of Allah (God) delivered to Mohammed by the angel Gabriel. Mohammed considered himself as the ultimate prophet of Allah and gave his followers a simple creed. The believer was obligated to propagate this creed, to visit the holy city of Mecca, and to destroy the unbeliever through waging holy war (jihad). Islam has no ordained ministry.

Islam's first great achievement was to unite the nomad Arabs of the desert. Mohammed's successor, Omar (581-644), was a great warrior and had managed to conquer the Arabian Peninsula within ten years of Mohammed's death. By the time of Omar's death, the Moslems were also masters of Persia, Egypt, Palestine and Syria. Moslem expansion had been phenomenally quick. Fifty years later, their conquering advance was renewed and Roman Africa, in 695, the Mediterranean islands (conquered gradually), and Spain, in 711, became part of the vast Moslem Empire. They also overran southern France. They laid siege to Constantinople in 717 but the Emperor Leo III (717-741) resisted them. In the West, the Frank-

---

[4] The main books utilized by Mohammed were the Pentateuch, the Psalms, and the Gospels.

ish warrior Charles Martel (c. 690-741) defeated them at the battle
of Poitiers in 732. The siege of Christendom had begun and war
would last for the next nine hundred years or so.

---

21. The Donation of Pepin

(a) Charles Martel was not a Frankish King when he defeated the
Moslems at Poitiers in 732, saving France and most of Western
Europe from Islamic expansionism. He was the chief of a family
who, in fact, ruled the Franks while the descendants of King Clovis
were still kings. Charles' son, Pepin (751-768), with the blessing of
Rome, replaced the puppet rulers in 751, and established himself
as the new Frankish King. St. Boniface[5] first anointed him king in
752, and three years later, Pope Stephen III (752-757) personally
anointed Pepin anew in Rome along with his two sons, Carloman
(768-771) and Charlemagne (768-814). This act forged an alliance
between the Franks and the Popes that would last for centuries.
It became the cornerstone of building up Medieval Europe and
establishing the Papal States.

(b) The Papal Monarchy[6] did not begin as some well thought
out plan. Political and social pressures brought it about. Since
the time of Pope St. Gregory the Great's youth, in the middle of
the sixth century, Italy had been the scene of long wars between
the Lombards and the Byzantines. The latter grew weaker and
weaker in their hold of Italy. Furthermore, the Byzantines had
very little interest to defend what was still theirs in Italy due to
the establishment of the Islamic states on their side of the empire.

---

[5]   St. Boniface (680-755) was an English missionary monk who is called the *Apostle
     of Germany*. Boniface's original name was Winfrid. He changed his name in Rome
     while a guest of Pope St. Gregory II in 732. He was ordained a bishop that same
     year.

[6]   The reason why it is called Papal Monarchy is because the Pope was the sovereign
     of the Papal States.

The Byzantine emperors perceived these states as the real threat to their sovereignty.

Pope Stephen III found himself torn between two forces: the Franks, who had become good Catholics, and the Byzantines who, though Catholic, had ongoing tensions with the Roman Church. The Lombard King Astoif (749-756) invaded Rome in 749. He was following his tribe's long-standing quest for Lombard domination of all of Italy. Emperor Leo III had no intention to defend the Pope and the City. Eventually, the autocratic emperor simply told Pope Stephen III to order Astoif to retire. The Pope instead sought help from King Pepin, who invaded Italy, drove out the Lombards, and handed their territory in sovereignty to the Pope. The grant of these lands became known as the Donation of Pepin. These lands, which covered about one third of the Italian Peninsula, would eventually form the core of the future Papal States. Thus, the Pope became also a secular sovereign,[7] with an aristocracy made up mainly of clerics. But the older lay military aristocracy in the new papal territories made numerous and limited successful attempts to have elected as Pope their own candidate rather than the candidate of the rightful papal electors, the clergy of Rome. It was just a matter of time before real trouble began.

22. Charlemagne

(a) King Pepin died in 768, and by 771 his younger son Charlemagne was sole ruler (771-814) of his vast lands. Adrian I (772-795) was elected Pope the following year. The first event to mark the peaceful cooperation between Charlemagne and the Popes was the Frankish conquest of the Lombards (773-774), by which Charlemagne became their King. This assured the papal territories of

---

[7]   Modern Popes are recognized in international law as the sovereigns of the (civil) Vatican City State that was established at the Lateran Treaties of 1929 between Pope Pius XI and the Italian Dictator Benito Mussolini.

protection and security. Pope St. Leo III (795-816) succeeded Pope Adrian I. Pope St. Leo III wrote to Charlemagne to notify him of his election and asked him to send a deputation to accept the oath of fidelity from the Romans. Charlemagne replied by counseling the Pope to be a wise ruler. This innocuous act was the first subtle establishment of the Frankish power over the Church. It was an omen of future interference at the highest level in Church affairs by the Frankish rulers, and of the dependence of the Church on the State.

Charlemagne's dream was to establish a great united empire, similar to that of Constantine the Great, with one Catholic Faith, to build on that Faith, to reform and reorganize the Church, and to expand the Catholic Faith into other lands. He became Europe's protector against Islam in the south and the pagan Saxons in the north. He was considered as the "ideal" Christian king. Consequently, on Christmas Day 800, Pope St. Leo III crowned Charlemagne as Holy Roman Emperor[8] in Rome. It had taken Charlemagne almost thirty years to make his dream come true.

(b) Charlemagne undertook the intellectual reform of the schools attached to monasteries and to cathedrals within his empire. This endeavor led to a brief Carolingian Renaissance. Charlemagne's reformist efforts were proposed and carried out by two outstanding churchmen: the Englishman Alcuin (c. 735-804), a Benedictine monk from York, and the prime motivator for this intellectual renewal, and the Spaniard Theoduif (c. 750-821), bishop of Orleans and a leading theologian of his day. Both men were Charlemagne's chief advisers. Originally, these three men combined their efforts to enact educational legislation that would elevate the low level of education among the Frankish clergy. Alcuin began by establishing a monastic school in Tours. It was the first time that boys were allowed to study alongside clerics. He also established a palace scholastic academy for Charlemagne's children, his nobility

---

[8]   The Holy Roman Empire lasted from 800 to 1806. The last Holy Roman Emperor was Francis II of Austria (1792-1806).

and their children, and the children of peasants. He envisioned an academic system that provided learning opportunities for all the peoples in the Frankish Kingdom. On the other hand, Theoduif established the cathedral school of Orleans, most renowned in its time for the scholarly training of the clergy.

(c) There was, however, a dark side to this picture. Charlemagne appointed his clever men to church positions, such as that of bishoprics. He also appointed clever churchmen to important political offices. Some of these churchmen turned out not to be model clerics. Charlemagne's son, Louis the Pious (814-840), followed his father's system of appointments, but suffered opposite results. The reign of Louis the Pious saw a lot of political upheaval that led to a brief establishment of the Popes' domination over the emperors during the ninth century. Louis the Pious was a weak ruler who loved to interfere with local politics and Church policy. He not only nominated bishops but also attempted to nominate Popes. His weak personality and imperial policy of intrusion brought him much personal grief. His three sons rebelled and defeated him at Colmar and the Assembly of Compiègne deposed him as emperor in 833. The Frankish bishops forced him to wear a penitent's robe, after which he was restored as emperor at Menz in 835. He did not seem to have learned anything from his disastrous career. He continued his attempts to interfere with the See of Rome until his death. He perceived himself to be above the Church. The far-reaching result of this posture forced the Popes of the ninth century to take effective action against imperial rulers and their possible interference.

---

23. Conversion of Northern European Tribes

The boundaries of Christendom during the Middle Ages continued to expand. The conversion of the Frisians and Hessian Germans occurred in the seventh and eighth centuries. Unfortunately, these conversions were forced upon these tribes.

The early attempts to Christianize the fiercely pagan Frisians were unsuccessful. It was not uncommon for the Frisians to murder Christian missionaries, the most famous of whom was the English monk and bishop, St. Boniface (680-755). The Frankish leader Charles Martel effectively subjugated all of Frisia in 734. He forcibly reintroduced Christianity in Frisia. By the time that Frisia reclaimed its independence from the Frankish grip in the early 800s, Christianity had already taken root.

On the other hand, the Hessian Germans, also known as the Chatti tribe, were incorporated in the Frankish kingdom of Clovis I at the beginning of the sixth century. St. Boniface had had more success in his efforts to Christianize this tribe. In 723, he felled their sacred tree, Thor's Oak, near Fritzlar, as part of his efforts to compel their conversion and that of other northern Germanic tribes.

Charlemagne forced the German Saxons to convert in the eighth century. Missionaries from both East and West had been active in Prussia since the ninth century. The northern Germans were converted by many missionary efforts from the ninth to the eleventh centuries. Denmark and Norway became Christian in the eleventh century. Pagan Sweden was the most resistant, but due to the conversion of the neighboring Denmark and Norway, it, too, became Christian at the end of the eleventh century. The Baltic peoples of Livonia and Lithuania became Christian during the thirteenth and fourteenth centuries.

24. Conversion of the Slavs

The term "Slavs" is a common genus used to encompass all Slavonic tribes. They migrated in hordes and occupied central Europe, including Poland and Bohemia. Their conversion to Christianity took place between the ninth and the eleventh centuries.

(a) Mojmír I of Greater Moravia (c. 795-846) was succeeded by his nephew Rastislav (846-870) in 846. Although he was originally appointed to the realm by the Frankish King Louis the German (804-876), the new monarch pursued an independent policy. Following his victory over a Frankish attack in 855, he sought to weaken the influence of Frankish priests in his realm by asking the Byzantine Emperor Michael III to send missionaries who would interpret the Christianity in the Slavic vernacular. The Emperor sent the brothers St. Cyril (826-869) and St. Methodius (c. 815-885) as his officials and missionaries in 863. As a means to help in their missionary activities among the western Slavs, St. Cyril invented the Cyrillic alphabet. The brothers journeyed to Rome a few years later, where they were ordained bishops by Pope Adrian II (867-872). St. Cyril died in Rome in 869. Subsequently, St. Methodius returned to Moravia. The missionary efforts of the two brothers had met with some success in converting Moravia. But it was not until the tenth century that Christianity made real progress among the many Slav tribes.

(b) The Bohemian princes looked to Germany for protection from the fierce Hungarian (Magyar) invaders of the ninth century. The conversion of the Hungarians took place during the tenth and eleventh centuries. One of their very first Christian rulers was King St. Wencelaus (921-935), martyred by his brother Boleslaus I the Cruel (935-972). It was during the latter's reign that Pope Benedict VI (973-974) erected the diocese of Prague in 973. From there Christianity spread to Poland. Prince Mieczyslaw (Mieszko), the Polish ruler of Posen from 962 to 992, was baptized in 966 and firmly established the Polish Kingdom as a Christian realm. For a while it looked like Russia would accept the Latin rather than the Greek form of Christianity, but it was not to be so. The Russian Grand Prince Vladimir of Kiev (c.958-1015) was baptized in 988 and Christianity was officially adopted under his rule. Vladimir had considered himself as being somewhat of a philosopher, and it was only after he had discussed religion with the representatives of the Pope, of the Patriarch of Constantinople, of Moslems and of Jews, that he decided to accept baptism in the Byzantine Church. Russia would side with Constantinople in the Great Schism of 1054.

25. The Approach of the Dark Ages

(a) St. Ambrose's affirmation in the fourth century that the emperor was not above the Church was put into practice during his lifetime. He publicly rebuked Emperor Theodosius the Great for being responsible for a massacre in Thessalonika. The emperor accepted the rebuke and did public penance at the entrance of the doors of the cathedral of Milan in 390. St. Ambrose's affirmation was essentially restated some one hundred years later by Pope St. Gelasius I (492-497) in a letter to Emperor Anastasius (491-518), where he affirmed the superiority of the Church's authority over that of all civil power. Pope St. Gelasius I affirmed that the Pope had the right to direct and lead all Christendom, including its secular leaders, toward eternal salvation. The emperor's role was merely to protect the temporal welfare of the Church and of its members. In line with this claim, the Popes of the ninth century tried to assert their supremacy over Christendom. Thus, when Pope St. Stephen V (816-817) crowned Louis the Pious as emperor in Rheims in 816, he made it very clear that the crown itself was derived from the successor of Peter. The papal position was strengthened when Emperor Louis' son, Lothar I (840-855), went to Rome to be crowned emperor by Pope Gregory IV (827-844). Successive Popes upheld their right to intervene in the affairs of the state, for they claimed the state was an agent of the Church. This policy reached its zenith under Pope St. Nicholas I (858-867). In crowning Louis the German (855-875) as emperor, the Pope declared that it was the emperor's duty to protect the Church, thereby dictating imperial policy. Pope John VIII (872-882) advanced the cause of papal supremacy by asserting the papal right not only to crown but also to choose the emperor. This happened in 875, when the Pope offered the imperial crown to Charles the Bold (875-877). The whole issue faded away as both empire and monarchical papacy began to disintegrate. However, the Popes had come a long way from the time of Louis the Pious' attempts to nominate Popes.

(b) While the struggle for political control was going on between emperors and Popes, the boundaries of Christian Europe were being threatened by outside forces. The followers of Islam regrouped. They ruled the Mediterranean and invaded south France and Italy by sea. They managed to land in Italy and sacked Rome and desecrated the Tombs of St. Peter and St. Paul in 844. From the north came the barbarous Norsemen who established their kingdom in Dublin, Ireland, in 795. They attacked England and northern France for the next century. With Islam's threat in southern Europe and the Norsemen's threat in northern Europe, the rest of Christian Europe down-spiraled into chaos. Both civil and Church systems collapsed. It was the height of the *Dark Ages.* Learning simply disappeared,[9] the clergy was illiterate, good bishops became rare, and corrupt laymen took over episcopal and abbatial nominations. There were plenty of scandals in the Church. Many bishops ignored Church Law, lived openly in concubinage, bought Church offices for their sons, and passed their episcopal sees to offspring as if these were their personal property. The See of Rome itself was not spared any kind of scandal. The powerful lay nobility disposed of one Pope after another, replacing one immoral Pope with yet another, and sometimes the Papacy itself was sold either to the highest bidder or to the most powerful noble family of the time.

There were thirty-seven Popes between the murder of Pope John VIII in 882 and the Council of Sutri in 1046 that marked the end of this dark era in the Church and Christian Europe. The nadir of this era occurred when the powerful Roman House of Theophylact and their relatives, the House of Crescentii, took over the See of Rome and, for the next century,[10] appointed at will some of the worst Popes in Church history, draining the papacy of its spiritual and moral authority. Nevertheless, in the midst of this

---

[9] The exception was in the Irish monasteries where scholarship was kept alive.

[10] The House of Theophylact and the House of Crescentii dominated entirely the papacy from 904 to 1012, except for the years 965-1003 during which time the Holy Roman emperors were in control of papal affairs.

chaos a great Pope arose to protect the Church, St. Nicholas I. In a couple of years he managed to curtail the schism in the East under Patriarch Photius of Constantinople, and resisted the divorce of King Lothair of Lorraine (863), even though the papal territories were threatened by an invasion.

On the other hand, Germany managed to produce a great Holy Roman Emperor, Otto I (936-973), during this period of great social, political and religious turmoil. Otto I was successful in temporarily restoring the unity within his empire. He intervened in the Papacy and (unlawfully) deposed the wicked Pope John XII (955-964). The subsequent interference of his son, Otto II (973-983), and his grandson Otto III (983-1002), secured for the Papacy the nomination of some good Popes.[11] Nevertheless, though such interference brought some measured good results, it was a bad system in that laymen interfered at the highest levels in Church life. Eventually, since some of the subsequent German emperors[12] were personally very corrupt, things reverted to chaos, especially during the reigns of Emperor Conrad II (1024-1039) and his grandson Emperor Henry IV (1056-1106). Even so, during this time, the Church was producing reforming churchmen from within. A great reform movement was begun by the Abbey of Cluny in Burgundy and by some holy bishops and monks. They would lead the Church into a great renewal.

---

[11] The Popes during the reigns of Otto II and Otto III were Pope Benedict VI (973-974), Pope Benedict VII (974-984), Pope John XIV (984), Pope John XV (985-996), Pope Gregory V (996-999), and Pope Sylvester II (999-1003).

[12] The titles *Holy Roman Emperor* and *German Emperor* were interchangeable titles until 1806 because most of the Emperors were of Germanic extraction.

Reforms

26. Monastic Reform

(a) Cluny, situated in France, was founded as a reforming Bene-dictine Abbey in 910. The Abbey was established as independent of all bishops and not subject to any other authority except that of the Pope himself.[1] The monks never left the cloister and aimed at attracting men by a way of life dedicated to personal holiness and complete service to God. Cluny began something new. Slowly, the abbey found itself being called upon to reform and even to establish other monasteries that began to affiliate themselves with the motherhouse of Cluny. Soon, there were thousands of monks living in different monasteries and priories all over continental Europe, all of them subject to one single common superior, the Abbot of Cluny.

A source of blessing for the Cluniac Reform was the fact that its first abbots were outstanding holy and learned men who lived very long lives. While there were forty-eight Popes in the two hundred and fifty years following the foundation of Cluny, the abbey had only eight abbots[2] during the same period! Within one

---

[1] This privilege came to be known as *religious exemption* and is still enjoyed by numerous religious communities to this day.

[2] The eight Abbots of Cluny between 909 and 1156 were: St. Berno (909-927), St. Odo (927-942), Aylward (942-965), St. Mayeul (965-994), St. Odilo (994-1049), St. Hugh (1049-1109), Pons (1109-1122), and St. Peter the Venerable (1122-1156).

hundred years of its foundation, Cluny became not only a symbol and source of Church reform, but also a universal counselor for Popes and secular rulers alike.

(b) Besides Cluny, there were other Benedictine reforms, mainly in Flanders, Germany and France. During this time there was also a new monastic reform movement led by the nobleman, St. Romauld (c. 950-1027) from Ravenna. St. Romauld, as a young man, had been shocked by his father's cruelty. As a result, he left home and became a monk at the Venetian Abbey of St. Apollinare in Classe. Within three years, he was living as a hermit on one of the Venetian islands and subsequently traveled to Spain, where he continued to live as a hermit. Emperor Otto III, in 998, persuaded him to become the abbot of St. Apollinare in Classe, but because he was very dissatisfied with the lifestyle at his abbey, he resigned his office in 999 and resumed a hermit's life. He founded the eremitical Order of Camaldoli in Italy in 1012.

There were foundations of other eremitical communities, such as the Carthusians who were founded in 1084 by St. Bruno of Cologne (c. 1031-1101) as a strictly contemplative order for both men and women. St. Bruno personally established its first foundation, the Grande Chartreuse, north of Grenoble, in 1084. The hermits' lifestyle reflected that of the early Fathers of the Desert. All of these monastic reforms were encouraged and supported by the contemporary reigning Popes. But it was Cluny that flourished the most.

27. Attempted Reform in the Papacy

The saintly Emperor Henry II (1002-1024) succeeded Emperor Otto III. He collaborated very well with Pope Benedict VIII (1012-1024) in matters pertaining to Church reform. Both men died the same year, in 1024, and both of their successors were immoral rulers: Emperor Conrad II (1024-1039) and Pope John XIX (1024-1032), Benedict's brother. Soon there was utter confusion in the supreme leadership of the Church. John XIX died in 1032 and was succeeded by his very corrupt nephew, Pope Benedict IX (1032-1045), who, having been invalidly deposed in 1044, sold the papal office to Pope Gregory VI (1045-1046), and then resigned. Some time later Benedict IX resurfaced and tried to reinstate himself as Pope. Meanwhile, there was another claimant to the papacy, Sylvester III. He had been invalidly elected Pope in 1045, after the dethronement of Benedict IX in 1044. There was utter confusion in Christian Western Europe as to who was the true successor to the Chair of Peter. Emperor Henry III (1038-1056) tried to clarify the situation by another imperial interference. Initially, he sided with the retired Pope Benedict[3] and marched on Rome in 1046. The emperor then called the Council of Sutri, deposed all three Popes, and nominated his own invalid appointee, a German bishop who took the name of Clement II (1046-1047). The emperor had hardly returned to Germany when the former Benedict IX reappeared on the scene and reestablished himself as Pope. Then Clement II died in 1047 from poisoning. The emperor was able to intervene again a year later, in 1048, and had another German elected, Pope Damasus II, who lived for only three weeks. Shortly afterwards Benedict IX disappeared. Another conclave was called in 1049 and the emperor nominated another German bishop, Bruno of Alsace (1002-1054). He took the name of Pope Leo IX (1049-1054). The election of Pope St. Leo IX was canonically valid. His pontificate began a new era for Church reform.

28. Free Papal Elections

(a) Pope St. Leo IX brought to Rome a huge number of reformers who were ready to deal with the issue of simony, clerical scandalous living, and the abusive right of laymen to appoint men to Church offices. The reformers, however, were not of one mind as to the

---

[3] Pope Benedict IX's resignation was canonically valid. Thus, his claim to the papacy in 1046 had no canonical foundation.

means that should be used to bring about reform. This was especially evident when reform touched the role that princes and the emperor had regarding the internal policies of the Church. One party, which had the support of the Pope, wanted the old tradition of Charlemagne to continue and, thus, to have the emperor nominate Popes, bishops and abbots. Another party thought that one of the major roots of the evil of abuses in the Church was the royal and imperial interference in such appointments. They argued that nominations to such Church offices should be restored to the local clergy, and that monks should elect their own abbots. Pushing aside these differences, Pope St. Leo IX began a Church reform process by touring Europe, holding local Councils in many places, preaching reform, deposing decadent bishops, and punishing simony and clerics involved in scandalous living. St. Leo IX died defending southern Italy against the Normans in 1054.

Another German bishop, Pope Victor II (1055-1057), was nominated by the emperor. He was the last Pope to be nominated by Emperor Henry III and any of his successors. Emperor Henry III died in 1056 and was succeeded by his son, Emperor Henry IV (1056-1106), a child six years of age. Pope Victor II died in 1057 and the reformers availed of their chance to have the Roman clergy elect a new Pope. They elected Pope Stephen X (1057-1058). Though the new Pope was also German, it was the first time in many centuries that the Roman clergy was able to freely elect the Bishop of Rome.

(b) Pope Stephen X died within a year after his election. The Roman nobility returned to its old corrupt ways and appointed Benedict X.[4] The Roman clergy and the imperial court refused to recognize Benedict X, and a new Pope was elected, Nicholas II (1059-1061). Although the reign of Pope Nicholas II, a Frenchman, was only for about two years, it proved to be crucial to papal elections. He called a Council in Rome in 1059 and passed the law that henceforth only Cardinals could elect validly a Pope. The Council also established an alliance with the Normans, shutting out the

---

[4]   The election was canonically invalid and Benedict X was in fact an antipope.

Holy Roman Emperor from papal elections and assuring Rome's protection against the emperor were he to attempt to interfere with future papal elections.

---

29. Clashes between Popes and German Emperors

The reform movement was gaining lots of enemies from deposed bishops, immoral bishops who were about to be deposed, and the dissatisfied Roman nobility and imperial court who were effectively shut out of papal elections. Matters came to a head in 1061 when the Cardinals elected an Italian, Pope Alexander II (1061-1073). The imperial court elected its own antipope and sent an army to invade Italy and install its candidate. It took three years for Pope Alexander II to end the schism. By the time he died in 1073, Church reform was well established.

(a) The greatest reformer of the Middle Ages succeeded Pope Alexander II. He was the Benedictine monk Cardinal Hildebrand, who took the name of Gregory VII (1073-1085). He had been associated with every legitimate Pope since the time of Pope Gregory VI who had made him his secretary. Pope St. Gregory VII knew exactly what the fundamental issues in Christian Europe were. He had a great determination to settle them. He believed that only the Papacy could save the Church. Therefore, he restored clerical scholarship, insisted on freedom of episcopal elections, prohibited *Lay Investiture*,[5] rooted out simony, and insisted on clerical celibacy. He always wanted to cooperate with the emperor, but not at the cost of having the Church subject to secular authority. When Emperor Henry IV (1056-1106) ignored the papal decree against

---

[5] The technical title for the custom or law that empowered lay authorities to make appointments for church offices. The *Lay Investiture Controversy* is the title given to the struggle between the papacy and diverse European emperors and kings where the Church did its best to free itself from the interference of civil authorities in the appointments to Church office. The struggle went on for a number of centuries.

lay investiture, St. Gregory VII excommunicated him in 1076, and did something new: he deposed the emperor and absolved all of his subjects from their allegiance to him. St. Gregory VII put into action the theory of Pope St. Gelasius I that had been expressed previously by St. Ambrose. The emperor initially resisted, but he had to capitulate because he ended up being completely isolated, even by his own bishops, and was faced with a revolt in his empire. The emperor was forced to make his personal submission to the Pope at Canossa on 28th January 1077. The Pope absolved the emperor and reinstated him in his imperial office. But the revolt in Germany continued and the rebellious nobility elected Duke Rudolf of Swabia as the new emperor in March 1077. Civil war was inevitable. The Pope remained neutral. When Emperor Henry IV returned to his old practice of appointing bishops, the Pope excommunicated him again and recognized as emperor the rival Duke Rudolf.[6] This time, however, the German bishops sided with Emperor Henry IV. They declared the Pope deposed in June 1080 and Henry IV appointed his own antipope, Clement III, that same month. Soon thereafter, on 15th October 1080, Henry IV defeated and slew in battle Emperor Rudolf. He invaded Italy in March 1081 and headed for the Papal States with the singular intention to capture and punish Pope St. Gregory VII. Those bishops and clergy who were discontented with the papal reform program welcomed the emperor and his antipope. But the people of Rome rallied to St. Gregory VII's defense during 1081 and 1082. He fled to Castel Sant'Angelo as the invading German army approached the city. Rome surrendered in March 1084, after a very long siege. The emperor installed his antipope in Rome almost immediately. Count Roger Guiscand (c. 1015-1085) led the Normans, the emperor's antagonists, who came to St. Gregory VII's rescue two months later, in May 1084. The emperor withdrew just in time for the Normans to sack Rome. When they retreated, they took with them St. Gregory VII. The Pope died on 25th May 1085 in Salerno as a semi-prisoner of his own allies.

---

6   The Pope declared Emperor Henry IV deposed on 7th March 1080.

(b) After the departure of the Normans, the antipope Clement III returned to Rome, while the faithful Cardinals were scattered. The Holy See remained vacant for almost three years, except for a very short time in 1087 with the canonical election of Pope Blessed Victor III, who lived only for a few months. Many came to believe, and some were very happy to do so, that the reform movement in the Church was dead. But, thanks to St. Peter Damian (1007-1072),[7] the reform movement had taken deeper roots than they thought. On 12ᵗʰ March 1088, the Cardinals were able to elect the French Abbot of Cluny, Odo, who took the name of Urban II (1088-1099). The new Pope continued the reform within the Church. Like Pope St. Leo IX before him, Pope Blessed Urban II summoned local Councils in Italy and France, and personally presided over them. The most famous of these was the Council of Clermont of November 1095 when the First Crusade was called. Meanwhile, the ordinary people had come to understand and accept the Pope's determination to reform the Church. The laity, united with faithful clergy, began to expel simoniac bishops and married priests. The Pope had achieved popularity among his faithful, and this would pay off during the struggle between Emperor Frederick Barbarossa (1152-1190) and Pope Alexander III (1159-1181) for the liberty of the Church.

(c) The weak Pope Paschal II (1099-1118), who almost wrecked the papal advancements in the victory over lay investiture, succeeded Pope Blessed Urban II. He was succeeded briefly by Pope Gelasius II (1118-1119). He, in turn, was succeeded by the Frenchman, Pope Calixtus II (1119-1124). It was this Pope who settled, once and for all, the issue of lay investiture through the Concordat of Worms in 1122. The German imperial electors had met in Wurzburg the year before, in 1121, to work out a compromise between Pope Calixtus II and Emperor Henry V. In the Concordat of Worms, the Pope dealt directly with the emperor. The Con-

---

[7] St. Peter Damian was declared a "Doctor of the Church" by Pope Leo XII on 27ᵗʰ September 1828.

cordat[8] stated that henceforth all elections to all Church offices would be freely made by the proper ecclesiastical authority, that before new bishops were ordained and new abbots were installed, that they were to take the oath of homage to the emperor for the temporalities they held for him, and that they were to be invested with these by the touch of the imperial scepter. The emperor was not to invest a bishop or an abbot with either crosier or ring for these ceremonies related to spiritual matters. This compromise meant that the emperor could still exercise great influence during the nomination process of bishops, but the Pope gained much more ground in this struggle. There was a new kind of relationship between the one who upheld the cross and the one who upheld the scepter. Pope St. Gregory VII's dream began to materialize.

There was also a new kind of papacy symbolized by the right of the Pope to wear the imperial insignia, including the tiara, a conical shaped head cover with a crown surrounding it.[9] The Pope had become, in fact, a great temporal ruler who would influence the life of Europe for succeeding centuries.

---

30. Emergence of the Supremacy of the Roman See

The Popes of the modern era still make the same claim that Popes had made centuries ago, namely, that the See of Rome is not the first among equals but has real primacy over every diocese in the universal Church.

(a) The official claim to supremacy by the See of Rome can be traced back to the fourth century. In practice, however, the See of Rome has had a very unique and special place in Christendom from the early years of the Church. For example, Pope St. Clement I had intervened in the inner affairs of the Church in Corinth

---

[8] A Concordat is an international treaty, with the force of law, between the Holy See and a specific secular power, usually a country.

[9] Pope Innocent II (1130-1143) changed the one crown to two, and Pope Boniface VIII (1294-1303) changed them to three crowns.

and St. Ignatius of Antioch had stated that the See of the Apostles Peter and Paul, that is Rome, was to be given a special place of reverence among all the Christian Churches. St. Irenaeus made a similar statement in 185. The dates and the persons who made these affirmations are important in themselves because they indicate that from the end of the first century, the Church of Rome did in fact, on some occasions, intervene in the inner life of other Catholic Churches. While there might be some allegation that St. Clement had a personal interest to intervene, because he was the Bishop of Rome, it should be borne in mind that St. Ignatius was the immediate successor of St. Peter as Bishop of Antioch, the Church that Peter founded before he went to Rome. Although the Church of Antioch was older in establishment than the Church of Rome, and thus one would expect some claim for special recognition of Antioch, St. Ignatius pointed to Rome as the Church that occupied a very unique position among all of the Churches. On the other hand, St. Irenaeus' statement regarding the special role of the Church in Rome was devoid of all self interest because he was Bishop of Lyons, a diocese physically far removed from Rome.

(b) The institutional structure of the Church followed the Roman imperial administration model. By the end of the third century, the union among all the Christian Churches was founded on the principle of subsidiarity among bishops. This was based on the different levels of autonomy and authority, beginning at the level of the local churches, moving upward to the level of metropolitan and then to the primatial sees, with Rome occupying a very special place at the top. The bishops in different Roman imperial provinces usually met in synods or Councils to exercise their collegial responsibility to regulate the inner life of their Churches and establish new dioceses and even new ecclesiastical provinces. This administrative method explains why, for example, the Church in Roman Africa frequently tried to affirm its jurisdictional independence from the See of Rome. Nevertheless, by the end of the third century, it was evident that the diverse Christian Churches, in matters of grave doctrinal importance, always consulted Rome and sought some kind of ratification for their decisions, such as the re-baptism of the *lapsi* in Roman Africa. This did not mean that there was no tension between the Church of Rome and some local Churches.

(c) Once the Christian Church was emancipated by Constantine the Great, the structural development within the Catholic Church took on a more rapid pace because the Catholic Faith could be practiced without any fear of civil persecution. The bishops were soon given civil recognition of their decisions. When St. Leo the Great became Pope in 440, he gave a very definite theoretical form to the centralization system within the Church. The Church was perceived as a pyramid that had at its bottom all Catholic believers, and moved upward by including priests, bishops, archbishops, primatial sees and patriarchates. The chain of authority culminated in the See of Rome. This concept was at odds with the conciliar approach of the Roman African and Eastern Churches. The latter Churches would resist Rome's hierarchical approach for many centuries.

As time went by, successive Popes were so successful in concentrating Church authority in the See of Rome that the ancient concept of collegiality and the idea of unity in plurality were lost and were not to be recovered until Council Vatican II (1962-1965). In time, the entire Catholic Church came to be identified with the See of Rome. Eventually, in Western Europe this identity would have, as normative, the Roman liturgical and disciplinary customs.

(d) There were many secular, political, social and religious reasons that assisted the Popes to establish the supremacy of Rome in the Catholic Church. The Eastern Roman Empire was collapsing; the civil power of the Byzantine emperor faded away; the Roman African Church, which frequently resisted Rome, was lost first to the Arian and than to the Moslem faiths; appeals to papal intervention began to be made by bishops in trouble or in conflict with local Church or civil authorities; the Christian faithful, at different times, called upon Popes[10] to deal and rescue them from

---

[10] This is especially true in the case of Pope St. Leo the Great and Pope St. Gregory the Great.

the barbarian invaders, and, in turn, the laity perceived the Pope as the chief political authority throughout Italy; Popes sent missionaries in Western Europe to establish the Faith in pagan lands and to erect dioceses under the primacy of the See of Rome.

A further development of the centralization of the See of Rome took place through the reorganization of the Western Church under Charlemagne. The new wave of converted peoples and the ecclesiastical reform under Charlemagne, saw the papal establishment of new ecclesiastical provinces and the restoration of old ones. As a symbol of the new reorganization, Popes began to confer the *pallium* to metropolitans as a visible sign that the new metropolitan was in union with Rome.

(e) The development of the Roman Primacy in the Catholic Church was not smooth, by any means. It was interrupted by a number of events, such as the disintegration of empires and of society; corruption within the papacy itself; and the control over the papacy by diverse, very powerful noble families. A number of Popes, nevertheless, stand out as having been very instrumental in the establishment of the absolute supremacy of the See of Rome throughout the Catholic Church.

Pope St. Nicholas I, in the ninth century, made great efforts to establish absolute papal control in the Church. For example, he deposed the archbishops of Cologne and Trier for resisting papal authority. He also forced the most powerful contemporary archbishop, Hincmar of Rheims (c. 806-882), to yield to the right of a bishop to appeal to the Pope. Pope St. Leo IX revived papal supremacy and leadership in the middle of the eleventh century by beginning a process of reformation within the Church. He traveled all over Western Europe, convened and presided over many local Councils, insisted on the independence of the Church from civil powers, and stopped episcopal and clerical abuses. He reorganized the Roman Curia and brought to it some of the brightest and most faithful minds of the day. He also laid the foundation for free papal elections by Cardinals alone, thus giving the Church complete control over the elections of its supreme bishop. This Pope set the stage for the appearance of Pope St. Gregory VII in 1073.

Pope St. Gregory VII established papal supremacy over the emperor and practiced it within the entire Catholic Church. He affirmed that no one had the power to judge the Pope; that the Pope had the right to depose and restore bishops; that the Pope alone could pass new Church law and call a General Council; that the Pope alone could set up new dioceses and divide old ones; that the Pope was the final court of appeals in the entire Catholic Church; and that papal legates had precedence over all other bishops. The supremacy of the Roman See, though it would still be challenged in succeeding centuries, was established once and for all under this Pope. This state of affairs required the rapid development of administrative and judicial machinery in Rome to meet the Pope's vast responsibilities in governing the Catholic Church. The Popes and their administrative assistants became the busiest people in Western Europe, for papal intervention reached down to the lowest person in Western society. This administrative machinery did not only involve the Pope's supremacy in spiritual matters, but it encompassed the Pope's role as the sovereign of the Papal States. The effects of the supremacy of the See of Rome were numerous and frequently advantageous, but not without wrinkles.

(f) One other area where Popes had to establish the supremacy of the See of Rome in Church matters was *Lay Investiture,* that entailed a lay person, be he an emperor or a king or a powerful nobleman, would nominate his own man for the episcopacy or some other important Church office. The Popes did not originally claim the exclusive right to name bishops. Rather, they fought to reestablish the ancient custom that the local clergy had the right to nominate their bishop. It can be stated that by the twelfth century the custom of the local clergy electing their own bishop was restored through most of Western Europe. Unfortunately, however, a lot of episcopal elections ended in dispute or controversy. It was not unusual in such instances that the Bishop of Rome was requested to step in and act as arbiter. The process turned out to be very complicated. Many dioceses were left vacant or had two concurrent contesting bishops for a considerable amount of time due to drawn-out quarrels between electors. The Pope found himself attempting to persuade the parties to compromise on a candidate or he finally had to settle the matter by appointing his own candidate as bishop. The situation became so commonplace that, by the fourteenth century, the Pope reserved exclusively to himself the right of the appointment of all bishops. The big drawback with such a system was that often the Pope needed the assistance of civil authorities to install a papal appointee. This, in turn, led to the privilege that different Popes bestowed on different monarchs to propose a list of candidates from which the Pope would choose one as the new bishop.[11]

The strong Popes of the twelfth century devoted themselves to the spiritual supervision of Christendom. When Popes clashed with secular rulers during this time, Popes usually, but not always, came out victorious. Thus, Pope Alexander III was victorious against Emperor Frederick Barbarossa, one of the most able emperors since Charlemagne, and against King Henry II of England in the matter of the murder of St. Thomas Becket, archbishop of Canterbury, which took place on 29th December 1170. On the other hand, Pope Innocent III chose Otto IV (1198-1212) as emperor, who soon thereafter betrayed him. Consequently, the Pope declared Otto deposed and chose Frederick II (1212-1250) as emperor in his stead. The same Pope was victorious against King John of England (1199-1216), forced the king to his knees in 1213, and secured papal appointment of bishops in England. Pope Innocent III won also the struggle with King Philip Augustus of France (1180-1223) in the royal divorce case. The Pope forced the king to restore his rightful Queen Ingeborg (1175-1236) to her royal position. It was this Pope who, for the first time in the history of the Church, promulgated Canon Law to have the force of universal law within the Church.

---

[11] These privileges were listed in Concordats or treaties or accords or accommodations, all with the force of international law, between Popes and specific secular rulers.

Division in Christendom

The Orthodox Churches eventually would end up paying a very heavy price due to the misfortune of a divided Christendom and devious personal interests. Some four and one half centuries after the final major break between Rome and Constantinople, lands which adhered to the Orthodox Faith in Eastern Europe fell to Moslem invaders. If there had been a united Christendom and mutual trust between West and East, the history of the Byzantines, the Crusades and the Ottoman Moslems might have been quite different. There had been tension between Latin-speaking and Greek-speaking Catholics for centuries. By the passage of time, obedience to Rome by the East was first weakened, then challenged and, finally, eliminated.

31. Iconoclasm

(a) The first serious clash between a Pope and a Byzantine emperor during the eighth century was the result of religious and secular reforms introduced by Emperor Leo III about 725. He considered himself supreme not only over his Empire but also over Church matters, because he had successfully defended the Byzantine Empire and Church against Islam in 717. Leo's most striking legislative reforms, however, dealt with religious matters, especially iconoclasm. He forced all Jews and Montanists, in 722, in the empire to be baptized (722), he issued a series of edicts against the worship of images beginning in 726. The emperor decreed that no images of saints should be venerated. Thus, he ordered every church to destroy them. It was the beginning of the heresy of *Iconoclasm*. The emperor's edicts found strong resistance from both Byzantine clergy and laity alike. He dealt with dissidents by their deposition from Church offices, imprisonment, and, in some instances, execution. The majority of theologians and all the Byzantine monks opposed the edict. The western lands of the Byzantine Empire simply refused to obey the edicts.

Pope St. Gregory II (715-731) strongly condemned Emperor Leo III's policy and threatened him by asking for the assistance of barbarian Lombards. The emperor, in response, sent his army in an attempt to capture the Pope. But a storm destroyed the Byzantine fleet before the army, which it carried, could execute the imperial orders. Emperor Leo III was succeeded by his son, Constantine V (741-775). The new emperor proved to be a first class iconoclast and persecuted everyone who did not agree with his designs. The Church in the East was in great turmoil.

(b) The first imperial move to restore the veneration of images came when Empress Irene[1] became regent for the infant Emperor Constantine VI in 780. The imperial restoration of the veneration of images was formalized at the *Seventh Ecumenical Council*[2] in 787. Pope Adrian I (772-795) sent a letter with his legates to the Council containing the authentic Catholic teaching on the subject matter. Nevertheless, the heresy managed to survive. The imperial army, being comprised mostly of iconoclasts, staged a successful revolt and managed to hold on to Iconoclasm for the next twenty years. It took Empress Theodora[3] and Patriarch Methodius of Constantinople (843-847) to finally reestablish the Catholic veneration of sacred images and have it accepted by the people, as well as by the army. This brought healing to a very serious division that existed

---

[1] Irene was born in 752 and died in 803. She became Regent in 780 and reigned as Empress from 797 to 802.

[2] This Ecumenical Council was called Nicaea II.

[3] Empress Theodora was regent for her infant son Emperor Michael III from 842 until 855. She died as a nun in 867.

between the Eastern bishops and Rome for most of the previous one hundred and thirty years.

---

32. The Photian Schism

(a) When Patriarch Methodius died in 847, he was succeeded by one of the sons of Emperor Michael I (811-813). The new Patriarch of Constantinople, Ignatius,[4] ran into political difficulties. He resigned and was succeeded, through compromise, by Photius (c. 815-897), a great scholar who was still a layman at the time of his appointment as Patriarch. The compromise proved to be unsuccessful. Before long, the Ignatian faction began speaking about electing a new Patriarch. The Eastern Church became split into two major partisan factions. Finally, Pope St. Nicholas I intervened and sent two legates to the local Council of Constantinople, held in 861, which was primarily assembled to settle the dispute. The papal legates sided with Patriarch Photius and the imperial government solemnly condemned Patriarch Ignatius. The Pope, still in Rome and having been persuaded by the Ignatian faction, disavowed his legates and declared for Patriarch Ignatius. There were two other factors that played an important part in the Pope's decision. First, there was the issue of restoring jurisdiction to the Pope in his capacity as the Patriarch of the West. The issue involved jurisdiction over the churches of the region of Illyricum that, since the days of Pope St. Leo III, had been usurped by the Patriarch of Constantinople. Second, there was the delicate issue of whether the Latin or the Byzantine missionaries should evangelize Bulgaria. Pope St. Nicholas I hoped that by supporting Ignatius, Rome would get its way.

---

[4] Patriarch Ignatius of Constantinople had a tempestuous career. He was deposed as Patriarch in 855, imprisoned in 861, released in 863, was one of two concurrent Patriarchs between 863 and 867, and reinstated as sole Patriarch in 867. He remained Patriarch until his death in 877.

The results of the local Council of Constantinople were that Patriarch Ignatius was held prisoner for the next two years and that Patriarch Photius published a series of anti-Roman writings and created a schism. Once again, Constantinople had two concurrent patriarchs. The Pope supported Patriarch Ignatius and the emperor supported Patriarch Photius.

The importance of the Photian schism laid in the fact that for the first time the Byzantine Church made a formal charge against Rome for tolerating the addition of the *Filioque* in the Nicene Creed. The term had been inserted by the West to describe the procession of *the Holy Spirit from the Father and from the Son*. The Byzantines stated that *the Holy Spirit proceeded from the Father through the Son*. Patriarch Photius, and centuries later the Orthodox Churches, objected to its insertion into the Nicene Creed and to the doctrine it implied.

(b) The Byzantine Emperor Michael III (840-867) was murdered in 867. His murderer succeeded him as Emperor Basil I (867-886). Patriarch Photius was forced to resign his patriarchal office and Patriarch Ignatius was restored in his stead. Pope Nicholas I died the same year that Emperor Michael III was assassinated. The new Pope, Adrian II (867-872), was requested to send two papal legates for the new General Council, held in 869.[5] The Council confirmed the restoration of Patriarch Ignatius and from that time on Patriarch Ignatius and Patriarch Photius lived in peace. Ironically, Patriarch Ignatius exhibited anti-Roman sentiments, refused to give up the jurisdiction over Illyricum, and sent Byzantine missionaries to Bulgaria. The new Pope, John VIII (872-882), reacted adversely and only the timely death of Patriarch Ignatius in 877 saved him from being excommunicated.

Photius became sole Patriarch again in 877. He immediately petitioned that a Council be convened to evaluate whether his original election and consecration in 858 and the decisions of the local Council of 861 were correct. Pope John VIII agreed to the proposal

---

[5]   This Ecumenical Council was called Constantinople IV.

and sent two legates. The new Council, assembled from 879 to 880, determined that the proceedings of the Council of 861 were not correct. The Pope ratified the decision. Patriarch Photius spent the rest of his life in communion with Rome. However, Emperor Leo VI (886-912) deposed him as Patriarch and installed his imperial son, Stephen I (886-893), as the new Patriarch.

33. The Great Schism

Some one hundred and fifty years after the death of Patriarch Photius, doctrinal dissent in the East rose again. This time it was due to the personal ambitions of the Patriarch of Constantinople, Michael Cerularius (1000-1059), and to the ignorance of the papal legates.[6]

Patriarch Michael Cerularius had begun a sudden campaign against Rome in 1053. In order to justify the closing of the Latin churches in Constantinople, he revived the old Photian accusation regarding the *Filioque*. The papal legates, who had been sent to Constantinople to settle the question once and for all, reacted by excommunicating the Patriarch, in the name of the Pope, on 16th July 1054. The entire Byzantine Church went into schism when Patriarch Michael Cerularius excommunicated the papal legates in retaliation to his own excommunication. But the excommunications of both the Patriarch and the papal legates were interpreted as the mutual excommunication of the Eastern and Western Churches. The tragedy was further complicated by the fact that, unbeknown to all parties involved, the papal legates did not have the authority to excommunicate anyone, because at the time the papacy was vacant due to the death of Pope St. Leo IX that took place three months earlier. The schism brought a definite and permanent

---

[6] The papal legates were Humbert of Mourmoutiers, a French Cardinal and Benedictine oblate, sent as the head of a legatine mission with Frederick of Lorraine, later Pope Stephen IX, and Peter, archbishop of Amalfi, to Constantinople.

rupture in the Church by the time the Crusades were under way. The Latins and the Byzantines would nurture mutual hostility and contempt for succeeding centuries. Then came the fatal sacking of Constantinople and the desecration of Hagia Sophia by the Crusaders in 1204 and the establishment of a Latin emperor and a Latin Patriarch in Constantinople. From that year onwards, to be an anti-Latin meant to be a Byzantine patriot. In fact, the reunions between East and West, made at the Council Lyons I, in 1274, and at the Council of Florence, in 1438, were short lived.

The Great Schism still exists today as an open wound in Christendom, although there have been many attempts since Council Vatican II to come to some kind of healing and understanding between the two great Churches.

Constantinople fell to the Ottoman Turks, who were Moslems, in 1453. It continues to exist under secular Moslem rule to this day. The Moslem authorities changed the name of the city from Constantinople to that of Istanbul. The Ottoman Empire disintegrated after World War I (1914-1919). The new Republic of Turkey was carved out of the old Ottoman Empire and recognized as an independent country in 1923. The headquarters of the Orthodox Patriarch is located in Istanbul.

The mutual excommunication was lifted in 1965. The Roman Catholic-Orthodox Joint Declaration of 1965 was read out on 7th December 1965, during a simultaneous public meeting of Vatican Council II in Rome and at a special ceremony in Istanbul (Constantinople). The joint Declaration withdrew the exchange of excommunications of 1054. However, the Declaration did not end the Great Schism, but rather showed a desire for greater reconciliation between the two churches represented at the time by Pope Paul VI (1963-1978) and Ecumenical Patriarch Athenagoras I (1948-1973).

The Issue of War

34. Western and Eastern Theories of War

The barbarian invasions of the West and the lifestyle inherent in the feudal system made war a fact of life throughout the Middle Ages. The medieval Popes aspired to control Western civilization. It meant they had to find a compromise between the demands of the Gospel and the issue of war. The Gospel unequivocally required forgiveness and love of the enemy.[1] On the other hand, successive Popes were faced with constant discord in and among Christian nations, including wars involving the Papal States, and the ongoing deadly threats to Christendom from the followers of Islam.

There was a very clear-cut contrast between the way Eastern and Western Christendom evaluated the topic of war. The position of the Byzantine Churches was consistently against war, except for St. Athanasius of Alexandria who had taught that it was lawful, and perhaps meritorious, to kill one's enemies during war. The Latin Church, however, has had a very inconsistent attitude toward war down the centuries. Despite the established Augustinian theory of a just war, there was always a strong peace movement in the Medieval Latin Church. Those medieval clerics who were magnates, however, engaged in wars as frequently and with similar zest as their secular counterparts. There were instances when even Popes

---

[1]   See, for example, Matthew 5:44, 6:15; Mark 11:26; and Luke 6:27, 35.

had to lead armies into war in order to defend papal territories. It was reasoned that war in the service of the Church and the Papal States was permissible.

35. The Peace and Truce of God

(a) The bishops of France were the first to lead a peace movement amid the anarchy of feudalism. The bishops of Aquitaine initiated it at the Synod of Charroux, assembled in 989, and proposed the *Peace of God*. The edict dealt with the Church's perpetual protection of consecrated persons, who were clerics, monks, virgins and cloistered widows; of consecrated places, which were churches, monasteries, and cemeteries, with their dependencies; and of consecrated times, which were Sundays and ferial days. Violators were to be excommunicated. The Church's protection, bestowed through the Peace of God, was later extended to include the poor, pilgrims, crusaders and even merchants on a journey. The clear object of this approach was to control medieval violence and to curtail bloodshed.

(b) On the other hand, the Church of the eleventh century inspired the *Truce of God*. While the Peace of God was perpetual, the Truce of God involved a temporary suspension of the epidemic hostilities between feuding lords. The Council of Elne, held in 1027, prohibited hostilities from Saturday night until Monday morning in recognition of the sacredness of Sunday, as well as on holy days. The prohibition was subsequently extended to include Thursdays and Fridays, and the entire liturgical seasons of Advent and Lent. Ultimately, there were only eighty days left in each year that allowed for possible warfare. However, the killing of a person during a battle, waged only for secular purposes, was labeled as a grave sin. The peace movement also gave knighthood some strong religious overtones. At his consecration, the knight pledged himself not to abuse clergy, women, children, the poor, traders and peasants; not to lay waste to crops and orchards; not to fight on holy days and specified liturgical seasons and, when necessary, fight only between Tuesday afternoons and Thursday evenings.

The theologians of the twelfth century, in their attempts to justify some kind of warfare, revived St. Augustine's theory of a just war and permitted secular rulers to do battle when, even indirectly, it involved papal interests. The Crusades, violent as they were, should be examined and evaluated within this historical and religious milieu. The original pure purpose was to re-conquer the Holy Land. But, many crusaders, being made of flesh and blood and often having their own personal schemes and ambitions, also had many ulterior motives for taking up the Cross and going on a Crusade.

36. The Crusades

(a) Pope Blessed Urban II set the Crusades in motion at the Council of Clermont, held in 1095. He told the assembled knights that they should dedicate their energies to rescue the Holy Land from the Moslem infidels and that those who died in the process would be assured eternal salvation as martyrs for the Faith. Past wars against the infidel Moslem Moors carried out by the Normans,[2] the Italians, the Spaniards,[3] and the Franks, and contemporary ideological and social forces formed the backdrop of the Crusades. There were many, however, who went on a Crusade for personal gains rather than for religious reasons. Such intentions would be played out with very ominous results in the centuries that followed. For example, some of the European nobility saw the possibility of

---

[2] The Normans, under Count Roger Guiscard, defeated the Moslems in Sicily and conquered first Messina in 1061 and then Palermo in 1072.

[3] For example, during the eleventh century, the kingdoms of Aragon and Castile initiated a very successful anti-Moslem campaign to recover those parts of the Iberian Peninsula that had fallen to Islam some centuries before. The legendary El Cid (1045-1099) lived and fought during these campaigns. He captured Toledo in 1085 and Valencia in 1094.

acquiring land in the East, and the growing population in Europe made some peasants look for relocation. There were plenty of opportunists. Ultimately, the Crusades became devoid of any semblance of Christian values and some Crusades were starkly brutal and blatantly political in motive.

(b) The Crusades were a series of military expeditions from Christian Western Europe to the Eastern Mediterranean. Their original intent was to stop the harsh treatment that Christian pilgrims received in the Holy Land, and to recover and hold the Holy Land from Islam. Later, they were called to counteract the expanding power of the vast Moslem Ottoman Empire.

The First Crusade was proclaimed by Pope Blessed Urban II on 27th November 1095 with a double intent, namely, to relieve the pressure that the Byzantine Empire was experiencing from the Seljuk Turks and to secure free access to Jerusalem for Christian pilgrims. A major part of Syria fell to the Crusaders in 1098. Jerusalem was captured in 1099. The Frank nobleman Godfrey of Bouillon (c. 1060-1100) was appointed thereupon as custodian of the Holy Sepulcher and this saw the establishment of the Latin Kingdom of Jerusalem (1099-1291). After his death in 1100, his brother Baldwin became the Latin King of Jerusalem (1100-1118). There followed some twenty years of Western expansionism in the Middle East. In the meantime, the Moslems began to regroup and grow in strength. Gradually, the Latin Kingdom of Jerusalem became surrounded by all kinds of military pressure as a result of the growing power of militant Moslems and the fall of Edessa to them in 1144.

Western Europe became alarmed and the Second Crusade (1145-1149) was proclaimed in 1147. St. Bernard of Clairvaux (1090-1153)[4] preached this Crusade. King Louis VII of France (1123-1170) and Holy Roman Emperor Conrad III (1137-1152) led it. It resulted in complete failure. Then, in 1187, Prince Saladin of Damascus (1170-1193) led his Moslem forces into victory at

---

[4] St. Bernard was declared a "Doctor of the Church" by Pope Pius VIII on 20th August 1830.

Hittim, capturing Jerusalem and the surrounding territory. These victories provoked the calling of the Third Crusade (1189-1192). Emperor Frederick Barbarossa, King Richard the Lionheart of England (1189-1199), and King Philip II of France (1180-1223) led it. Although the Crusaders recovered some territory that had been lost to Saladin, mostly through the bravery of Richard the Lionheart, Jerusalem was not retaken.

The Fourth Crusade, which took place between 1202 to 1204, was a disaster from the start and ended with the sacking of Constantinople and the short establishment of a Latin Kingdom there (1204-1261). Although there was a temporary reunion of the Catholic and Orthodox Churches under Pope Innocent III, the Crusade's long term adversarial effects were to deepen the Greeks' bitterness against Rome and to weaken the Byzantine power against future Moslem assaults.

Subsequent Crusades attempted to maintain the Frankish hold on Syria and to regain the Holy Land. Emperor Frederick II led the sixth Crusade in 1228, signed a treaty with the Sultan of Egypt in 1129, and managed to crown himself King of Jerusalem that same year. Jerusalem remained in Latin hands until 1244.

The two largest Crusades, during this period, were the failed fifth Crusade of 1217, and the seventh Crusade of 1248 led by St. Louis IX of France (1241-1270) which brought about the conquest of Egypt in 1249. Both Crusades ended disastrously. The first of these two Crusades did not ameliorate the preexisting conditions for Christians in the Holy Land and ended in defeat, while the second one saw St. Louis IX being taken prisoner by the Saracens in 1250. The saintly king led his second and last Crusade in 1270, but caught dysentery after he landed in Tunis and died there shortly thereafter. What was left of the Middle Eastern territories in Latin hands slowly succumbed to Islamic power by 1291.

The Western European Christian rulers organized other Crusades between 1291 and 1464. This time they were led against the rising star of the Moslem Ottoman Turks in Eastern Europe. The call for the last Crusade, made in 1464 by Pope Pius II (1458-1464), fell on deaf ears.

37. Religious Military Orders

The rise of the Military Orders was a direct result of the Crusades. Their original members were Crusaders.

(a) The Military Order of the Knights Hospitallers has been known in history under different titles. Originally they were known as the *Knights of the Order of the Hospital of St. John of Jerusalem* (c. 1099-1310), then as the *Knights Hospitallers of St. John of Jerusalem and Rhodes* (1310-1522), and finally, since 1530, they have been known with the more popular title of *Knights of Malta*.

The origins of the Order date back to around the year 1048 when the Caliph of Egypt, Abu Tamin Bonesor, gave permission to some merchants from the Republic of Amalfi to build a church, a convent and a hospital in Jerusalem to take care of any kind of pilgrims, Christians and non-Christian alike. Blessed Brother Gérard Tonque (c. 1100-1120) transformed the Knights from being a secular fraternity of noble knights into a religious fraternity of knights with vows, and added to their mission the promise of hospitality to pilgrims and Crusaders. Thus, they established themselves as a religious community of armed knights who offered protection to pilgrims in the Holy Land. He was already the community's Grand Prior by 1099. Pope Paschal II (1099-1118) approved the foundation of the Hospital on 15th February 1113 and erected it into an autonomous religious Order under the aegis of the Holy See. Blessed Brother Gérard's successor, Brother Raymond du Puy (1120-1158/60), who became the first Grand Master, furthered the Knights' mission by including the caring for sick pilgrims at St. John's hospital in Jerusalem.[5] The community was organized into two groups: the military brothers and the infirmarian brothers. The Order experienced a rapid growth throughout Europe, and shared in the successes and defeats of subsequent Crusades. After the fall of Acre in 1291, they escaped to Cyprus from where they conquered

---

[5]   For this reason they were called *hospitallers*.

the island of Rhodes in 1310. They established themselves in Rhodes under Grand Master Foulques de Villaret (1305-1319). It was during their two hundred-year stay in Rhodes that the Order took a definitive militant character, retaining a few infirmarian brother-knights to care for the sick. The Order was governed by a Grand Master, who was also the Prince of Rhodes, and the Council; minted their own coins; and maintained diplomatic relations with other States. The Order's wealth and sea power became legendary. In the early fourteenth century, the members of the Order were divided into seven groups, each according to the native language the Knights spoke. In 1492, the eighth *Langue* was established.[6]

While in Rhodes, the Knights harassed the Ottoman Turks, defeated them in war in 1480, but were in turn honorably defeated in 1522 by Sultan Suleiman the Magnificent (1520-1566). The Sultan, in recognition of the bravery of the Knights, allowed them to leave Rhodes with full honors. After wandering for seven years, Holy Roman Emperor Charles V gave them the sovereignty of the island of Malta where they established themselves in 1530 under Grand Master Philippe de Villiers de l'Isle Adam (1521-1534). They would remain on the island as its sovereign rulers for more than two hundred and fifty years.

The Knights, led by the legendary Grand Master Jean Parisot de la Vallette (1557-1568), encountered Sultan Suleiman again in battle. This time they defended Malta against his Ottoman army and navy in the Great Siege of 1565. The last time that the Knights engaged the Turks in battle was through their participation in the Battle of Lepanto in 1571. The Turks were utterly defeated and their expansion in the West was decisively stopped.

The Knights did not escape but succumbed to the full-blown decadence of the seventeenth and eighteenth centuries. Emperor Napoleon Bonaparte (1799-1814), assisted by the oppressed Mal-

---

[6] The original Langues were Provence, Auvergne, France, Italy, Aragon (Navarre), England (including Scotland and Ireland) and Germany. Eventually, Castile and Portugal split off from the Langue of Aragon and was established as the eighth Langue. Each Langue included Priories or Grand Priories, Bailiwicks and Commanderies.

tese natives, expelled the Knights from Malta in 1798. At the time, Ferdinand von Hompesch zu Bolheim (1797-1802) was the ruling Grand Master. Even though the Treaty of Amiens of 1802 reaffirmed the Knights' sovereign right in Malta, the Maltese people opted for the British monarchy as its ruler. Thus, the Knights were unable to reclaim their sovereignty over the island. Consequently, after a number of residences, the Order settled permanently in Rome in 1834, enjoying extraterritorial status.

The Knights of Malta continue to exist today as a religious community on a very small scale. They are dedicated completely to the cause of the sick. Many secular branches of the Knights of Malta have emerged, consisting of members, without vows, dedicated to charitable work.

(b) The second renowned Military Order was the *Poor Knights of Christ and of the Temple of Solomon,* more commonly called the Knights Templars. The Frenchman Hugh de Payens (c. 1070-1136), a knight of Champagne, and his eight companions founded the community in 1118, when the nine of them took a vow to protect Christian pilgrims from bandits in the Holy Land. They approached King Baldwin II of Jerusalem (1118-1131), who allowed them to set up headquarters on the southeastern side of the Temple Mount, which was believed to be the location of the ruins of the Temple of Solomon. Being a very important site not only for Jews and Christians but also for Moslems, Caliph Abd al-Malik (646-705) had built on this location a major Islamic shrine, the Dome of the Rock Mosque (*Al Aqsa)*, in the seventh century. The Crusaders turned it into a church, calling it the *Templum Domini.* The Knights took their name from this site.

Hugh went to the West in 1127 to obtain Church approbation of his small community. The Council of Troyes, held in 1128, gave him quick approval and the Order was formed. The Order had a great patron and defender in St. Bernard of Clairvaux, the leading churchman of the time, and a nephew of one of the original nine knights.

The history of the Order was a record of one controversy after another. The Templars quickly became very politically influential, numerous, wealthy, and extremely socially powerful because of their elitist membership. The Knights were fierce warriors and every one of them took a vow that he would never retreat. They were deeply involved in the Crusades. It was not only once that a Crusade failed because of some Templar Grand Master's personal ambitions and pride. There was constant tension and competition between the Templars and the Knights of St. John, once the latter established itself on a par with the Templars. The Templars were frequently at odds also with those European rulers who participated in different Crusades.

The great wealth the Order accumulated was regularly deposited in Paris and London. Thus, the Templars assumed another activity: banking. They, in effect, invented the notion of international banking.

The fall of Acre to the Moslems in 1291 forced the Templars to relocate on the island of Cyprus.[7] Soon, the Templars became an Order lacking a clear purpose or support, but still enjoying enormous financial power. This unstable situation was a major contributing factor to their eventual downfall. The Council of Lyons, held in 1274, failed in its attempt to unite the Templars and the Knights of St. John into one Order. This led to further friction between their respective members. The Templars' great wealth stood in the way and proved to be a major incentive to bring down the Order. The very greedy and cunning King Philip the Fair of France, who had made a formal treaty with the French Templars against Pope Boniface VIII (1294-1303), had set his mind on finding a means to acquire the Templars' wealth and cancel his great debts with them. He was quickly flexible in his allegiances, especially in matters relating to self interests. The opportunity arose when a renegade Templar denounced his Order to Pope Clement V (1305-1314) and charged it with homosexual activity, blasphemy and heresy. For

---

[7]   King Richard I of England sold the island of Cyprus to the Knights Templars after he conquered it in 1291.

all practical purposes, Pope Clement V, residing in Avignon, was under the complete control of the French king. King Philip saw his moment to confiscate the Order's great wealth and to abrogate his extreme financial debt to the Knights. He invited the Inquisition in France to examine the charges. Torture was used to extract confessions and many innocent Knights were executed along with those who were guilty. Although their papal trial declared the Templars to be innocent of the charges of heresy in 1308, Philip cajoled Pope Clement V and forced him to declare the Order suppressed in 1312. Its last Grand Master, Jacques de Molay (c. 1244-1314), was burnt in Paris on 18th March 1314. The wealth of the Order, except for that in Spain and Portugal, was transferred, in title, to the Knights of St. John. But, ultimately, King Philip found a way to get hold of the Templars' wealth in France.

Roman Centralization and Church Innovations

38. Papal Legates

(a) Medieval Popes were able to centralize further their leadership in the Church through two major efforts: papal legates and Church Law.[1]

The Concordat of Worms, signed by Pope Calixtus II and Holy Roman Emperor Henry V on 23rd September 1122, gave the Roman Pontiffs a limited victory in that kings and emperors could no longer control the Church through a direct appointment of bishops. The Concordat was a compromise, following a struggle that had been undertaken by several Popes for over two generations to take away the right from secular authorities to nominate bishops. The effects of this struggle were new papal initiatives in all Church matters in order to procure a stronger centralization of papal authority. Since different Popes were instruments of Church reforms and supported good bishops, the latter, in turn, made recourse to Rome to fend off the intrusion of tyrannical rulers and to resolve local problems. Such events led to the establishment of two very important means of Roman centralization: the permanent role of papal legates and a newly scientifically organized canon law.

(b) Papal legates participated in all of the local, regional and national Councils that began to be held on a very regular basis throughout Western Europe in the late Middle Ages. These legates

---

[1] Church Law is usually referred to as *Canon Law* and its laws are called *canons*.

were the personal representatives of the Pope, who vested them with plenty of authority. There were three kinds of papal legates. The papal *legates a latere* were persons deputized for important papal missions of a temporary nature. Nowadays, legates of these kinds continue to exist in the form of Cardinal legates appointed by the Pope for a specific mission or celebration as his personal representatives. The *legati nati* were prominent native archbishops or Cardinals in a given country who performed specific duties that today are confined to the third kind of papal legate, the *apostolic nuncio*. This third kind of legate was and remains a permanent diplomatic papal representative to the Catholic Church in a country and to the civil government in that same country.[2] Originally the apostolic nuncio was expected to collect papal tithes and other contributions for Rome. Eventually, he was given much jurisdiction over the local bishops. The functions of the nuncio became restricted to diplomacy since the Council of Trent (1542-1564), and his authority could no longer override completely that of the local bishops. Further definitions of the role of the nuncio were enforced through a number of successive papal decrees and pontifical norms in subsequent centuries.

---

39. Canon Law

(a) Canon Law is a body of Church laws imposed by the competent Church authority in matters of faith, morals, discipline and church legal procedures. Church law traces its roots to Apostolic times.[3] When Church Councils began to assemble, it was not unusual for the Council Fathers to settle matters of uncertainty or dispute and to issue pronouncements on faith and discipline. The weight of the decrees depended on the importance of a given Council, be it on a

---

[2]   There are some instances when more than one country has the same apostolic nuncio.

[3]   For example, see St. Paul's regulation on marriage in 1 Corinthians 5:1-5 and 7:12-16.

local or regional or national or universal level. The first Ecumenical Council to pass such canons or norms was the Council of Nicaea in 325. Many other Councils have passed canons since that time. Side by side the conciliar canons stood the legal norms issued by prominent bishops through their canonical letters to their respective dioceses. A very special weight was bestowed on canonical letters issued by the Bishops of Rome,[4] beginning with the letter Pope St. Siricus (384-399) sent to Himerius of Tarragona in 385. The letter is considered to be the most ancient decretal in Church history. Other collections of canons were ascribed to fictitious authors to give them some weight in authority.

The first attempt to systematize these canons took place under the direction of Charlemagne. The Latin Church, from that time onwards, has had trained canonists in the interpretation and application of such canonical legislation.

(b) A new authoritative system of canon law appeared in the *Decretum* of Gratian,[5] a canon law professor at the University of Bologna. The *Decretum* was not merely a systematic collection of prior Church canons formulated in Councils, canonical letters, patristic texts and papal decrees, but the work also offered a discussion whereby apparent contradictory or conflicting canons in the aforementioned documents were reconciled. The *Decretum* quickly became the text taught by Church lawyers at universities and served as an authoritative tome in the practice of the papal curia.

Gratian's *Decretum* was revolutionary. His masterpiece elevated canon law to the level of a science. For the next seven hundred years or so, the subsequent collections of canon law became a supplement to the *Decretum*.

(c) When all of the aforementioned canons were put together, they formed the principal collection of canon law.[6] It remained in force in the Latin Church until 1917 when the first universal Code

---

[4]   These papal laws were called *Decretals.*

[5]   Gratian lived during the twelfth century and died no later than 1159. Practically nothing is known of his life except that he was a Camaldolese monk and a professor of canon law in Bologna.

[6]   It is called in Latin *Corpus Iuris Canonici.*

of Canon Law[7] was promulgated by Pope Benedict XV (1854-1922)[8] for the entire Latin Church. Pope John Paul II (1920-2005)[9] promulgated a second Code of Canon Law for the Latin Church on 27th November 1983.

---

40. The Canonist Popes

There were four Popes in the Middle Ages who stood out as great canon lawyers and, as Popes, gave great value to canon law: Alexander III (1159-1181), Innocent III (1198-1216), Blessed Gregory IX (1127-1241), and Innocent IV (1243-1254). All four, during their respective pontificates, had to deal with the issue of papal supremacy and independence. They fought strenuously against the encroachments of their contemporary Holy Roman Emperors.[10]

(a) Cardinal Ronald Bandinelli was elected Pope in 1159 in the midst of a war between Emperor Frederick Barbarossa (1122-1190) and Pope Adrian IV (1154-1159) that had been initiated the previous April. The emperor wanted to make himself ruler of Rome and of the Church. Pope Adrian IV, the only Englishman to be elected Pope, resisted him and the emperor invaded Italy for a third time. Pope Adrian IV died on 1st September 1159, within five months of the initiation of war. The emperor's partisans, on 7th September 1159, elected their own antipope, Victor IV (1159-1164), creating a schism in the Church that lasted for the next seventeen years. The schism ended with the unconditional surrender of the emperor in

---

[7] It is called in Latin *Codex Iuris Canonici*.

[8] Cardinal Giacomo della Chiesa was elected Pope in 1914 and took the name of Pope Benedict XV. He died in 1922.

[9] Cardinal Karol Wojtyla, a native of Poland, was elected Pope in 1978 and took the name of Pope John Paul II. He is the first Slav to ever be elected Pope, and the first non-Italian Pope since Pope Adrian VI (1522-1523). He died on 2nd April 2005.

[10] The Holy Roman Emperors who opposed these Popes were Frederick Barbarossa (1152-1190), Henry VI (1190-1197), Frederick II (1212-1254) and Conrad III (1250-1254).

Venice in 1177. The majority of the Cardinals, despite the election of the emperor's antipope, had elected Cardinal Bandinelli as the legitimate Pope. He, too, was elected on 7th September 1159. Bandinelli took the name of Alexander III (1159-1181). He was a great reformer, a scholar, and one of Gratian's most distinguished students. The Pope spent most of his time in France during the said schism. Throughout his pontificate, he rendered an immense number of scientifically legally termed decisions in reply to appeals made to him from all over Europe. Like all of the medieval Popes, Alexander III was greatly anxious for Christians living honorably. His most serious problem was how to get his decrees obeyed. His laws were more pastoral than punitive in both word and spirit. His activity as a constructive reformer reached its climax when he summoned and presided over Council Lateran III in 1179. One of the greatest achievements of the Council concerned papal elections. A law was passed which stated that henceforth the right to elect a new Pope was exclusively restricted to Cardinals and that a two-thirds majority was needed for a valid canonical election. Another important law was that every cathedral had to establish a school for the training and education of clerics.

(b) Cardinal Lotario dei Conti di Segni, a renowned theologian and canonist, was elected Pope at age thirty-seven on 8th January 1198. Since he was still not a priest at the time of his election, he had to be ordained at once. He took the papal name of Innocent III (1198-1216). This Pope is credited with saving medieval civilization. The greatest danger that threatened civilization, at the time, was the revival of Manichaeism that had re-emerged during the prior one hundred years. It had spread from southern France to northern Italy. Its stronghold was in Provence, France, where its secular rulers patronized it.

The old heresy of Manicheism re-appeared under the names of Cathari and Albigenses. They taught that evil was matter and matter was evil, for they were one and the same thing. Along with this notion was the belief in two gods, a good god and an evil god, and the practical teaching of abstinence, that is abstinence from food and from marriage and, especially, from conception. Starvation, suicide and abortion were considered virtuous acts because they were acts that freed the spiritual from matter, that is, from evil. Free love and homosexuality, though considered bad, were less vicious than the fruitful intercourse of marriage. The Albigenses even opened schools to instruct people in their heretical faith. They developed a new anti-Christian culture, actively and militantly hostile. The Pope turned first to the Cistercians, and then to the Dominicans to give missions throughout the heretical regions. But preachers and papal legates sent to the region were systematically murdered. Finally, the Pope called for a Crusade in 1209. It resulted in the first major defeat of the Cathari and Albigenses in 1215. The political result of this Crusade, which ended in 1229, was that the King of France became established as king of both north and south France in 1229.

Two direct products of the papal defense of religion and civilization were the establishment of the Inquisition[11] and the papal recognition of the Order of Preachers. The Inquisition was a tribunal set up by the papacy and responsible to the Pope. The inquisitor traveled around the country to discover and to punish Catholics who adopted heresy. If the accused was found guilty, he or she was excommunicated. In 1252, the inquisitor was given power not only to excommunicate heretics but also to punish them by use of instrumental torture.

The Lateran Council IV, held in 1215, was the culminating event of Pope Innocent III. Heresies were condemned and doctrine, especially the doctrine of Transubstantiation of the Eucharist, was clearly defined. In addition, reform decrees were passed. There were laws on annual confession, on preaching in cathedrals, on bishops' duties as authentic Teachers of the Catholic Faith, on the foundation of schools, and on a higher standard of conduct for the clergy. Since royal and not so royal persons from all over Europe sought

---

[11] The Inquisition properly so called was established in 1233 when Pope Gregory IX entrusted it to the Dominicans and had Papal Inquisitors officially appointed. Eventually, the Inquisition would acquire an ominous connotation particularly due to the Spanish Inquisition that was controlled by King Philip II of Spain.

judicial consultations and decisions from the Pope, he contributed a vast amount of canonical decisions. Finally, he is the first Pope to call himself *Vicar of Christ*, and witnessed the zenith of Papal Monarchy.

(c) Count Ugolino of Segni was the nephew of Pope Innocent III and a Cardinal when he was elected Pope on 19th March 1227. He took the name of Gregory IX (1227-1241). He was a scholar, a canonist, and a practical diplomat. At the time of his election, he had a considerable amount of experience as a papal legate in Germany and the northern Italian city-states. He was a personal friend of St. Francis of Assisi and protector of the Franciscan Order from its early beginnings. The Franciscans drew up a more detailed rule for their communities under the inspiration of Pope Blessed Gregory IX when he was still a Cardinal.

Cardinal Ugolino was also a friend of St. Dominic and the Dominicans to whom he entrusted the Inquisition. As Pope, he commissioned the Dominican St. Raymond de Peñafort (1185-1275) to collect all papal decretals, and was the first Pope to issue an official compilation of canon law in 1234. He also directed William of Neauvais to examine the works of Aristotle. Finally, he labored unsuccessfully throughout his pontificate to bring a union between Rome and the Eastern Churches and to bring about a healing of the Great Schism.

(d) The papacy had been vacant for some eighteen months before the Cardinals, in flight at Anagni, elected Cardinal Sinibaldo Fieschi as Pope on 28th June 1243. He took the name of Pope Innocent IV (1243-1254).

The new Pope had risen to fame by being a renowned canon lawyer while he was professor at the University of Bologna, and by his commentary on the Decretals. The reason for the long papal vacancy was that Emperor Frederick II had occupied Rome and held two of the eleven Cardinals as his prisoners. Finally, through the intervention of St. Louis IX of France, the emperor released the Cardinals and the conclave to elect a new Pope was held.

Frederick II's singular resolve was to be master of the Church.

With this in mind, he invited all princes of Christendom to help him dismantle the Church's independence from the civil state. Pope Innocent IV made it very clear that he would not only resist the emperor's plan, but would try to obliterate the emperor's power. Thus, in 1245, the Pope called the Council Lyons I to deal with what he called the five wounds of the Church, namely, the corruption among the clergy and the faithful, the danger of the Moslem Saracens, the Greek Schism, the invasion of Hungary by the Tartar tribes, and the situation of Emperor Frederick II regarding his treatment of the Church. The principal achievement of the Council was the deposition and another excommunication of the emperor. The Pope followed the strategy of his predecessor, Pope Innocent III, in his dealings with the Counts of Toulouse during the Albigensian Crusade. War broke out between the papacy and the emperor, with each party experiencing successes and defeats over the next four years. Frederick II died on 13th December 1250. His son, Emperor Conrad IV (1250-1254), died four years later, leaving his baby son Conradino (1252-1268) as his successor and, ironically, naming the Pope as the child's guardian. One would think that hostilities should have ended at this point. But Conrad IV's younger half-brother, Manfred (c. 1232-1266), would hear of no peace. He went to war and delivered a great defeat to the papal armies in 1254. Pope Innocent IV died within a week. His successor, Pope Alexander IV (1254-1261) was no match for Manfred, who moved from one victory to another and divested the papacy of its influence. The next two Popes, Urban IV (1261-1265) and Clement IV (1265-1273), reorganized the Papal States and the Roman Curia and began the road for the recovery of papal influence.

Pope Urban IV had offered Charles of Anjou (1226-1285), brother of St. Louis IX of France (1215-1270), the Crown of the Two Sicilies in 1262.[12] It was at this time that Manfred's power began to disintegrate. Manfred was killed at the Battle of Benevento on 20th January 1266, and Charles of Anjou became, in fact, the

---

[12] The two Sicilian Kingdoms were comprised of the Kingdom of Naples and the Kingdom of Sicily.

King of the Two Sicilies. Unlike his saintly brother, Charles was a very cruel king who forced his new subjects to rebel against him. They called upon the sixteen-year-old Conradino to be their new ruler. Charles, with the help of the papacy, defeated decisively the young leader, whom he subsequently had beheaded publicly in Naples in 1268. The German influence over the Papal States came to an abrupt end, but from now on the Popes had to deal with a mad Frenchman.

Pope Clement IV died on 29th November 1268, and the Holy See was to remain vacant for the next three years. It was a first class calamity for the Church.

41. The Emergence of a New Religious Lifestyle

The ideal of the ancient monastic Orders was to withdraw completely from the world. However, a new type of religious lifestyle arose in the thirteenth century — the Mendicant Orders. One of the brilliant ideas of Mendicant Orders was that their members were not restricted to spending their entire life in one specific and stationary place, an abbey or monastery, as was required of monks. The mendicant's aim was to profess renunciation, chastity, poverty and obedience while staying in the world in order to convert the world. They were called friars.[13] Their communities were called Mendicant Orders because they begged for a living. It was mainly the Franciscans, Dominicans, Carmelites and Augustinians who represented this new brand of religious. They were a godsend for the Church because, at the time, vast numbers of people were moving away from the country into the cities. The Church was running the risk of lacking pastoral service and losing touch with great numbers of people who populated numerous slums outside the city walls.

---

[13] The title is taken from the Latin word *fratres*, meaning brothers.

---

42. The Franciscans

The origins of friars can be traced back to St. Francis of Assisi (c. 1181-1226). The baptismal name of Francis was John. He was the son of the wealthy cloth merchant Pietro Bernardone and his wife Pica. John helped in the family business until age twenty. He was nicknamed Francis, or the Frenchman, because of his love for French fashions and way of life. He would be called by that name for his entire life and throughout history.

Francis never hesitated to live to the fullest the life of his social status. He was gallant, high spirited, poetic, generous, and dreamt of being a brilliant soldier. With this in mind, he joined other young Assisi soldiers in the war against Perugia in 1202. But Francis was captured and held prisoner for some months. He returned home after his release and, during a subsequent serious illness, he underwent a radical spiritual conversion.[14] As a result, he dedicated himself completely to God and stripped himself totally of all his possessions. He stood barefoot and penniless in the streets. He preached repentance, proclaimed a simple message of trust and joy in God, and spoke of love for God's creation. He devoted himself exclusively to the service of the poor and lepers. Before very long, he had gathered round him a small group of like-minded disciples for whom he drew up the First Rule based on short statements from the Gospels. While visiting Rome during 1209 to 1210, Francis presented himself to Pope Innocent III and managed to procure a reluctant verbal papal approval of his community. The community took the name of the Order of Friars Minor. It increased in number and spread rapidly.

Francis' ideal was shared by St. Clare (1193-1253), a noble woman of Assisi, who accepted his charism and, along with Francis, founded a similar community for women in 1215.

---

[14] Something similar would happen to St. Ignatius of Loyola some three hundred years later.

Francis was in southern France and Spain from 1214 to 1215, hoping to convert the Moors. He intended to go on to Africa, but illness prevented him from doing so. The Order grew so much that, in 1217, it was organized into Provinces with friar ministers as provincials. Francis made a preaching tour of Eastern Europe and Egypt in 1219. During his absence in the East, the Order underwent a radical change, and its leadership was taken away from him and given to other friars. He never contested the change. His simple rule was adjusted by down-to-earth men who realized that a more practical rule had to be enacted for the Order to survive. The drawing up of this Second Rule took place in 1221 and was inspired by Cardinal Ugolino,[15] a friend of St. Francis. The rule would undergo several revisions before it was finally given papal approval by Pope Honorius III (1216-1227) in 1223.

Francis was already a blind middle-aged man when he received the gift of the Stigmata during a retreat in September 1224. He died in the chapel of the Portiuncula on 3rd October 1226 and his friend Ugolino, by then Pope Gregory IX, canonized him less than two years later.

43. The Order of Preachers (Dominicans)

The Order of Preachers, commonly known as Dominicans, was founded by St. Dominic de Guzman (c. 1170-1221), the son of the Castilian nobleman Felix Guzman and (Blessed) Joanna of Aza, in connection with his efforts to convert the Albigensian heretics. Dominic began his advanced studies at the University of Palencia at age fourteen. He sold all of his possessions, including his books, and used the proceeds to help the poor during a famine in 1191. He became a canon of his diocese of Osma in 1199, where the bishop had established a very strict discipline among his cathedral's

---

[15] He was the future Pope Gregory IX.

chapter of canons, following the Rule of St. Augustine. Dominic became the head of this community and, in 1203, he went with his bishop, Don Diego d'Azevedo, on a mission to preach against the Albigenses in Languedoc, France. When Pope Innocent III declared a Crusade against the Albigenses in 1209, he initially entrusted it to the Cistercians. During the next seven years, Dominic, at the risk of losing his life, did his utmost best to win over heretics but met with little success.

Count Simon IV de Montfort (1160-1218) put his castle of Casseneuil at Dominic's disposal in 1214. It was during that year that Dominic's plan to found a community to preach for the conversion of the Albigenses took definitive shape. Several volunteers joined him. He obtained permission from Foulques, Bishop of Toulouse (1205-1231), to establish a convent at Prouille in 1206. He based his community's lifestyle on the ancient Rule of St. Augustine. Dominic went to Rome in 1216 and, through his friendship with Cardinal Ugolino, obtained formal recognition of his Order from Pope Innocent III. Since the charism of the Order was that of preaching, it was called the Order of Preachers.

Dominic was a man of great sanctity, humility and courage. His aim in life was to convert souls from error by preaching pure Catholic doctrine. Accordingly, he insisted on the need that his followers be trained at a high intellectual level. He was a great leader and organizer. He journeyed all over Italy, Spain and France to establish new friaries and to organize the expanding Order. He attended the Order's first chapter at Bologna in 1220. In 1221 he set out to preach to the pagans in Hungary, fell ill on his journey, was taken back to Bologna, and died there soon thereafter.

44. The Carmelites

The Order of Our Lady of Mount Carmel, whose members are better known as Carmelites, was founded in Palestine around 1154. It claimed continuity with hermits who had settled on Mount Carmel many centuries before.[16] The Order's Primitive Rule was drawn up in 1209 by St. Albert of Vercelli, the Latin Patriarch of Jerusalem (1205-1214). It was a very harsh rule in that it demanded total solitude, absolute poverty, extreme asceticism, and abstinence from all meat. After the collapse of the early Crusades, many hermits belonging to the community migrated to Europe. Soon thereafter, the Order was reorganized by its sixth General, St. Simon Stock (c. 1165-1265), along the lines of the Mendicant Orders. He had procured prior papal approbation for changes in the Primitive Rule to meet the new conditions in Europe.

St. Simon Stock had been one of the first Englishmen to join the Carmelites after they settled in England. It was during his leadership that the Order changed from an eremitical to a communitarian Order. Two and one half centuries later, a group of pious women pledged themselves to follow the Carmelite charism. The cloistered Carmelite nuns were founded in 1452 in the Low Countries and spread rapidly through France, Italy and Spain.

45. The Augustinians

The Order of the Augustinian Hermits has an unusual beginning. Though its roots are eremitical and can be traced back to St. Augustine and his Rule, the Order became mendicant in the Middle Ages. It was formed by the amalgamation of several Italian Augustinian congregations of hermits. Pope Alexander IV (1254-1261) estab-

---

[16] This claim is very dubious and cannot be historically established.

lished the Great Union of some 180 religious houses as an Order in 1256. They were to follow the Rule of St. Augustine. Lanfranc Septala of Milan was chosen as the first General Prior of the united communities. The Augustinians soon began to relocate from remote areas to towns and cities and spread throughout Western Europe. They undertook extensive pastoral and educational apostolates.

Faith and Reason

46. The End of the Dark Ages

The Dark Ages, also known as the Early Middle Ages, began drawing to a close in the tenth century. It witnessed new migrations and invasions. The era was marked with the coming of the Vikings from the north, the Magyars from the Asian steppes, and a series of inner struggles within the Holy Roman Empire. European cohesion and expansion were weakened further still. The ensuing violence and dislocation caused a decline in population, left lands uncultivated, and monasteries once again became outposts of civilization. Nevertheless, the cultural work of assimilating the legacy of antiquity had been done, and it was not to be lost.

Charles Martel (c. 688-741) in Gaul, then King Alfred in England (849-899), and, finally, Henry the Fowler of Germany (c. 876-936) enlisted cavalry soldiers to withstand and repel foreign raids into their lands. To support his cavalry soldiers, Martel gave them estates of land farmed by dependent laborers. He already had wrestled the land away from the Church. The estates, called benefices, were given for the duration of a soldier's service. These soldiers were their lord's vassals. Under the leadership of their feudal lords, the united vassals fended off invaders and created feudal principalities of different sizes and complexities. Toward the year 1000 the term "fief" began to replace "benefice." The change in term reflected a change in the institution. Feudalism became a political as well as a military establishment, one based upon a contract between two individuals, both of whom held respective rights in the fiefdom. The estate given to a vassal was hereditary, provided the vassal's heir was satisfactory to the lord and paid an inheritance tax called a "relief."

Meanwhile, the Popes, by the sixth century, had become the de facto rulers of the city of Rome and the surrounding area. Through their alliance with both King Pepin and his son, Charlemagne, the Popes emerged as powerful landowners, who would play a major role in the emerging new social order.

Following the fall of the Western Roman Empire, the loose confederation of tribes began to coalesce into independent kingdoms, but lacked the necessary machinery of government. Political and economic development was local in nature, while regular commerce ceased to a minimum. The culmination of this process was that peasants became bound to the land and came to depend on their landlords for protection and the rudimentary administration of justice. This social reality eventually evolved into Seignorialism. It was a system of political, economic and social relations between seigneurs, or lords, and their dependent farm laborers during the Middle Ages. This became the norm for the common man throughout medieval Western Europe. This system should not be confused with Feudalism. Rather, simultaneously, and in a parallel process, feudal connections were also emerging to form the roots of Feudalism. These ties, which traded land for military and other services, may have been rooted in the old Roman patron-client relationship or in the Germanic *comitatus,* groups of fighting companions. All connections that emerged from both processes impeded any tendency toward political consolidation.

By the year 1050, Europe stood on the verge of an unprecedented period of development. The era of migrations had come to a close. In the meantime, Europe experienced the continuity and dynamic growth of a settled population. Town life, and along with it a regular and large-scale trade and commerce, was revived. The society and culture of the High Middle Ages became complex, dynamic and innovative. Modern medieval scholarship refers to this period as the renaissance of the twelfth century. The Church, through some of its brilliant Popes and churchmen, would shape and dominate European society in the intellectual sphere.

47. Intellectual Reawakening

Learning, except that done in a few monasteries during the seventh and eighth centuries, disappeared in Western Europe with the fall of the Roman Empire. The ninth century saw the short-lived rise of the Carolingian Renaissance. But, the eleventh century witnessed the rise of the universities. With them arose a great debate in the Church in the West.

The intellectual reawakening in Europe originated in the monastic schools and then moved to the cathedral schools in northern Europe. Beginning around 1170 the newly founded universities began to replace slowly the cathedral schools and became the most vital places for learning.

While the great conflict between the Popes and the German emperors was going on, there was another conflict being waged in the intellectual life of the Church: the debate between Faith and Reason. Which one of these was to lead the other? Which one was supposed to be the basis to enlighten the other? The cause of this controversy was due to the gradual discovery of the entire works of Aristotle, completed by 1220. This discovery was accompanied by the masterful commentaries of the Arab secular philosophers: Avicenna (980-1037) and Averroes (1126-1198). Both of them emphasized the non-religious and non-spiritual aspects of Aristotelian thought. Secular philosophy was being presented as a complete rational guide to life as an alternative to the one offered by the Church's teachings. While Aristotle offered it through reason, the Church offered it through faith.

Initially a number of papal bans were issued against secular philosophy. But in time, Church leaders saw the wisdom in confronting the issue and bring secular philosophy within the realm of Christian studies by giving it a Christian character. The Church had to come to grips with the new philosophical discoveries and show that faith was above reason. It was an undertaking that would take centuries to iron out. It would involve some of the greatest minds of all ages.

48. The Emergence of Universities

Several universities in Italy, England, France and Germany emerged in the Middle Ages. There were the Italian universities of Salerno,[1] Bologna,[2] Siena,[3] and Vicenza.[4] There were the English universities of Oxford[5] and its perennial competitor, Cambridge.[6] France had its famous University of Paris officially established in 1150,[7] and was followed much later by the universities of Toulouse,[8] the Sorbonne,[9] and Montpellier.[10] Germany had a number of schools and the formation of German universities came much later.[11] The

---

[1] The University of Salerno has a very long and intricate history. It began as a regular school of learning in 850, then became a medical school in 900, and was established eventually as a full university around 1200.

[2] The University of Bologna was officially founded in 1119. Its medical faculty was established in 1150.

[3] The University of Siena was officially established in 1203. The university was originally a Cathedral School.

[4] The University of Vicenza was established in 1204.

[5] The University of Oxford was established in 1167, with a number of independent colleges forming the university.

[6] The University of Cambridge was established in 1200.

[7] As in the case with the universities of the time, the University of Paris emerged from the Cathedral School in Paris.

[8] The University of Toulouse was established in 1229.

[9] The Sorbonne is the Paris School of Theology, founded in 1254.

[10] The University of Montpellier was founded in 1289.

[11] The first formal and official German university was that of Heidelberg, founded in 1385, which was soon followed by the establishment of the University of Cologne in 1388.

universities of Paris and Bologna, by the end of the twelfth century, had overshadowed the rest of the universities and attracted students from all over Europe. Initially, both teachers and students were clerics,[12] all of whom enjoyed clerical protection and privileges. University life was not a bad lot, but, as time went by, university students brought havoc to the local citizenry.

Three branches of knowledge were regarded as worthy of specialized or advanced studies: law, medicine and theology. These, together with the preparatory liberal arts, formed the four university faculties. Law comprised both canon and civil laws. Canon law was established as a science by Gratian's *Decretum*. Civil law came to prominence by the rediscovery of Emperor Justinian's *Code*. The University of Bologna led the field in law. Medicine, for a very long time, was practiced by quacks. The study of medicine as a science began by the introduction of Greek and Arabic medical texts in the eleventh century, such as those of Avicenna. The progress in medicine was hampered by the students' rigid attachment to the Greek and Arabic sources. But the University of Salerno made real progress in surgery, hospitalization, and the use of quarantine. Salerno became the prominent university for medicine. Paris and Oxford were originally prominent in the experimental and physical sciences. But the real queen of all medieval thought was theology.

---

49. Philosophy and Theology Debates

(a) During the twelfth century, a new interest toward philosophy began to appear and its influence on theological thinking was tremendous. Philosophy was considered the handmaid of theology. The ground for a new way of thinking was tilled by St. Anselm of Bec (c. 1033-1109), the Italian Benedictine Archbishop of Canter-

---

[12] One became a cleric by undergoing the religious ritual of tonsure.

bury (1093-1109). Anselm was born in Lombardy. He wasted his early youth with aimless living. He went to France in 1056 and entered the Benedictine monastic school of Bec, in Normandy, in 1059. He was persuaded to take monastic vows in 1060 and shortly afterwards, in 1063, became prior of the Abbey of Bec. He was readily recognized for his great ability as a teaching scholar and spiritual director. His philosophical writings earned him high regard among current intellectuals. He was the one to establish the program of Scholasticism. Following the traditional teachings, he asserted: *I believe that I may understand.*[13] This meant that reason had a right to inquire into revealed Truths so that the mind, as much as its limited capacity allowed, would begin to understand those Truths revealed by faith. The mind was to probe even in those Truths which, by definition, remain beyond human understanding. Faith was the precondition for the right use of reason, but it was the duty of a believer to attempt to apprehend revealed Truths, no matter how limited such an understanding might be. Anselm spent the rest of his life attempting to put into practice what he taught, preferring to defend the Faith by intellectual reasoning rather then by simply quoting past authorities. As a philosopher and theologian, his mind stands as the most precise and insightful between that of St. Augustine and St. Thomas Aquinas.

Anselm became Abbot of Bec in 1078. After he had reluctantly become Archbishop of Canterbury in 1093, he entered into a series of disputes with King William II of England (1037-1100) over royal interference in Church affairs. This clash led to his first exile. During these years of conflict, Anselm managed to write many theological works, *Cur Deus Homo* being the most famous of all his works. The treatise was a theological breakthrough in the theology of Redemption. Anselm rejected the well established theory that Christ's death was one of ransoming man's soul from the devil and interpreted it in terms of the justice and mercy of God. He attended the Council of Bari, assembled in 1098, to de-

---

[13] *Credo ut intellegam.*

fend the Double Procession[14] against the Greeks. His defense was to appear later in one of his other theological works.[15] He learned about the papal decree against lay investiture while attending the local Vatican Council of April 1099.

King William II died in 1100, while Anselm was still in exile. The new English king, Henry I (1100-1135), recalled Anselm, but the latter insisted that the king accepted the said papal decree without compromise. Nevertheless, more controversies ensued between the archbishop and the king due to lay investiture. Anselm had to contend himself with a second exile from 1103 to 1107. He spent the last two years of his life in England and died there in 1109. He was declared a "Doctor of the Church" by Pope Clement XI on 3rd February 1720.

(b) Peter Abelard (1074-1142) was the first great mind to tackle the issue of the Aristotelian method toward theology. He was a brilliant philosopher and theologian who, due to his arrogance and insolence, ran into great difficulties with his teachers, religious superiors and, finally, Rome. He showed a lively, restless, and independent mind from a young age, and was frequently at odds with his teachers. He was a very popular lecturer in Paris, first in dialectics and, later, in theology. His brilliant teaching career was cut short when his love affair with Heloise was discovered in 1118. He retired to the monastery of St. Denis and soon thereafter he was charged with heresy for his dialectic teachings. The dialectic method consisted in quoting what seemed to be contradictory statements and in then attempting to reconcile them. Abelard applied this method to Sacred Scriptures, the Church Fathers, and the doctrine on the Trinity. The latter earned him his first condemnation at the Council of Soissons in 1121. Not long afterwards, he ran into conflict with the monks at the monastery of St. Denis and fled. He resumed his teaching in Paris in 1136. His theory of Atonement was presented in terms of love: Christ's atoning death

---

[14] This was the controversy of the *Filioque.*

[15] The work was called *De Processione Sancti Spiritus* ("On the Procession of the Holy Spirit").

was effective primarily through its exemplary value, that is, through the exemplary love that Calvary evoked in the sinner. This new approach evoked suspicion and was highly criticized by St. Bernard of Clairvaux, who denounced his teachings to the bishops of France. Archbishop Henri le Sanglier called the Council of Sens in 1140 and condemned Abelard's teachings. Abelard appealed to Pope Innocent II against the condemnation, but the Pope confirmed the condemnation later that same year. Abelard eventually reconciled with St. Bernard and spent his remaining years at the Abbey of Cluny under its abbot, St. Peter the Venerable.

(c) St. Albert the Great (c. 1193-1280) was the next great mind to tackle the issue of reconciling Aristotle with Christian teachings and to incorporate the scientific method within the realm of Christian thought. He was a medieval theologian, philosopher and scientist.[16] He was born in Lauingen, Swabia around 1193, the eldest son of the Count of Bollstädt. St. Albert joined the Dominicans as a young man in 1222. He possessed a great knowledge and understanding of the Greek and Arabic philosophers. He was the first to draw a scientific distinction between philosophy and theology. He also led a very active life. He was originally the resident teacher for the German Dominicans. He taught in Paris from 1241 to 1248, where St. Thomas Aquinas was one of his students. He responded to an imperial summons to Cologne in 1248, and St. Thomas Aquinas followed him there. He went to Rome in 1256 to defend the Dominicans against the attacks of the secular teachers at Paris. While in Rome, at the request of Pope Alexander IV, he held a disputation on the unity of the intellect, directed against the views of the Arab philosopher Averroes. St. Albert also lectured on the Gospel of John while still in Rome. Afterwards, he returned to Cologne. At the insistence of the Pope, he was ordained Bishop of Ratisbon in 1260, but resigned two years later, and resumed his teaching at Cologne for the better part of the rest of his life. He participated in the Council of Lyons in 1274. He died in Cologne

---

[16] Some of St. Albert's scientific method is still in use today.

on 15th November 1280. He was declared a "Doctor of the Church" by Pope Pius XI on 16th December 1931.

(d) Theology was considered the queen of all the sciences. This was the field in which some of the greatest medieval minds made their most significant contributions. Up to this point in intellectual history, the traditional method in both the cathedral and monastic schools involved the critical reading[17] of Sacred Scriptures, and/or an exegesis of one or more pericopes accompanied by the commentaries of the Church Fathers on those specific scriptural passages. Over the centuries, these commentaries began to be categorized according to theological themes. The most famous person who raised this approach to a very refined level was Peter Lombard (c. 1100-1160), called *the Master of the Sentences*. Peter began teaching in the Cathedral School of Paris around 1134. He stayed there until his death, shortly before which he had been appointed Bishop of Paris. He wrote commentaries on the Psalms and the Pauline Letters, but he is most renowned for his *Sentences*. The tome was arranged into four parts: the Trinity, Creation and Sin, the Incarnation and the Virtues, and the Sacraments and the Four Last Things. The tome contained a great wealth of quotations, particularly from Sacred Scriptures and the Latin and Greek Church Fathers, all arranged according to the subject matter. Peter made great headway in sacramental theology and is the one who insisted that there were seven sacraments.[18] Notwithstanding, his scholarly approach was based on the acceptance of tradition and authority, but the speculative aspect of theology was minimal.

By the middle of the thirteenth century the study of Aristotle was in full bloom. During this time a good number of Christian theologians began to harmonize with Church teachings everything perceived valid in Greek and Arabic philosophical thought. This scholastic approach was soon to change.

---

[17] This intellectual exercise was called *lectio* and was aimed at moving one's heart to God after one's mind has been enlightened by the contents of Sacred Scripture.

[18] Peter Lombard settled on this number by distinguishing the proper sacraments from acts that were sacramentals.

50. Medieval Theologians

Two great theologians stand out in the Middle Ages as eminent scholars who tackled the issue of secular philosophy through a theological approach.

(a) The first medieval theologian to attack secular philosophy, specifically that of Averroes, was a brilliant Italian Franciscan, St. Bonaventure (1221-1274). He stands out in a singular fashion among his contemporary great Franciscan intellectuals such as Alexander of Hales (d. 1245), Roger Bacon (c. 1214-1294), William of Ockham (c. 1288-1348) and Blessed John Duns Scotus (c. 1266-1308).

Bonaventure was the son of Giovanni di Fidanza and Maria Ritella. He was given the name of John at his baptism and it is still uncertain as to how his name changed to that of Bonaventure. He begun studying the Arts at the University of Paris in 1242, and he entered the Roman Province of Order of Friars Minor around 1243. He returned to the University of Paris to complete his studies under Alexander of Hales. His theological studies were undertaken also at the same university. Having received the "licentiate" in 1248, he began to teach publicly at the university. Though he was a great success as a professor, he was compelled to discontinue teaching in 1256, owing to the then violent outburst of opposition to the Mendicant Orders on the part of the secular professors at the university. The latter sought to exclude the Franciscans and Dominicans from teaching publicly. The Holy See intervened, and Pope Alexander IV reaffirmed the Mendicants in all their privileges. Accordingly, St. Bonaventure resumed his teaching until 1257, at which time he was elected, at age thirty-six, as the Minister General of his Order.[19] It was a time when the Order was fighting for its very survival due to bitter internal dissension. St. Bonaventure was the right person at the right time and in the right position to bring about peace among his Franciscan brethren.

---

[19] St. Bonaventure was elected Minister General on 2nd February 1257.

St. Bonaventure is considered as the second founder of his Order because of his success in uniting and revitalizing the Franciscans. He was created Cardinal Bishop of Albano in 1273, and took a prominent part in the Council Lyons II in 1274, which attempted to heal the Great Schism. He died while the Council was still in session.

St. Bonaventure contested the philosophy of Averroes by using natural dialectics. He was the first to construct a cohesive theological system based on a very clear relationship between faith and reason as proposed by St. Augustine and reasserted by St. Anselm. His natural inclination, however, was to approach issues from a mystical illumination perspective. He taught that it is God who sheds light on the faithful Christian as the mind travels toward God, who is Light of lights. His greatest and most systematic work was his *Commentary on the Sentences of Peter the Lombard*. He was declared a "Doctor of the Church" by Pope Sixtus V on 14th March 1588.

(b) Perhaps the greatest of all Catholic thinkers is St. Thomas Aquinas (c. 1125-1274). He was the youngest son of Landulph, Count of Aquino, and Theodora, Countess of Teano. He was related, through both sides of his family, to the German Emperors[20] and to the Kings of Aragon, Castile and France.[21] His parents, intending for him an ecclesiastical career by becoming a Benedictine monk, sent him to school at Monte Cassino when he was five years old. In 1240, while on his way to Naples to continue his studies, he became enamored with the Dominicans. His family resisted his wishes to the point of holding him prisoner for over a year. But the son won the day and joined the Dominicans in 1244. While still a student at the University of Paris (1245-1248), he came under the influence of St. Albert the Great, and forged an admiration and friendship which made him follow St. Albert to Cologne. Aquinas returned to Paris in 1252 where he began teaching his fellow Dominicans.

---

[20] Emperor Frederick II and Conrad IV.
[21] Kings Louis VIII, St. Louis IX, and Philip III.

He taught in Italy between 1259 and 1269. Then he was sent back to teach in Paris. He went to teach in Naples in 1272 and died on his way to the Council Lyons II on 7ᵗʰ March 1274.

St. Thomas Aquinas understood perfectly Aristotelian thought and consequently he was able to "Christianize" the Greek philosopher. He distinguished Aristotle from his commentators, pinned down where the philosopher's thought was incomplete or inadequate, and, in the spirit of Aristotle, was able to develop Aristotelianism and harmonize it with Catholic teaching. In developing the Aristotelian thought, Aquinas proved to be a first class philosopher. In relating the Aristotelian thought to Church teachings, Aquinas proved to be an eminent theologian. The distinction between faith and reason is fundamental to Aquinas' crystal clear, precise, and compact writings and commentaries. He taught that although many of the revealed Truths cannot be established by reason, they cannot be considered contrary to reason. These revealed Truths were given primarily in Sacred Scriptures and through the consistent teachings of the Fathers. His philosophical and theological works are voluminous. He was declared a "Doctor of the Church" by Pope St. Pius V, himself a Dominican, on 11ᵗʰ April 1567.

The Age of Scandals and
the Papal Babylonian Exile

51. Papal Elections and Ecclesiastical Appointments

(a) The medieval Popes had managed to procure free papal elections and maintained the upper hand in the lay investiture controversy. Unfortunately, a new abuse slowly crept within the Church in its elective system of nominating bishops, abbots and other Church offices. Many candidates were outright very ambitious men. For such men, election to a Church office meant competing with other candidates. Thus, they introduced the practice of secular politics in its worst form. Rivalries, feuds, factions, riots, promised favors, etc., became commonplace, especially when some very important Church office became vacant. Several Popes tried to defuse these incidents by insisting on free elections, and also by proposing nominees. The latter generated a most unfortunate scheme. Men who were hungry for power, desirous of advancing themselves in the Church, went to Rome, befriended some powerful curial official, lavished many gifts upon him, made many promises, and then waited, looking forward to the opportune time to be appointed to a very promising diocesan or monastic office. Some men were so bluntly corrupt that they asked for a specific diocese or abbey or canonry. These men were not only after the power inherent in a Church office, but were also after the income that its possession generated.[1] Eventually, they would not be content with one source of income alone but wanted more. Consequently, there arose a time when a man occupied a number of Church offices at one given time. On the other hand, the papal court gradually became a place of great intrigue, ambition, deception, corruption, and personal financial gain. Even some Popes themselves were not immune from such vices. On the other hand, there were instances when a Cardinal went so far as to buy from his electoral colleagues the papal throne itself.

(b) Another scandal that left the papacy morally and politically weak was the interregnums in the papacy over a period of about ninety years (1241-1334), as well as the imprisonment of a Pope. These interregnums, accumulatively speaking, left the See of Rome without its Bishop for almost twelve out of these ninety years! Pope Celestine IV died in 1241, after a sixteen days' reign. Due to the political ambitions and intrigues of Emperor Frederick II, the Cardinals were unable to elect a new Pope for the next sixteen months. Then, they elected Pope Innocent IV. The next interregnum lasted three and one-half years. It began with the death of Pope Clement IV on 29 November 1268, and was not over until the Cardinals elected Teobaldo Visconti (1210-1276) on 1ˢᵗ September 1271, who took the name of Pope (Blessed) Gregory X (1271-1276). The next major interregnum, which lasted two years and three months, followed the death of Pope Nicholas IV (1288-1292). Then, there was the unspeakable capture of Pope Boniface VIII (1295-1303), on 7ᵗʰ September 1303, by mercenary soldiers in the pay of King Philip the Fair of France. Not so long afterwards, there was another interregnum, this time for about one year, following the death of Pope Boniface VIII's successor, Pope Blessed Benedict XI (1303-1304). Finally, there was an interregnum of

---

[1] This was the *benefice system* where certain duties were performed and, in turn, their discharge provided certain revenues or the Church office had attached to it some land or other source of income. The benefice system remained in effect until 1983. The *1917 Code of Canon Law* revised the benefice system and attempted to make it equitable. The *1983 Code of Canon Law* basically called for its abolition.

almost two and one-half years between the death of Pope Clement V (1305-1314) on 14th April 1314 and the election of his successor, Pope John XXII (1316-1334), on 7th August 1416.

(c) A further scandal was associated with papal taxation and tithes imposed on every kind of Church land and salary throughout Christian Europe. Every source of income attached to a Church office was appraised and a papal tax was imposed. In order to keep current the financial records, a new brand of Church tax-collectors emerged as papal centralization became more vigorous. Many of these people could be easily bribed to doctor documents and lower taxes for a kickback. At the same time, the papacy found itself relying more and more on income from papal taxation, especially when the Popes set up their residence at Avignon from 1309 to 1377. During those years, Popes usually could not collect any income from their Papal States in Italy. Nonetheless, the Popes at Avignon needed money for the upkeep of their curia, to enrich their many relatives,[2] to fund the papal wars against the rebellious Christian rulers, and to subsidize armies that fought heretics. Eventually, when Christendom had two Popes concurrently reigning from 1378 to 1417, one in Rome and one in Avignon, each Pope needed money for his personal upkeep and that of his respective papal court. Lack of ready income would force respective Popes to borrow very heavily from bankers at unbelievable interest rates. The situation, in turn, forced a reigning Pope to levy more taxes. It was a vicious circle of intrigue and corruption.

In the end, what all of the above came down to was the fact that one direct consequence of rigid Roman centralization was that the Pope needed more and more income to be able to meet all the demands that such an administrative system brought with it. On the other hand, money had to come not only from taxes on Church offices and tithing, but also by directly taxing every member of

---

[2] The very abusive custom of *nepotism* had taken roots by the beginning of the thirteenth century. It should be noted, however, that not everyone who utilized or benefitted from nepotism was corrupt.

Christendom. When the Pope and his agents were virtuous, the great majority of the faithful felt some kind of benefit from the highly centralized Church system. But, when a Pope and/or his agents were weak and (eventually) corrupt, people became resistant to donate, begrudgingly paid their taxes, and turned very resentful toward the Pope and his agents.

(d) The period between 1370 and 1517 in the Catholic Church was one of a steady, gradual down-spiraled decline. The medieval Popes had established the Church as a sort of super power that stood above the delineated boundaries of the Western European nations. Different Popes had played a dangerous political game by allying themselves with different nations at any given time or played one nation against another so that the reigning Pope would hold the reins in European politics. One detrimental result of such a dangerous political policy was that the papacy was dragged into intra-national hate, the papal curia became suspect, and some Pope's or Cardinal's or bishop's political promises were just as vague or devious or deceptive as those of any other secular ruler. The papacy gradually became very secularized. Particularly during this time, there was also a number of Popes, Cardinals and bishops who practiced nepotism. They worked very diligently to install their illegitimate children or relatives as ruling princes in some small or larger principalities in Italy. Others attempted to do so by marrying off such blood relatives to some reigning principality. This political scene provided its own lists of papal Leagues and Alliances, along with their anxieties, intrigues and wars. Yet the picture of the Church was not so bleak since there were great reformers, including Popes and Cardinals and bishops, in every generation that lived during this period. Nevertheless, the Church lost most of its prestige as the spiritual leader in the West. Furthermore, there were times when both good and bad Popes used the spiritual weapons of interdict and excommunication in order to either subdue a rebellious ruler or rouse his subjects against him. At times such spiritual weapons brought the desired effects. But there were other times when the common folk perceived the Pope as abusing spiritual weapons for sheer political reasons, and so they ignored the papal sanctions.

The atmosphere became such that many secular rulers sought an opportune time to strike against the Church, and to curtail papal interference in what these rulers perceived to be their nation's internal interests. The rise in the consciousness of a national identity among the European nations hastened the process.

52. Popes and French Interests

Pope Innocent IV was elected at the end of a conclave that lasted sixteen months. The election was held in the midst of a long drawn out war between the papacy and the empire. Rome had learnt that in order for it and the Papal States to survive with some kind of independence from the German emperors, the Kingdom of the Two Sicilies had to remain entirely separate from the empire. Thus, Charles of Anjou, the papal candidate, was offered and accepted the Crown of the Two Sicilies, in 1262, with the solemn proviso that he would keep separate the politics of his new kingdom from those of the empire. On the other hand, with the public beheading of Conradino in 1268, the last of the Imperial House of Hohenstaufen died and the imperial crown, after a very long interregnum of nineteen years, was given to the pious Rudolf I of Hapsburg (1273-1291).[3] Pope Blessed Gregory X recognized Rudolf as emperor and induced King Alfonso X of Castile (1221-1284) to resign his claims to the imperial crown in 1273. At first blush things seemed to have worked according to the papal designs. But, in fact, things were very unsettled. The Sicilians hated their new French masters and organized secretly for the overthrow of their cruel ruler, Charles of Anjou. They successfully rebelled against the French on Easter Monday 1282, during the reign of Pope Martin IV (1281-85), and massacred many of the French in Palermo. Since the signal for the rebellion was the tolling of the bell for vespers, the event was

---

[3] The House of Hapsburg was to occupy the imperial throne practically for the remaining existence of the empire, that is until 1806.

called the *Sicilian Vespers*. It marked the beginning of the end of the French very brief rule of the Two Sicilies. On the other hand, the papacy tried its best to uphold the French authority against the Sicilian rebels, unwisely throwing its lot with the cruel French and against the very proud, resourceful, and independent Sicilian people. The papacy ended in losing not only huge amounts of war funds and many soldiers, but more importantly, the papacy lost its spiritual prestige. Christian Europe was dismayed in seeing a Pope using his spiritual weapons for political gains. The respect for papal authority began to erode.

53. Papal Autocracy

The papacy fell vacant with the death of Pope Nicholas IV on 4th February 1292. The College of Cardinals was bitterly divided between those who supported French interests, led by the powerful Orsini faction, and those who supported the interest of Spanish Aragon, led by the powerful Colonna faction. Secular politics were blatantly present throughout this papal conclave (1292-1294), and the Cardinals reached an impasse. Then, Latino Malabranca, the aged and infirm dean of the College of Cardinals, suggested the nearly eighty-year old saintly hermit Peter Morrone (1209-1296) as the next Pope. Surprisingly, everyone agreed on the proposed candidate who was then brought from his mountain hermitage and ordained Bishop of Rome on 29th August 1294. He took the name of Celestine V. It was a disastrous choice. St. Celestine V was utterly inept for the office and was under the complete control of Charles of Anjou. The new Pope, however, had enough sense to resign his papal office on 13th December 1294, about five months after his election.[4] The Cardinals immediately convened and, on 24th December 1294, elected Cardinal Benedict Gaetani, who took

---

[4] Pope St. Celestine V, who was canonized sixteen years after his death, is, as to date, the last Pope to canonically resign the papacy.

the name of Boniface VIII (1294-1303). He turned out to be one of the most energetic Popes to exercise papal autocratic authority and, in his case, at a great cost to papal prestige. He proclaimed the first papal jubilee in 1300. He constantly interfered with the local affairs of dioceses. He acted as the arbiter in European affairs. He insisted on the independence of the Papal States by waging wars against principalities and making alliances with others. He, however, lost face in the Sicilian War in that he was forced to seek a peace settlement with the Kingdom of the Two Sicilies. He was also forced to compromise with the new awakening of nationalism throughout Europe. Ultimately, his very ambitious papal program forced the papacy to lose its spiritual and political grip over many European nations due to the emergence of nationalism.

54. The Papacy Battles France

(a) The French monarchy, always a valiant supporter of many Popes, turned against the papacy at the end of the thirteenth century and delivered to it a great defeat. The traditional antagonist of the papacy had been the Holy Roman Emperors. There was nothing new in Church history when powerful secular leaders opposed Popes. The innovation lay in the identity of the opposing country, France, and particularly in the person of King Philip IV who contested Pope Boniface VIII. King Philip IV was a very greedy and shrewd man. He needed a lot of money to consolidate his kingdom. This put him constantly in debt, especially with the Knights Templars. He had his eye on two entities, the Church and the wealth of the Knights Templars.

(b) The conflict between the Pope and French king arose over clerical taxation in 1296. The king had levied a heavy tax on the clergy. The Pope responded by excommunicating anyone, without naming the king, who imposed extraordinary taxation on Church property without prior sanction from Rome. The king responded by blocking all transport of French gold and money to Rome. The parties agreed to a compromise, which proved to be very temporary (1297-1301). The king, however, was determined in his resolve to make the Church in France subservient to the state. He saw his opportunity in 1301 when he arrested the papal legate, Bishop Bernard de Saissert (1297-1317), and had him tried in violation of clerical immunity. The Pope reacted by condemning the king's action and summoned him and the French bishops to a council in Rome, scheduled for 1302. The king rallied popular opinion and even managed to procure the support of half of the French clergy. Nationalist consciousness, by this time, had already taken root in France. Meanwhile, the Pope issued the famous bull, *Unam Sanctam* on 18th November 1302, listing all papal prerogatives. In essence the papal declaration stated nothing new. It simply reiterated what had been stated by previous Popes in their traditional claim of ultimate papal supremacy in Christendom, including its social order. It stated that Christ gave this supremacy to Peter and to all of his successors. Thus, no one was competent to judge a Pope since every human being was subject to the Power of the Keys. King Philip IV openly defied the Pope and was determined to bring him to trial. With this in mind, one of the king's mercenaries, William de Nogaret (d. 1314), held the Pope prisoner for three days at Anagni, from the 7th to the 9th of September 1303, and the unthinkable became history. The prestige of the papal office hit a new low. Although Pope Boniface VIII was liberated by Italian troops, his spirit was broken and he died in Rome the following month, on 11th October 1303. He was succeeded by Pope Benedict XI (1303-1304), who lived for nine months. The new Pope excommunicated de Nogaret because of the rough and scandalous treatment Pope Boniface VIII had received at his hands and under his command. But, no one dared punish the French king for he was gaining ground in bringing the papacy to his feet.

(c) King Philip IV was more vicious and vindictive than his great uncle, Charles of Anjou. He wanted to destroy completely any hint of anything good about Pope Boniface VIII. It did not matter whether the poor Pope was alive or dead. Consequently, the king continued to pursue his vicious determination to bring Pope

Boniface VIII to trial, even after the Pope's death! Following the demise of Pope Blessed Benedict XI on 7th July 1304 and an interregnum of eleven months, the Cardinals elected the weak Frenchman Bertrand de Got (1264-1314) on 5th June 1305. He took the name of Clement V. The new Pope was crowned in Lyons, on 14th November 1305, in the presence of the French king. Out of the twenty-four Cardinals he created during his pontificate, twenty-three of them were Frenchmen.

Pope Clement V was subservient to the French king in all things but one, the posthumous trial of Pope Boniface VIII. The king had vehemently insisted that his papal countryman exhume the body of Pope Boniface VIII so as to stand trial on charges of heresy and immorality![5] The Pope passively resisted the royal plans and, in exchange, acquiesced to the king's demand for the suppression of the Knights Templars in 1312. King Philip immediately laid his hands on the Knights Templars' possessions, although the Pope had given their title to the Knights Hospitallers. The latter did not offer any real resistance to the royal act. It was one of the most scandalous defeats ever experienced by the papacy. Pope Clement V, who designated as his papal residence the Dominican priory in Avignon in 1309, established the Roman Curia there, and lived and died as Pope in France in 1314.

---

55. From Rome to Avignon

Avignon became papal property in 1348. The Italian poet and humanist Francesco Petrarch (1304-1374) was the first to perceive the papal stay at Avignon (1309-1377) in terms of a papal exile and referred to this period in Church history as the *Babylonian Captivity.*

---

[5]   King Philip IV tried to emulate a previous infamous posthumous trial of a Pope. The remains of Pope Formosus (891-896) had been exhumed in 897, vested with papal attire and sat on a throne. Then, he was put on trial in the notorious Cadaver Synod.

(A) Fourteenth century Avignon was not part of France, but was an imperial fief held by the King of Sicily. There were many reasons why Pope Clement V and his immediate six successors extended their stay in Avignon for so long. Some Popes, as in the case with many of their predecessors, had to face the traditionally antagonistic Holy Roman Emperors. These Popes had to rely on the good will of the French kings who, in turn, saw the papal residence in Avignon as an effective means to forward French interests. Consequently, political barriers were erected that prevented the Popes from returning to the City. There was also the fact that a number of Popes had become subservient to the French kings.[6] The situation was coupled with the overwhelming number of French Cardinals in the papal curia that assured an absolute French control over every new papal election.[7] The majority of the French Cardinals did not wish to leave their homeland and neither did they wish for their papal countryman to depart from France. On the other hand, some of the Popes in Avignon had every intention of returning to Rome, but were too ill to do so. Finally, there was constant war among the Italian principalities, coupled with the political instability and unpredictability that went, hand in hand, with such a scenario.

(b) The French Cardinal Jacques Duèse (1249-1334) had the misfortune to succeed Pope Clement V, after an almost two and one half year interregnum. He chose the name of Pope John XXII (1316-1334). He had been the candidate proposed by Robert of Anjou (1277-1343), Count of Provence and Forcalquier and King of Naples (1309-1343). The new Pope fixed his residence at Avignon. His papacy was overwhelmed with political and theological turmoil. One of the final acts of Pope Clement V, upon the death of Emperor Henry VII (1308-1313), had been to reassert the supremacy of the papacy over the empire. The Pope also determined that he would

---

[6] The French kings during the Papal Babylonian Captivity were Philip IV the Fair (1285-1314), Louis X (1314-1316), Philip V (1316-1322), Charles IV (1322-1328), Philip VI Valois (1328-1350), John II (1350-1364), and Charles V (1364-1380).

[7] There were one hundred and thirty-four Cardinals created when the Papacy was in Avignon. Of this number, only twenty-one Cardinals were not Frenchmen.

rule the empire during an imperial interregnum. This determination was rather strange due to the fact that the Pope was of a very weak character. In any case, Clement V outlived Henry VII by just eight months. Following the death of the Pope, the papacy had a long interregnum, that is, until the election of Pope John XXII.

The new Pope found the imperial electors divided and waging a civil war that was led by two opposing imperial claimants, Louis of Bavaria (1314-1347) and Frederick of Austria (1314-1330). Pope John XXII immediately told both claimants not to consider themselves emperors and that he would administer the empire until he judged the case himself. He then proceeded to appoint an administrator. But war continued to be waged, particularly in Italy and, in 1322, Louis decisively defeated Frederick. Since the Pope refused to recognize Louis as emperor, the latter waged war against the Papal States.

---

56. Popes and Holy Roman Emperors

(a) While Pope John XXII had to come to grips with politico-military issues, there was also a theological war being waged within the Church itself. The Pope had dissolved the Franciscan Spiritualists in 1317. He had denounced their extreme doctrine of absolute poverty as heretical. Several of the more fanatical Spirituals fled to the protection and support of Emperor Louis of Bavaria. The emperor perceived the Spiritualists as an added force against the Pope. The Pope, in turn, declared the emperor a heretic in 1324. The emperor next invaded Italy, installed himself in the Vatican, declared the Pope deposed on grounds of heresy and treachery, and set up his own antipope, the Franciscan Spiritualist, Pietro Rainallunni, who assumed the name of Nicholas V.[8] The new an-

---

[8] Nicholas V was antipope from 12th May 1328 until his submission, on 25th August 1330. He died in 1333.

tipope crowned Louis as emperor in 1328. Although the antipope submitted to Pope John XXII in 1330, the war between Pope and emperor dragged on, even after the Chair of Peter fell vacant not only once, that is through the death of Pope John XXII in 1334, but also upon the death of his successor, Pope Benedict XII (1334-1342). Meanwhile, the princes, religious orders and faithful in Germany were divided into two camps, one supporting the Pope and the other supporting the emperor. All the imperial electors, however, had agreed to issue a declaration at Rense, dated 16th July 1338, affirming the dignity of the emperor as coming directly from God, that it fell to whoever procured the majority of the electoral votes, and that the duly elected emperor had no need of papal confirmation to assume the exercise of his imperial office. In effect, the declaration made it very clear that the emperor was completely independent of the Pope.

(b) Pope Clement VI (1342-1352) had been Pope just for two years when the pugnacious Emperor Louis was forced to abdicate the imperial throne. The papal candidate, Charles IV of Bohemia (1344-1378), was elected emperor after pledging the empire's subordination to the papacy. But once he had established himself as emperor, Charles IV proved to be as independent as his predecessor, though more respectful toward the papacy. He re-issued the declaration of Rense in 1353, accompanied with the *Golden Bull*, specifying the procedure for subsequent imperial elections. The document identified seven princes as having an electoral right and specified how the empire would be administered when a vacancy occurred. Emperor Charles IV left the papal role completely out of the document and asserted that the empire was a secular society independent of the papacy. The Pope at that time, Innocent VI (1352-1362), did not raise any protest. He simply followed the road of political concessions to Christian secular rulers that his predecessors had begun. The triumphs of Pope St. Gregory VII were gradually and steadily disappearing.

57. End of the Papal Babylonian Exile

(a) The first serious attempt ever made by a Pope at Avignon to return the papacy back to Rome was Blessed Urban V (1362-1370). The saintly French Benedictine monk, Guillaume de Grimoard (1309-1370), was the abbot of St. Victor at Marseilles, not even a bishop or a Cardinal, at the time he was elected Pope on 16th October 1362. He took the name of Pope Urban V. His election had broken the deadlock that had existed between the polarized Cardinals at the conclave, following the death of Pope Innocent VI on 12th September 1362. The new Pope was immediately consecrated in Avignon as the Bishop of Rome. In many ways, Blessed Urban V was the best of the Popes at Avignon. He continued to lead the life of a monk throughout his pontificate, and seriously undertook the reform of the Church, especially in the area of just distribution of benefices. He was a great benefactor to universities and to poor scholars. During his short time in Rome, from 16th November 1367 to 5th September 1370, he received into communion with the Roman Church the Byzantine Emperor John V Palaeologus (1341-1391) in 1369.

Continued troubles in Italy, as well as pleas from figures such as Petrarch and St. Bridget of Sweden (1303-1373), led Pope Urban V to express his wish to return the papacy to Rome in 1366. There was an immense negative reaction from the French King Charles V (1364-1380), the Cardinals, and the entire papal court at Avignon. Overcoming all obstacles that the French put in his way, Pope Urban V set out for Rome, which he reached on 16th November 1367. However, although well received by both clergy and people, Rome resumed being a very unsafe place in just over two years after his arrival, and no secular ruler came to his aid. Unable any longer to resist the urgency of the French Cardinals, and with numerous cities of the Papal States in revolt, the Pope decided to return to Avignon despite the prophecy of St. Bridget that he would died soon after his return to France. He arrived at

Avignon on the 24th September 1370, fell sick a few days later, and died the following 19th December.

(b) Eleven days after the death of Pope Blessed Urban V, the Cardinals had a very brief conclave and elected as Pope the renowned canonist Pierre Roger de Beaufort (1329-1378), the nephew of Pope Clement VI. The new Pope took the name of Pope Gregory XI (1370-1378). He proved to be the last French Pope to be elected and to reside in Avignon. His first resolve as Pope was to return to Rome, having been convinced to do so during a personal visit of the mystic St. Catherine of Siena (1347-1380). He also realized that if he did not return to Rome soon, the papal authority over the Papal States would be lost completely. His departure was postponed many times due to political obstacles. The Pope finally left Avignon in September 1376 and arrived at Rome in January 1377. The Pope survived in Rome for fourteen months[9] and died before he was able to follow his resolve and return to Avignon.

(c) On 8th April 1378, while the Cardinals were in conclave for a second day, an antagonistic Roman mob threatened the Cardinals with death if an Italian was not elected as the new Pope. The terrified Cardinals, mostly French, hurriedly elected Bartolomeo Prignano (1318-1389), who took the name of Urban VI (1378-1389).

Pope Urban VI had been a respected administrator, but soon after his election as Pope, he proved to be suspicious, overbearing, and prone to violent outbursts of temper. The Cardinals who had elected him became very fearful. Soon, most of the Cardinals fled to Anagni, where they elected Robert of Geneva as a rival pope on 20th September of the same year. Robert took the name pope Clement VII (1378-1394).[10] He reestablished a papal court in Avignon, where he became completely dependant on the French court. His election threw the Church into turmoil because, for the first time,

---

[9] Pope Gregory XI died in Rome on 27th March 1378.
[10] The legitimate Pope Clement VII (Giulio di Giuliano de' Medici) reigned as Pope from 1523 to 1534.

the same legitimate Cardinals had elected both popes. In the past antipopes, rival claimants to the papacy, had been mostly appointed by various rival factions. The election proved to be the beginning of the Great Western Schism (1378-1417), which would last for almost forty years and which would create a lot of confusion within the Universal Church.

---

58. European Population in Crisis

Much of the reform efforts that some Popes at Avignon tried to undertake were undermined by the appearance of the immense catastrophe brought about by the Black Death. This pandemic disease, the deadly bubonic plague, invaded Europe through the trade routes from China and India. Infected black rats spread this rapid, highly contagious and usually fatal disease. It attacked particularly the young, who died within a few hours of contracting it. Superstition was rampant and medicine was very inadequate during this fearsome time. There was no known remedy for the bubonic plague at the time.

The Black Death decimated Western Europe, claiming as its victims between twenty and thirty million people over a period of less than two years. Some historians have estimated that up to forty-five per cent of the European population succumbed to the disease.[11] No country escaped its deadly grip.

The Black Death first showed its deadly head in Italy in early 1348. It spread rapidly through France, Spain, Germany, Austria and Holland. By summer it reached England, Iceland and Greenland. England, for example, lost about half of its population to the disease. The Black Death profoundly disrupted religious life by depleting abbeys, monasteries and convents. It claimed most of the

---

[11] See Robert Gottfried, "Black Death" in *Dictionary of the Middle Ages*, Charles Scribner's Sons (1989), volume 2, pp. 257-67.

dedicated clergy because, in the process of attending to the dying, they fell victim to the disease.

The disastrous social, economic and spiritual effects of the Black Death can hardly be overestimated. No one felt safe. People began to despair and to live only for the day. Bands of degenerates attacked and sacked monasteries, convents and abbeys. The economy of every European nation was on the verge of total collapse. On the spiritual order, the common man lost his faith. All kinds of abhorrent people banded themselves together in a spirit of carelessness and reckless defiance to all that had spiritual overtones. Saintly and highly committed pastoral clergy, fallen to the plague, were replaced by many who were simply unprepared and unsuitable. There was a foreboding of chaos for the Church.

The Great Western Schism and Its Aftermath

---

59. Church in West Divides

(a) The Great Western Schism refers to the most confusing and regrettable forty year period in the Catholic Church between 1378 and 1417 when two, and eventually three, individuals simultaneously claimed to be the legitimate Bishop of Rome.[1] The term *schism* is applied loosely to this historical situation since, technically speaking, a schism involves the formal and willful separation from unity of the Church. Upon analyzing what happened during the Great Western Schism, it is evident that there was no rebellion in the Church against any lawfully perceived Pope, there was no rejection of papal powers or negation of obedience due to the one perceived as the legitimate Pope. Thus, the division, though very real, was not a schism in the strict and technical sense of the term.

(b) There were many reasons as to why the Great Western Schism took place. The immediate reason for the schism, however, was due to the circumstances under which Bartolomeo Pregnane was elected as the successor to Pope Gregory XI. The Cardinals,

---

[1] The claimants to the papal office during the Great Western Schism were: (1) *Roman Popes*: Urban VI (1378-1389), Boniface IX (1389-1404), Innocent VII (1404-1406), and Gregory XII (1406-1415), all four considered legitimate Popes; (2) *Avignon Popes*: Clement VII (1378-1394) and Benedict XIII (1394-1423), both considered antipopes; (3) *Pisan Popes*: Alexander V (1409-1410) and John XXIII (1410-1415), both considered antipopes.

while in conclave and for fear of their lives, gave into the demands of an antagonistic Roman mob. They elected as Pope, on 8th April 1378, the Italian archbishop Pregnano of Bari, who was not a Cardinal at the time. The seventy-four year old took the name of Pope Urban VI (1379-1389). He had been a model official as vice-chancellor at the papal court in Avignon. He was well aware of the need for Church reform. Consequently, the Cardinals thought that they had elected the right person under those extraordinary circumstances. But, soon after his election, Pope Urban VI began to show signs of insanity. He was tactless and tyrannical in his manner of introducing Church reform. Within a very short time, he succeeded in completely alienating the Cardinals who had elected him a few months earlier. By June 1378 most of them, including all the French Cardinals, had fled Rome to declare their doubt in the validity of the papal election due to the pressure the Roman populace had exerted over them while in conclave. Ironically, the same Cardinals expressed their doubt after they had already repeatedly and publicly acknowledged Urban VI as Pope. In August 1378, the fleeing Cardinals unanimously declared as invalid the recent papal election and, meeting in conclave in Anagni, elected Cardinal Robert of Geneva as the new Bishop of Rome. He took the name of Clement VII (1378-1394).[2] There were now two Popes, elected essentially by the same College of Cardinals, simultaneously claiming to be the valid Bishop of Rome. Western Christendom speedily divided its papal allegiance, based on political motives. There was never a division in doctrine during the Great Western Schism, but only in papal allegiance. Those who were anti-French recognized Urban VI as the legitimate Pope, while pro-French rulers recognized Clement VII.

Clement VII was the first antipope of the Great Western Schism. Denmark, England, Flanders, the Holy Roman Empire,

---

[2]   The issue as to whether Cardinal Roger of Geneva was a legitimate Pope (as Clement VII) was ultimately decided in 1523 when Giuliano de Medici (1478-1534) was elected Pope and took the name of Pope Clement VII (1523-1534), thereby making it very clear that Roger of Geneva was an antipope.

Hungary, Ireland, Norway, Poland and Sweden declared for Pope Urban VI. On the other hand, France, Scotland, Castile and León, Navarre, Cyprus, Burgundy, the Kingdom of the Two Sicilies, and Savoy acknowledged the authority of Clement VII. The kingdoms of Aragon and Portugal were in the midst of internal conflicts and allegiances to either Pope fluctuated, while most of Italy remained in utter confusion, not knowing which claimant should be accepted as the true Pope. Eventually, when a ruler in one papal allegiance did not get his way with his Pope, the ruler would threaten to or simply switch allegiances. Such political maneuvering had a major detrimental effect on Church matters. Each Pope's popularity reached a new low.

Clement VII took up residence in Avignon in 1379. Soon, the Church had parallels of two Roman curias, two Roman administrations and two Colleges of Cardinals — one in Rome and one in Avignon. Each camp claimed to have the true Bishop of Rome, each camp produced its own bishops, abbots, priests, religious, theologians, and so on, and even saints.

(c) Pope Urban VI's serious mental imbalance became more intense by the passage of time. He became paranoid of the nineteen Cardinals he had created. He did not hesitate to put Cardinals to torture, with five of them dying as a result. After he had died, on 15th October 1389, his fourteen surviving Cardinals, on the following 2nd November, elected as his successor, Piero Tomacelli, who took the name of Pope Boniface IX (1389-1404). Clement VII died in Avignon on 16th September 1394. The schism could have ended at this junction by having the Avignon Cardinals re-elect or declare their acceptance of Pope Boniface IX as the legitimate Pope. Instead, the Avignon Cardinals came up with their own solution. Their plan, had it been followed through, would have effectively resolved the entire matter. Before they met in conclave, each of the Avignon candidates took a solemn oath, pledging that should he be elected pope he would resign the office soon thereafter and pave the way for a new joint Rome-Avignon conclave. The Avignon conclave was held and the austere canonist Pedro de Luna (1394-1417) was elected pope and took the name of Benedict XIII.

(d) Pope Gregory XI had created Pedro de Luna as a Cardinal in 1375. He would participate in the election of Pope Urban VI in April 1378, as well as in the election of the antipope Clement VII in 1378. As pope, Cardinal de Luna took the name of Benedict XIII.[3] Once he was enthroned in Avignon, he reneged on his pre-conclave oath and refused to resign. King Charles VI of France (1380-1422), for four long years, tried unsuccessfully to persuade the Avignon pope to resign his papal office. Finally, Charles VI lost his patience, France withdrew from its allegiance to Benedict XIII, the king laid siege to Avignon, and incarcerated the pope in his own papal prison. Meanwhile, negotiations were undertaken first with Pope Boniface IX in Rome and then with his two immediate successors, Pope Innocent VII (1404-1406) and Pope Gregory XII (1406-1415) to resolve the situation.[4] But Benedict XIII remained adamant in his refusal to resign as pope. After five years of resistance, France capitulated and returned to the Avignon obedience of Benedict XIII. The Great Western Schism continued.

60. Conciliarism

(a) The very long absence of the Popes from Rome was followed by the great scandal of the Great Western Schism. The Schism first entailed the simultaneous existence of two rival Popes, one with his independent headquarters in Rome and the other with his own in Avignon. Eventually, the schism led to the *Conciliarist Movement* that maintained that under very special and extraordinary circumstances, a General Council could be convoked without the Pope's approval, and even against his will, and issue decrees without his consent. In essence, then, according to this theory, a General

---

[3] Pedro de Luna (d. 1423) as Benedict XIII (1394-1417) was an antipope. Consequently, when Pietro Francesco Orsini (1649-1730) was elected Pope in 1724, he took the name of Pope Benedict XIII (1724-1730).

[4] Pope Gregory XII resigned the papal office on 4th June 1415 and died on 18th October 1417.

Council could enjoy authority over any Pope. It would take some time for Popes to re-establish their authority over General Councils, but, nonetheless, they failed to regain their powerful papal moral and spiritual leadership.

(b) The Council of Pisa was self-assembled in that the Cardinals from both the Roman and Avignon papal allegiances, independent of their respective Pope, convoked it in that city on 25th March 1409. Its primary purpose was to end the schism and introduce reform in the Church. Twenty-four Cardinals, many bishops, and some three hundred doctors in theology and canon law participated. At its very outset, the council proclaimed itself canonically valid.[5] Then, it proceeded to depose both pope Benedict XIII and Pope Gregory XII because both refused to respond to the conciliar summons. Next, they passed a number of decrees aimed at reforming Church life. These decrees benefitted the authority of bishops, decried the frequent episcopal transfer from one diocese to another, deplored the oppressive papal taxation system, and sanctioned the infringement by the Roman courts on lower Church courts. The Cardinals then elected a new Pope, Alexander V (1339-1410), on 26th June 1409. He was a former supporter of Pope Gregory XII. The Council of Pisa did not only fail to end the schism, but made things even more adversely complicated in that there were now three claimants asserting themselves as being the legitimate successor to St. Peter.

(c) The new pope, Alexander V, was formerly known as Pietro Philargi of Candia.[6] Born in Crete and raised in Venice, he had joined the Franciscans at a young age. He was a renowned theologian, canonist and diplomat. He had been appointed bishop to successive sees in Italy until he was appointed archbishop of Milan in 1389, and before he was unanimously elected as pope at the Council of Pisa. Alexander V's papacy lasted ten short months because he died in Bologna on 3rd May 1410 on his way to Rome.

---

[5] The Council of Pisa had no authority due to the fact that a lawful Pope did not convoke it.

[6] Candia was another name for the island of Crete.

At the time of Alexander V's death, the Church was faced with the identical situation that had existed at the time of his papal election, namely, there were still two claimants to the papacy. The claimant Pope Gregory XII was in the line of succession to Pope Urban VI of Rome, while the claimant pope Benedict XIII was in the line of succession to pope Clement VI of Avignon.

(d) The new papal conclave once again looked at the successors of Urban VI and Clement VI as deposed, and proceeded to elect a new pope in the person of Cardinal Baldassare Cossa. The Cardinal was the person who had originally taken the lead in calling the Council of Pisa. The new papal election provided Western Christendom for a second time with three concurrent Popes. Utter confusion at the Church's highest level continued to rule the day. The new pope took the name of John XXIII.[7] He was an antipope to both the Roman and the Avignon papal lines.

The Neapolitan Cardinal Cossa had a much checkered background. He had entered the military and was involved with piracy as a young man. Following a change in his lifestyle, though not in his morals, he studied law at the University of Bologna. He then entered the Roman Curia and Pope Benedict IX eventually created him a Cardinal in 1402. Of the three contemporary Popes, John XXIII had the greatest support in the Church and succeeded in entering Rome on 12th April 1411. He called a local council in Rome in 1412, which was soon dissolved due to poor attendance. As pope, John XXIII had every intention to continue in his intricate financial endeavors and blatantly promoted nepotism. It was obvious that he was not the right man to restore universal unity in Christendom.

(e) Sigismund of Luxembourg was elected Holy Roman Emperor the same year that John XXIII was elected pope in 1410. Emperor Sigismund (1410-1431) was determined to do whatever

---

[7]   Baldassare Cossa (d. 1419) was invalidly elected pope and took the name of John XXIII (1410-1415). He should not be confused with Cardinal Angelo Giuseppe Roncalli (1881-1963) who was elected Pope in 1958 and took the name of Pope John XXIII (1958-1963).

was necessary to bring about unity both within the Church and in Western Europe. Having seen the disastrous local council of Rome of 1412, and having grown very impatient with John XXIII's inability to unite Western Christendom, the emperor insisted that the latter convoke a General Council. John XXIII had no choice but to acquiesce to the emperor's demands. Therefore, he decreed that a General Council would begin in the imperial city of Constance on 1st November 1414. John XXIII arrived at Constance on 28th October 1414. He was greeted jubilantly by five patriarchs, twenty-nine Cardinals, thirty-three archbishops, hundreds of bishops and theologians and canonists, and thousands of clerics and lay persons. It was an assembly similar to the one that had taken place at the Council of Pisa but on a much larger scale, and this time a pope was present. In his opening address, John XXIII stated that the aim of the Council was unity and reform within the Church. Things begun moving at a very slow pace. The Council did not start to work seriously until the arrival of Emperor Sigismund on Christmas Eve 1414. One of the declarations of the Council was its explicit affirmation that a General Council had authority over a Pope. Church governance in the future was to be based on a parliamentary system and Popes would be accountable to regular General Councils. The result of this line of thinking would bring about the rebellious and disastrous Council of Basle (1431-1449). As history would prove, Popes Martin V (1417-1431), Eugene IV (1431-1447), and Nicholas V (1447-1455) never wavered in their resolve to destroy Conciliarism and to reestablish papal supremacy over General Councils.

61. End of the Great Western Schism

(a) The Council of Constance (1414-1417) was a very unusual Council from the very start. It reflected the utter confusion that reigned at the time in Western Christendom. There were many reasons that created this atmosphere. First of all, a pope convoked the Council at a time when there were three papal claimants. Second, it was convoked at the insistence of a Holy Roman Emperor. The emperors of the old Roman Empire[8] had convoked General Councils, but this time a Holy Roman Emperor[9] forced a pope to convoke one. Furthermore, after Pope Gregory XII initially refused to recognize the Council's canonical status because he claimed that the antipope John XXIII had had no authority to convoke the assembly, it was agreed to state that Emperor Sigismund had called the Council originally, and that subsequently it was recognized by Pope Gregory XII as being canonical. Third, the Council was convoked not to deal with some straight-forward schism, as had happened in the past,[10] but a schism that had divided Western Christendom into three religious camps and given the Church three bishops who simultaneously claimed to be the true and legitimate successor to St. Peter.[11] Fourth, the Council sought unity within the Church by removing three concurrent Popes in favor of a new one. Fifth, the members of the Council, in attempting to neutralize Nations[12] that had many representatives who were ready to put forward their Nation's views and interests, decided that voting would not be based on one bishop one vote, but was to be cast by equal representations from each Nation, that is from Germany, France, England, and Italy.[13] Sixth, the Council officially declared that it was upholding the tenets of *Conciliarism*, which meant even a Pope fell under the authority of a General Council. Seventh, in order to ensure its validity, the same Council was convoked by two differ-

---

[8] The Byzantine emperors considered themselves to be the true successors of the ancient Roman emperors.

[9] That is, Emperor Sigismund.

[10] This was the case, for example, with the Donatist, the Acacian, and the Photian Schisms.

[11] The three Popes were: Gregory XII in the line of Urban VI (Roman obedience); Benedict XIII in the line of Clement VI (Avignon obedience); and John XXIII in the line established by the Council of Pisa.

[12] This was especially true for the Nation of Italy who had a superabundance of bishops.

[13] At the time the Council met, the Nations of Spain and Portugal were still under the obedience of Avignon and, therefore, did not have any representation. This situation would change while the Council was still in session.

ent and contemporary reigning Popes.[14] Eighth, the Council held a papal election where the electors were not only Cardinals but also included six additional members from each Nation[15] represented at the Council, and that a papal candidate needed two-thirds of the votes of both the College of Cardinals and each of the five Nations to be elected Pope.

(b) Soon after the Council of Constance convened, John XXIII became very frightened when uncomplimentary rumors about his personal behavior begun to circulate. Consequently, he promised to resign if the other two Popes, Gregory XII and Benedict XIII, would do the same. Having made such an offer, he fled Constance under the guise of night on 20th March 1415, and declared that the Council of Constance was called under great duress and, therefore, lacked the necessary papal authorization. The Council participants panicked when the pope's flight was discovered. Emperor Sigismund managed to calm down the assembly. Then, the Council summoned John XXIII to appear and, in order to give itself judicial authority, issued the decree *Haec Sancta* on 15th April 1415, stating that the Council was acting in accordance with the conciliarist teaching. Meanwhile, the imperial army caught up with John XXIII, and brought him back forcefully. The Council deposed John XXIII on 29th May 1415 on grounds of immoral behavior. He was imprisoned by an imperial decree. He remained a prisoner in Germany for the next two years, that is, until he recognized Pope Martin V (1417-1431), whereupon he was created Cardinal Bishop of Frescati. He died of natural causes soon thereafter.

Once the Council had declared John XXIII deposed, negotiations got under way with the other two Popes. Pope Gregory XII of the Roman obedience abdicated on 4th July 1415, after he had convoked the Council anew because he refused to recognize the

---

[14] John XXIII convoked the General Council in 1414, and Pope Gregory XII convoked it in 1415.

[15] These were the five Nations: Germany, France, Italy, England and Spain. Portugal was consolidated with Spain to form one Nation.

earlier convocation by John XXIII. The retired Pope was nominated permanent papal legate to Ancona, where he died on 18th October 1417.

The situation with Pope Benedict XIII of the Avignon obedience proved more complicated. He and the King of Aragon met with Emperor Sigismund,[16] but the pope refused to abdicate. Subsequently, the Council of Constance deposed Benedict XIII on 26th July 1417. All of his adherents[17] abandoned him after his deposition. Benedict XIII eventually shut himself up in a castle in Valencia from where he claimed to be the rightful bishop of Rome until he died in 1423.

Emperor Sigismund successfully entered into an accord with the kings of Spain and Portugal after his failed negotiations with Benedict XIII. It was agreed that the kings of Spain and Portugal would send delegates to a local council, also to be held in Constance, to settle their countries' papal allegiance. After the successful conclusion of the local council, Spain and Portugal sent their consolidated delegates to participate in the General Council of Constance. Consequently, the make-up of the nationalities at the Council changed in that France detached itself from the Anglo-German bloc and joined the Italo-Spanish bloc.

Emperor Sigismund was personally present at the Council from 27th January 1417 onwards. His resolve for Church reform never wavered. He was determined to effect Church reform before a new Pope was elected. The Italian bloc resisted the imperial proposal. A compromise was worked out where all the decrees regarding Church reform already approved by the Council would be promulgated on 9th October 1417, and then a new Pope would be elected before further discussion on Church reform. A conclave was convened and three days later, on 11th November 1417, Cardinal Oddone Colonna was elected Pope. He took the name of Pope Martin V (1417-1431).

---

[16] The meeting took place on 18th September 1416.
[17] These were the kingdoms of Aragon, Scotland, Castile and the Kingdom of the Two Sicilies.

The Council of Constance had managed to finally end the scandalous Great Western Schism and to enact Church reform. It decreed that, in the future, there should be a General Council first after five years, then after seven years, and from then onwards, every ten years. It passed regulations regarding schisms, the transfer of bishops, and the prohibition of illegal confiscation of Church property. Furthermore, it condemned a number of contemporary heresies, particularly those of John Wycliffe (c. 1330-1384)[18] and John Huss (c. 1372-1415).[19] Due to the diversity of self interests emanating from the different Nations that participated at the Council, it was decreed that each Nation should enter independently into its own concordat with the Holy See.[20] The Council had also managed to do something that had never been done before, namely it had judged and deposed two Popes[21] and elected a new one. Pope Martin V dissolved the Council of Constance on 22nd April 1418.

---

[18] John Wycliffe, an Englishman, was the founder of the Lollards, a heretical sect. He was a philosopher, theologian, and reformer. He bitterly opposed the institution of religious life and clerical celibacy, denied the doctrine of Transubstantiation and the teaching of Indulgences, rejected papal and episcopal authority, taught that the validity of the sacraments was determined by the moral character of the priest, upheld the personal interpretation of Sacred Scripture and that Sacred Scripture was the sole authority in religion. Wycliffe's teachings were initially condemned by Archbishop William Courtenay of Canterbury at the Blackfriars Council in 1382. Wycliffe's teachings on the rejection of papal authority paved the way for the English Reformation. His heretical teachings had a great influence on Czech scholars, especially John Huss.

[19] John Huss was a Bohemian reformer, a very popular preacher, and an excommunicated Catholic priest. He was deeply influenced by the teachings of John Wycliffe, which he promoted at the University of Prague along with his own teaching of predestination and personal election by God. His unrelenting attacks on the morals of the clergy provoked hostility in Bohemia. His teachings were denounced at Rome in 1407 and Pope Innocent VII, through archbishop Sbinko of Prague, forbade Huss to preach. Huss was excommunicated by Pope John XXIII in February 1411. Huss appealed to the Council of Constance. Emperor Sigismund gave him safe conduct and Huss traveled to defend himself at the Council. He was imprisoned during the entire trial at the Council of Constance where his teachings were condemned. He was burned at the stake on 6th July 1415. His death made him a national hero in Bohemia and the University of Prague declared him a martyr.

[20] Pope Nicholas V established concordats with Germany, France, England, and Spain during the year 1418.

[21] Pope Gregory XII, the legitimate Pope had resigned.

62. Popes Battle Conciliarism

There were three successive Popes who vigorously fought Conciliarism: Martin V, Eugene IV, and Nicholas V.

(a) Cardinal Oddone Colonna was born in the Campagna region of the Papal States around 1368. He was a member of the powerful Colonna family who, by then, had already given the Church twenty-seven Cardinals. Oddone studied at the University of Perugia, and was subsequently entrusted with a number of papal assignments under Popes Urban VI and Boniface IX.[22] Pope Urban VI created him a Cardinal in 1402. Eventually, the Cardinal abandoned the Roman obedience and attended the Council of Pisa. He participated in the conclaves that invalidly elected popes Alexander V and John XXIII. Cardinal Oddone was unanimously elected Pope, at age forty-one and still a sub-deacon, at the Council of Constance on 11th November 1417. He took the name of Pope Martin V. He was immediately ordained deacon, priest and bishop, and then crowned Pope in Constance on 21st November 1417. This papal election effectively brought an end to the Great Western Schism.

Pope Martin V was a very simple man and a good canonist. He owed no favors to any member of the Council of Constance. Pope John XXIII submitted to his obedience on 23rd June 1419, but Benedict XII remained recalcitrant till the end. His successor, pope Clement VIII, submitted to Pope Martin V in 1429. A self-elected pope, Benedict XIV, who had no following, succeeded pope Clement VIII as antipope.

Although Pope Martin V dissolved the Council of Constance on 22nd April 1418, he did not immediately return to Rome. While in Constance, Emperor Sigismund tried to persuade the new Pope to reside in a German imperial city, while France begged him to transfer to Avignon. Pope Martin V rejected all offers, and made

---

[22] Both of these Popes belonged to the Roman obedience.

known his determinate intention to reside in Rome. Then, he proceeded slowly to Rome, negotiating peace treaties with different Italian city-states and Queen Joanna of Naples on the way.

It took Pope Martin V three years to reach Rome, entering the city on 28th September 1420. At the time, Rome was in a pitiful state. He immediately embarked on restoring churches and public buildings, and slowly re-established papal leadership in the Papal States. In order to do the latter, he employed the assistance of many of his relatives whom he promoted through the practice of nepotism. Pope Martin V dedicated most of his energies primarily to curtailing Conciliarism. During his pontificate, he managed to reform most of the blatant abuses in the Roman Curia and to curb the secular encroachments on the Church in France. He also tried to suppress the Hussites and to heal the division between the Roman Catholic and Orthodox Churches. He failed in the last two endeavors.

Pope Martin V opened the General Council of Pavia[23] in April 1423, in accordance with the provisions of the Council of Constance.[24] Then, the plague broke out and the Council was transferred to Siena the following June. Due to its poor attendance and the dissent among Cardinals, the Pope saw the opportunity to dissolve the Council on 26th February 1424. The Council members were highly displeased with the papal aggressive action, but were appeased with his agreement to convoke a new Council in Basle within seven years hence. He called the Council of Basle, but died on 20th February 1431 before the Council convened, though he had already appointed Cardinal Giuliano Cesarini (1398-1444) as president of the Council with plenipotentiary powers. The Cardinal would play a very important role in the history of this Council and in the Conciliarist Movement.

Giuliano Cesarini was a member of a noble Roman family and, as such, belonged to a family that had undermined papal su-

---

[23] The General Council of Pavia began on 23rd April 1423.

[24] The Council of Constance had decreed that a General Council be called sometime during the fifth year following the conclusion of said Council.

premacy in the past. Giuliano studied at the universities of Perugia and Padua. He was a friend of Nicholas of Cusa (1401-1464),[25] with whom he shared his passionate support for the Conciliarist Movement.

(b) Cardinal Gabriele Condulmaro, the nephew of Pope Gregory XII, was elected to succeed Pope Martin V. Gabriele was born into a wealthy Venetian family in 1388. As a young man, he distributed his wealth to the poor and joined the Augustinians in Venice. His uncle, Pope Gregory XII, created him a Cardinal in 1408. When the same Pope appointed his nephew bishop of Siena in 1412, the Sienese rejected the nomination. Consequently, Gabriele resigned his bishopric. Prior to the conclave of 1431, Gabriele promised in writing that, should he be elected Pope, he would consult regularly with the Cardinals on matters of importance affecting the Church and the Papal States and pledged to give them half of the Church's revenues. The Cardinals were very pleased with the arrangement and elected him Pope on the first ballot on 4th March 1431. Anticipating a stormy pontificate, like that of Pope Eugene III, he took the name of Pope Eugene IV. His pontificate proved to be indeed very stormy due to his anti-conciliarism, his avid rejection of nepotism, and his conflict with the house of the Colonnas.[26] Ironically, his successor, Pope Nicholas V, was a member of the Colonna family.

---

[25] Cardinal Nicholas of Cusa, a very influential German Churchman and philosopher of his times, was an intellectual forerunner of the Renaissance and a Church reformer. He originally advocated that a General Council was superior to the Pope. But once he saw the dissension and fiasco of the Council of Basle he changed his mind and became a great supporter of the Popes from 1437 onwards. Pope Pius II appointed him as his Vicar General (1459) during which time he reformed the governing of Rome and the Papal States. He promoted the papal cause at the Imperial Diets of Mainz (1440), Frankfurt (1442), and Nuremberg (1444).

[26] The Colonna family was a very distinguished Roman family that played a major role in Papal and European politics between the twelfth and eighteenth centuries. Although vassals to the papacy, it was not unusual for the Colonnas to revolt against the Popes. The Colonna family supplied the Church with a number of Cardinals, one of whom became Pope Nicholas V. The Colonnas were the centuries old adversaries to another powerful Roman noble clan, the Orsini family.

Pope Eugene IV was a genuine reformer. He abhorred nepotism and led an admirable lifestyle. His reform efforts began to bear fruit through the renewal of religious life. Benedictine abbeys and monasteries were renewed through the founding of the new Congregation of St. Justina. The Augustinian Canons Regular founded a reformed congregation in Windesheim, Holland. The Franciscans renewed their members under the leadership of St. Bernardine of Siena and St. John of Capistrano. St. Colette reformed the Franciscan nuns in Burgundy, and the Dominican nuns were renewed in the spirit of St. Catherine of Siena. Through his papal legates, the Pope also managed to summon many provincial councils in Italy, Spain, France and Germany. Pope Eugene IV also founded the first seminary for the secular clergy in 1436 in the city of Florence, where he lived as a refugee. Finally, the Pope was very careful in his selection of the members of the College of Cardinals whose privileges and jurisdiction he increased. But the Pope also experienced many disappointments. He had to deal with the rebellious Council of Basle and its eventual election of the anti-pope Felix V (1439-1449). He had to confront King Charles VII of France (1422-1461) and the German princes. These secular rulers, without refuting papal primacy, began to impose legislation on local councils, the administration of the churches and dioceses, and the appointments of bishops. The Pope vehemently protested such interference. Pope Eugene IV also exerted himself in attempting to rouse Western European princes against the advances of the rising power of the Ottoman Turks. The first successes of the Christians were followed by their utter defeat near Varna in eastern Bulgaria on 10th November 1444.

The Pope's harsh character made France politically alienated during 1438, but the diplomatic skills of the papal legate Cardinal Aenaeus Sylvius Piccolomini,[27] brought the Empire over to the papal side in 1447.

(c) The Council of Basle (1431-1449) is one of the most con-

---

[27] Cardinal Piccolomini was elected Pope on 19th August 1458 and took the name of Pope Pius II. He died on 14th August 1464.

troversial Councils in the history of the Church. The Council had the great misfortune to inherit the tasks and the difficulties of the Council of Constance. Pope Martin V had convoked the Council right before he died. The new Pope, Eugene IV, confirmed Cardinal Giuliano Cesarini as the president of the Council. At the time, the Council was comprised of some fourteen bishops and abbots and a number of lower clergy. Due to bad press about the assembly that was reaching the Pope, he dissolved the Council on 18th December 1431, and stated that it would meet in Bologna eighteen months later. Pope Eugene IV, by dissolving the Council, alienated public opinion which had concluded that the new Pope was against Church reform. The Council's response, led by Cardinal Cesarini, ignored the Pope's orders and reaffirmed formally the Conciliarist teaching, namely a General Council was superior to a Pope. The secular rulers and the great universities, led by the brilliant Nicholas of Cusa, supported the Council's rebellious declaration. Thus, the Council became a rebellious assembly. Its members behaved as if there had been no papal order to dissolve the assembly. Furthermore, they issued a summons, dated 29th April 1432, ordering the Pope and his Cardinals to appear in front of them within three months. The Pope was adamant in his resolve and held out against the rebellious assembly for the next two years. Emperor Sigismund averted another schism by defusing the situation while in Rome to be crowned Holy Roman Emperor.[28] Sigismund, along with the German electors, reinforced his arguments by pointing out the turbulent political situation surrounding the Papal States, and convinced the Pope to recall his Bull of the dissolution of the Council of Basle. Consequently, Pope Eugene IV, on 15th December 1433, issued a papal statement that revoked his previous dissolution of the Council and recognized the validity of all of its acts. Nevertheless, the Council continued in its anti-papal disposition.

A revolution broke out in Rome in May 1434. The Pope fled the city and sought refuge in Florence.[29] Meanwhile, over the next

---

[28] The coronation took place on 21st May 1433.
[29] Pope Eugene IV remained outside of Rome for the next ten years.

three years, the Council, led by Cardinal d'Allemand, was very busy issuing pronouncements. It reaffirmed the Conciliarist decrees of the Council of Constance. It prescribed an oath that every newly elected Pope had to take, in which he declared his submission to a General Council. It issued decrees that restricted the authority of papal legates, and attempted to pass norms regarding the nomination of Cardinals and the activities of the Roman Curia. The end result was that the norms of the Council practically relinquished the role of a Pope to that of a figurehead.

The choice of the place to meet with the Byzantines for a re-union between the two Churches proved to be crucial. The Pope wanted an Italian city, but the Council wanted a non-Italian city, lest the papal choice for the meeting-place might be perceived as a papal victory. The discussion lasted two years. Finally, the Pope ran out of patience. The Byzantine envoys at Basle broke their ties with the Council and sided with the Pope. The Pope transferred the Council to Ferrara, which was formally opened on 8th January 1438, under the presidency of the saintly Cardinal Niccolò Albergati of Bologna (1373-1443). Some members of the Council refused to leave Basle and formed another rebellious assembly. There were now two Councils in session: one under the legitimate authority of Pope Eugene IV and the other being the rebellious council of Basle.

Cardinals Cesarini and Cusa deserted the Basle assembly and went over to the Pope's side. Nevertheless, the assembly at Basle declared Pope Eugene IV deposed in 1439, established a schism, and elected Duke Amadeus VII of Savoy as antipope. He took the name of Felix V. The schismatic assembly continued to meet until 1449, despite the fact that it steadily lost the support of every Nation. Eventually, every Nation declared its obedience to Pope Eugene IV. But the Pope did not live to see the end of the rebellious council.[30] It was the Holy Roman Emperor Frederick III of Hapsburg (1440-1493) who, as a result of the Concordat of Vienna between the Holy See and the Empire in 1448, ordered the rebellious assembly to leave Basle. The assembly moved to Lausanne. The following

---

[30] Pope Eugene IV died on 23rd February 1447.

year the antipope Felix V abdicated[31] and the assembly dissolved. The short-lived schism had finally come to an end.

63. The End of Conciliarism

The Council of Florence, despite its traditional designated name, assembled successively in three cities: Ferrara (1438-1439), Florence (1439-1443), and Rome (1443-1445). Technically speaking, this Council is a continuation of the Council of Basle from the moment of papal dissolution of the latter in 1437. This Council of Florence was convoked after the majority of the members of the Council of Basle refused to accept the papal dissolution of their assembly. Pope Eugene IV appointed Cardinal Niccolò Albergati of Bologna as the president of the new convocation of the Council that opened in Ferrara on 8th January 1438. The designation of the Council as a General Council branded the ongoing council of Basle as rebellious and devoid of further authority.

The primary purpose of the Council of Florence was to seek the re-unification between the Roman and Byzantine Churches. The Byzantine Emperor John VIII Palaeologus (1425-1448), Patriarch Joseph II of Constantinople (1416-1439), Archbishop (later Cardinal) Bessarion of Nicaea,[32] and Metropolitan Mark of Ephesus represented the Greek side. The Roman side had Cardinals Albergati, Cusa and Cesarini, the Dominican theologian John of Montenero, and Pope Eugene IV. Some members from both sides were opposed to the proposed union between the two Churches.

---

[31] Antipope Felix V resigned on 7th April 1449.

[32] John Bessarion (1403-1472) was a Greek scholar, statesman, and churchman. His arduous work to bring about a union between the Byzantine and Roman Churches had made him very unpopular in Constantinople. Nevertheless, he made his profession of the Roman Catholic Faith and remained in Italy for the rest of his life. Pope Eugene IV created him a Cardinal in 1439. Bessarion was almost elected to succeed Pope Eugene IV at the next conclave. Subsequently, Cardinal Bessarion fulfilled many important papal assignments until his death.

Nevertheless, after long negotiations, commissions of equal representation of Rome and Constantinople were formed. Subsequently, the Council got to work on the major controversial issues: the *Filioque* clause, the Procession of the Holy Spirit,[33] Papal Primacy, the use of unleavened bread at the celebration of the Eucharist, and the doctrine of Purgatory.

The Council soon proved to be financially very burdensome for the Pope. Consequently, the city-state of Florence volunteered to bear the expenses. Thus, the Council was transferred to Florence on 26th February 1439. The discussions between Romans and Byzantines on the doctrine of the Procession faltered until Archbishop Bessarion declared that the Byzantines never denied that the Holy Spirit proceeds from the Son. The deadlock was broken and further discussions followed. Then, Pope Eugene IV personally addressed the Byzantines on 27th May 1439. The pro-union members among the Byzantines urged their brethren that the two phrases were neither contradictory nor inconsistent but were two correct ways of expressing the same faith. Each declaration affirmed the unity of faith with diversity of rite. The Roman and the Byzantine members of the Council, by the end of June, managed to agree on all of the major doctrinal issues between the two Churches. Both sides signed the Decree of Union, *Laetentur Coeli,* on 5th July 1439. It was promulgated the following day amid great joy. Metropolitan Mark of Ephesus (d. 1444) was the only Byzantine prelate who opposed the decree.

The Council of Florence continued its sessions after the Byzantines departed. The Council then turned its attention to the schismatic council of Basle, the issue of Conciliarism, and more attempts of union with other Eastern Churches. The Council excommunicated all of the members of the schismatic assembly at Basle in 1439, established the union of the Armenians that same year,

---

[33] The Roman Catholic Church professes that the Holy Spirit proceeds from the Father *and* the Son. The Orthodox Churches profess that the Holy Spirit proceeds from the Father *through* the Son.

and, on 20th April 1441, declared the Pope to be superior to every General Council, thereby giving a deadly blow to the Conciliarist Movement. Another union with Rome, that of the Coptic Church in Egypt, followed in 1442. The Council was transferred to Rome in 1443. There followed the union with the Jacobites later that year. The union of the Syrians, the Chaldaeans and the Maronites of Cyprus took place in 1444. The union of the Nestorians was declared in 1445.

The Renaissance and the Church

---

64. The Beginning of the Renaissance in Rome

(a) The humanistic spirit of the Renaissance was introduced into the papacy by Pope Nicholas V. At the same time, he attended well to the spiritual needs of the Church. Such an affirmation cannot be made of his immediate successors who lived more like Renaissance humanistic princes rather than spiritual leaders of the Universal Church. The Church, even at its highest spiritual authority on earth, had to pay a very heavy moral price for the glory and magnificence of the Renaissance. Some of the Renaissance Popes had come from a background that was immoral, corrupt, overwhelmingly secular, and devoid of spirituality. This sad state of affairs at the highest level in the Catholic Church had not been seen since the turbulent tenth century. Some Popes virtually practiced simony to ensure their papal election and avidly promoted nepotism. Some Popes, at the time of their papal election, had already fathered illegitimate children. Many of these Popes ensured that their progeny was established within dynasties in Italian princely States, crowded the College of Cardinals with their illegitimate sons and other relatives who were unworthy, incompetent, unsuitable, and corrupt. They turned the papal tiara into a pawn for blatant temporal gains. However, not everything was negative with the Church of Rome. A major consequence for the Renaissance spirit in the Church was that contemporary Popes were very successful politicians, though disastrous as spiritual leaders due to their private moral lifestyle. They gave Western civilization a great culture by managing to attract brilliant scholars, sculptors, painters, architects, and poets who produced some of the greatest works of art human history will ever see. They managed to establish the papacy as a great temporal power in European politics, but, in the end, rendered it devoid of moral fiber.

Within fifty years from the election of Pope Nicholas V in 1447, Rome would become the hub of moral corruption with some Popes at the helm. An evil lifestyle would run through the papal palace for forty years thereafter. Yet, this same period also produced great saints. The dark cloud over Rome had, after all, a silver lining.

(b) Tommaso Parentucelli was born at Sarzana, Liguria, in 1397. He showed brilliant scholarship from early youth, but was forced to abandon his studies at the University of Bologna due to the premature death of his parents. He was hired consecutively as a tutor by the powerful Strozzi and Albizzi families in Florence. Tommaso returned to the University of Bologna to finish his studies in theology in 1419. The saintly bishop (later Cardinal) Niccolò Albergati of Bologna took him into his service, where Tommaso stayed for the next twenty years. Pope Eugene IV appointed Tommaso bishop of Bologna upon the death of Cardinal Albergati in 1444. The newly appointed bishop, due to the widespread unrest in Bologna, was unable to enter the city and take formal possession of his diocese. Consequently, the Pope entrusted him with a number of important diplomatic missions in Italy and Germany. Their successes were rewarded with a Cardinal's hat in 1446. Pope Eugene IV died on 23rd February 1447 and Tommaso was elected as his successor the following 6th March. He took the name of Pope Nicholas V in memory of his great patron, Cardinal Niccolò Albergati.

Pope Nicholas V devoted himself to establish Rome as the center of Western civilization. Due to his cultural endeavors, he is considered the first, and the best, of the Renaissance Popes. By the time of his papal election, the new Pope had already established himself as a great humanist, imbued in the spirit of the Renaissance. Soon after his election, the new Pope reformed the governance of the Papal States and began ruling with a benign hand. He undertook the restoration and rebuilding of Rome and of the cities that peppered the Papal States. He welcomed all sorts of artists, irrespective of their private morals, and would lavish his generosity over scholars. He especially set his heart on rebuilding the Leonine City, the Vatican, and St. Peter's Basilica.[1] But the crowning glory of his humanist efforts was the establishment of the Vatican Apostolic Library in 1450. Traditionally, Pope Nicholas V is regarded as the founder of the Vatican Apostolic Library, because he was the one to conceive the idea of a public or "Vatican" library, as distinct, that is, from a purely papal or private one. The Vatican Apostolic Library remains one of the most famous, prestigious, and vast libraries in the world. It was a masterpiece in the world of the Renaissance Era.

Pope Nicholas V, while busy with his humanist undertakings, also attended to the needs of the Church. He carefully created new Cardinals. He established papal rights and reformed the Church benefices system[2] through the Concordat of Vienna in 1448 with Emperor Frederick III. The Concordat effected both the collapse of the rebellious assembly of Basle and the submission of the antipope Felix V in 1449. In commemoration of the union with the Byzantines and the restoration of a united Christendom under one papal authority, Pope Nicholas V declared 1450 as a Year of Jubilee. The celebration also served as proof that Rome was the center of Western civilization. At the conclusion of the Jubilee Year, the Pope sent papal legates to the majority of the European states, mandating them to root out ecclesiastical abuses and nepotism. Cardinal Guillaume d'Estouteville (1403-1483) was commissioned to his

---

[1] At the time of the election of Pope Nicholas V, St. Peter's Basilica still was the one that had been erected by Emperor Constantine the Great. It was in great need of repair.

[2] Papal attempts to bring equity in the benefice system had been made during previous pontificates.

native France, Cardinal Nicholas of Cusa was sent to northern Germany and England, St. John of Capistrano (1386-1456)[3] was dispatched to southern Germany. The latter two held successful provincial and local synods to promote papal authority and sound Church practices. Papal supremacy was further manifested by the coronation in Rome of Frederick III Hapsburg, in 1452, as Holy Roman Emperor.[4]

Nevertheless, despite many successes, Pope Nicholas V had to face many disheartening realities during his pontificate. He was not able to quell the spirit of rebellion in the Papal States.[5] Stefano Porcaro, who numbered Popes Eugene IV and Nicholas V among his mentors and benefactors, led a number of revolts to establish the Papal States as a republic. There was also a very serious assassination scheme to murder the Pope. There was the heart-breaking failure of the union between the Roman and the Byzantine Churches. The *Decree of Union* was not accepted by most of the Orthodox in Constantinople. Many Byzantines preferred to succumb to the rule of the advancing Ottoman Turks rather than to Rome. The Christian forces on the Eastern European front suffered a heavy defeat from the Ottoman Turks at Kosovo, waged between 14th and 20th October 1449. The imperial city of Constantinople fell to the Ottoman Turks on 29th May 1453 and the Byzantine Emperor

---

[3] John of Capistrano was a lawyer, the secular governor of Perugia, married and a soldier. When he was a prisoner of war of the Malatesta family, he experienced a vision of St. Francis of Assisi that, upon his release, led him to renounce his worldly aspirations and join the Franciscan Friars Minor after he had obtained a dispensation from his marriage vows in 1416. He was ordained a priest in 1420 and immediately began a series of missions throughout Italy. He was instrumental in bringing the union between the Franciscan Conventuals and the Franciscan Observants in 1430 and with his old friend, St. Bernardine of Siena, began the reform of his Franciscan Order. He was entrusted with several papal diplomatic missions in Austria and Hungary. He raised an army against the Turks and, having defeated them on 22nd July 1456, he died from the plague on 23rd October of the same year.

[4] The imperial coronation of Frederick III as Holy Roman Emperor was the last imperial coronation to take place in Rome.

[5] Pope Nicholas V, in order to secure peace within the Papal States, sowed discord and suspicion among his foes. This policy would come back to haunt him and his successors.

Constantine XI Palaeologus (1448-1453) perished in the process. The Pope's summons for a Crusade against the Ottoman Turks fell on deaf ears. To add insult to injury, some of the European city-states, like Genoa and Venice, befriended the Turkish enemy for political and economic reasons. This sad state of world affairs had a grave toll on the Pope's health. He died during the night of 24th March 1455. Like his immediate predecessor, Pope Eugene IV, Pope Nicholas V seriously attempted to reform the Church. These attempts had limited success.

---

65. Need for Inner Reform

(a) There are many complicated reasons that stood at the background of the Protestant Reformation. The Great Western Schism was history, but the effects of having two or even three concurrent Popes were long lasting. The Conciliarist Movement was defeated, but it had presented the opportunity for a new way of perceiving papal authority. The Popes of the first half of the fifteenth century had enacted reforming laws, but failed to eradicate abuse within the Church. The Church saw the rise of the Renaissance Popes in the middle of the fifteenth century and their dreams of aggrandizing Rome. Other reasons that led to the Protestant Reformation are being presented elsewhere.

The new historical situation had an old ring to it. Much money was needed to enact the new papal plans. There was grave disorganization and abuse at all levels within the Church. Despite initial papal efforts to wipe out abuse and nepotism, the Roman Curia managed to continue with its scandalous way of life. The Concordat of Vienna in 1448 allowed Popes to gain control over a vast amount of Church appointments. These appointments became a source of great evil within the Church, viz. simony. Church offices began to be sold. The bad curial practices of past centuries had come back with great gusto. Simony ruled the day. Some Popes, on the other hand, were, at best, passively compliant with simony because it assured papal financial power. Even a Cardinal's hat went to the highest bidder. Moreover, the Roman Curia leveled more taxes on newly conferred benefices.

Another grave abuse was pluralism. The system entailed that a person was able to possess more than one benefice or diocese at any given time so as to ensure he had enough income to maintain a regal standard of living in the spirit of the Renaissance. The fact that a person was simultaneously in charge of more than one benefice or bishopric meant frequent absenteeism. Some bishops never set foot in some of their multiple dioceses. The situation led to further abuses at the local level since there was no authority on hand to check them. The worldliness of the bishops was compounded with the fact that the European nobility, as a result of simony, was able to monopolize high Church offices. It was not unusual for a secular ruler to have one or more of his younger sons appointed to some bishopric, thereby assuring his child's regal comfort, irrespective of his suitability. Neither was it uncommon for regal boys to be appointed bishops in their childhood without receiving priestly or episcopal ordination. Many of these boys grew up to be worldly men, to live immoral lives and father children, and to live openly in concubinage. They were consumed with pleasure seeking, mesmerized by materialism, and disinterested in matters spiritual.

(b) It has been stated that some Popes, many Cardinals, many bishops, and many abbots were morally corrupt and led lives not conducive to their vocation. The same sad state of affairs was found among the majority of monks, the lower secular clergy[6] and the religious. The Hundred Years' War between England and France,[7] the ongoing struggles in Italy and Germany between the Popes and

---

[6] Secular clergy is a term for clergy who belong to a diocese and are not members of a monastic or religious community.

[7] The so-called *Hundred Years War* (1337-1435) began when King Edward III of England (1327-1377) claimed the French Crown and assumed the title of King of France in 1337 despite the fact that France was being ruled by King Philip (Valois) VI (1328-1350). The war was tragic for both countries. It ended when King Henry VI of England (1422-1461) gave up all of its English possessions in France, except for Calais, in 1453, during the reign of the French King Charles VII (1422-1461).

the Holy Roman Emperors and their consequent factions, the Great Western Schism, and the devastation from the Black Death had left the monastic life in a very bad state. Abbacies became political appointments, and abbeys became symbols of political successes and places where the ancient monastic rule was dead. Monastic vows were given lip service, community life was nil, community prayers were rarely said, and common property was replaced by personal possessions. Secular absentees and worldly abbots governed abbeys and monasteries.

The majority of the lower secular clergy mirrored their bishops and the Roman Curia. These men of God were in fact men of the world. They were after multiple benefices, negligent of their pastoral duties and responsibilities, worldly, pleasure-seeking, poorly trained, ignorant in matters of faith, superstitious, disinterested in instructing the young, and usually living in concubinage. Many members of the Mendicant Orders were caught up in a similar lifestyle.

(c) A trend evolved among some clergy and laity to perceive the reception of the sacraments of Holy Communion and of Penance as unnecessary for one's spiritual journey. They taught that one's own prayer life and meditation on Sacred Scripture sufficed.[8] Ultimately, the spirit of the Renaissance exalted man to a very high and exaggerated degree. Men and women considered themselves sophisticated if they were fascinated by the eminence of the individual rather than the community and if they sought a deeper quest for all that was secular. This attitude infiltrated a number of occupants of the papal throne. The result was that of a very deep void in the spiritual life of the Church at its highest level. The Christian notion of service to others was flipped and became the humanitarian notion of service to oneself. Nonetheless, the picture of the Church at the time was not altogether bleak. It would be incomplete if it were not stated that there were some very powerful churchmen and secular persons who occupied high offices in different countries and led a very holy life.

---

[8] This attitude toward one's spiritual life was successfully promoted by Martin Luther.

The majority of people, good and bad alike, knew that there was a great need for Church reform. The argument for reform regarded which means were to be used in order to achieve it. The most successful method of Church reform, on the universal level, had always been through a Church Council, even though the then recent record of such a Council had been very tarnished. It was generally agreed that a reforming Council had to be assembled and led by a Pope. Nevertheless, despite the obvious need and the collateral pressure for a reforming Council under the leadership of the Pope, there was no sign that such an undertaking was about to take place. Rather, the Renaissance papacy was more concerned in its political dealings with the various Italian city-states and the cultural aggrandizement of Rome than with the universal interests of the Catholic Church. Consequently, many Cardinals, bishops, abbots, pastors, priests, monks and religious were either unable or unwilling to provide spiritual leadership when the Protestant Reformation broke out. It took a religious revolution from the roots to force the Church's leadership at all levels to take the reform movement seriously.

---

66. Visions for Church Reform

(a) Attempts of inner reform before the Protestant Reformation showed some bright instances of renewal being carried out in many and varied ways. Reforming attempts and programs were either undertaken or proposed by different Popes, bishops and lower clergy, canonists and universities, monks, friars, secular princes, and the laity. The Popes who reigned from the middle of the fifteenth to the middle of the sixteenth centuries, although absorbed in politics and worldly matters, were acutely aware that the Church was in dire need of reform. Every one of them fully understood the havoc the Councils of Constance and Basle had imposed on the Church. They were conscious of the struggles some of their predecessors had

undergone to eradicate the Conciliarist Movement. Though Popes
Martin V and Eugene IV, in particular, had managed to suppress
the Conciliarist Movement, its embers were still hot. Various secular
princes and ecclesiastical bodies, supported by some universities and
canonists, still maintained that a General Council was superior to
a Pope. Although some Popes wished to initiate reform, they were
cognizant that absolute papal authority over a General Council had
not yet been accepted fully throughout the Church. Therefore, they
usually interpreted a call for a General Council as a call to revolt.
Thus, reform-minded Popes tried to initiate Church reform through
direct papal action in the form of papal bulls or decrees or through
their papal legates. Pope Pius II (1458-1464),[9] an adherent to the
Conciliarist Movement until 1445, was sincerely committed to
Church reform and drew up a papal bull, *Pastor Aeternus*, wherein
he laid out procedures in Church governance that bound even the
Pope himself. Unfortunately, he died before the papal bull was published. Even the worldly Pope Alexander VI (1492-1503)[10] showed

---

[9] Aeneas Sylvius Piccolomini (1405-1464) was elected Pope on the 19th August 1458
and took the name of Pope Pius II. He became one of the greatest humanists in
his time while still in his early twenties, leading a dissolute life for many years.
After being secretary to several Cardinals, he became a prominent leader at the
council of Basle, opposed Pope Eugene IV and supported the antipope Felix V.
He was an eloquent promoter of the Conciliarist Movement. Holy Roman Emperor Frederick III crowned him as the Imperial Poet in 1442 before appointing
him as his secretary. He reconciled with Pope Eugene IV in 1445 and became
his great ally. He reconciled the emperor and the Pope later that year. Shortly
thereafter, he reformed his immoral life and received Holy Orders in 1446. As
bishop of Siena, he enthusiastically promoted a crusade against the Turks after
the fall of Constantinople in 1453. Pope Callistus III created him a Cardinal in
1450. After being elected Pope, his papacy became consumed with promoting,
and subsequently proclaiming, a crusade against the menacing Turks. He formally
condemned the Conciliarist Theory in 1460. He died in Ancona on 14th August
1464, soon after he had put himself at the head of a crusade against the Turks.

[10] Rodrigo Borgia was a Spaniard by birth and a nephew of Pope Callistus III. The
Spanish spelling of the family name was Borja. He served in prominent positions
in the Papal Curia of his uncle, of Pope Paul II and, for a short time, of Pope
Sixtus IV. Rodrigo was elected Pope, mostly through bribery, on 11th August
1492 and took the name of Pope Alexander VI. Rodrigo never gave up his immoral lifestyle, embroiled the papacy in political and family intrigues, practiced
blatant nepotism and tried to secure princely positions for his children, par-

some interest in reform and went so far as to draw up another papal document. It contained the most comprehensive reform program between the rebellious Council of Basle and Council Lateran V. The papal document never saw the light of day because the Pope got distracted with political and family dynastic intrigues.

(b) The last papal attempt at reform before the Protestant Reformation was made at the Council Lateran V. It had eventually assembled under the warrior Pope, Julius II (1503-1513),[11] on 1st October 1512, and was concluded under the worldly Pope Leo X (1513-1521)[12] on 16th March 1517. The Camaldolese monks Giustiniani and Quirini drew up a radical reform program for the Council Fathers. They criticized harshly the papal fascination with secular politics and worldliness, the bureaucratic centralization at

---

ticularly Cesare and Lucretia. As Pope, he divided the New World between Spain and Portugal (1493-1494), prosecuted and condemned Savonarola (1452-1498) in 1498, called for a crusade against the Turks (1499-1500) and declared 1500 as a Year of the Great Jubilee.

[11] Giuliano della Rovere was the nephew of Pope Sixtus IV. His papal uncle lavished him with Church titles and benefices. Giuliano was very instrumental, through bribery, in the election of Pope Innocent VIII and continued to lead a prominent role in papal affairs that led him to become a deadly enemy of Cardinal Rodrigo Borgia. After Borgia was elected Pope as Alexander VI in 1492, Giuliano fled to France. Though the two churchmen were reconciled in 1498, Giuliano stayed away from Rome until Pope Alexander VI died in 1503. Following the very brief reign of Pope Pius III (8th - 18th October 1503), Giuliano was elected Pope on 1st December 1503 and took the name of Pope Julius II. He was the last Pope to personally lead a papal army into war. In between leading wars, Pope Julius II managed to initiate some Church reforms, particularly declaring as null and void any papal election procured through simony. The Pope called the Council, Lateran V, formed the Holy League against France, was a great Renaissance patron and recognized the genius of such artists as Raphael, Michelangelo and Bramante. He declared an Indulgence for the rebuilding of St. Peter's which eventually was instrumental for Martin Luther's open rebellion against Rome.

[12] Giovanni de Medici was elected Pope on 9th March 1513. He was the second son of Lorenzo de Medici, 'the Magnificent.' He was created a Cardinal at age 13 and, as a young teenager, led an immoral lifestyle in Germany, Holland and France, until he returned to Rome in 1500. He underwent a personal conversion in his early thirties. He was elected Pope at age thirty-seven and took the name of Leo X. Although one of the most extravagant Renaissance Popes, he had moral integrity and was sincerely religious. Nevertheless, he was not too concerned about Church affairs, very liberal with papal favors, a good administrator, and diplomat for the Holy See. Unfortunately, he failed to appreciate what was at stake for the Church with Luther's revolt.

all levels within the hierarchical structure of the Church, especially within the Roman Curia, and the regretful ignorance of the clergy. Their program called for the revision of canon law, for the proper training of the clergy, and for the Pope to convoke General Councils every five years. The program prefigured many reforms that were to be enacted by the subsequent Council of Trent (1545-1563). Unfortunately, the program was too spiritual and revolutionary for Pope Leo X and the majority of the Roman Curia. Thus, it was set aside quietly. The failure of Council Lateran V was the immediate background to the Protestant Reformation.

---

67. Attempts at Church Reform

A number of diocesan bishops and secular clergy, especially in Germany, made various reform attempts. The lay people of the imperial country, having witnessed the rising and fall of many reforming or corrupt Holy Roman Emperors, were undergoing a spiritual re-awakening on the eve of the Protestant Reformation. Many churchmen could no longer tolerate abuse within their local diocese and parishes. Martin Luther was one such person.

(a) Monastic communities undertook attempts to reform. The Carthusians, who exercised considerable power in favor of reform in Germany during the fifteenth century, never needed to reform. Nevertheless, these monks urged other monastic communities to undergo reform. The Benedictine monks who belonged to the Bursfeld and Melk German congregations had begun their own inner reform. There was the reestablishment of life and prayer in community. Unfortunately, the abbeys and monasteries that belonged to these congregations did not find much support among their Church leaders.

(b) Some of the Mendicant Orders tried to reform. As in the case with the reforming monks, these attempts were at the grass roots levels. They began with individuals and spread, though in a limited way, to other members of their religious congregations. Such efforts were carried out by persons like the great Franciscan preachers and saints, Bernardine of Siena (1384-1444) and John of Capistrano, who established the Franciscan Observants in an effort to recapture the spirit of St. Francis of Assisi.

St. Bernardine of Siena, born in Massa di Carrera, Italy, in 1380, became a Franciscan of the Strict Observance in 1402 and its Vicar General in 1438. A most eloquent preacher, he aimed at reforming the Italian Peninsula. He eventually managed, with the help of his friend St. John of Capistrano, to reform his order and unite it with the Franciscan Conventuals. By the time of his death on 20th May 1444, he had become one of the most influential persons in the moral renewal in the Church in Italy.

There were also the reformed Dominican congregation in Lombardy, and the reformed Augustinian Hermits in Holland and in Germany.

(c) Some secular princes, too, made an effort at reform. For example, Pope Innocent VIII (1484-1492) authorized the Dukes of Saxony, in 1485, to implement monastic reform in their German principality. The French Kings of the latter part of the fifteenth century also used their regal influence to initiate Church reform in France. The German and French reformist endeavors did not become widespread. But the royal rulers in Spain made much progress. Spain, at the time, was gifted with many powerful, energetic, prudent, and saintly bishops. All of them, under the leadership of Archbishop Ximénes de Cisneros of Toledo, found royal patronage and support in their reform efforts.

(d) Cardinal Francisco Ximénes de Cisneros (1436-1517) was one of the greatest religious and political leaders in Spain from 1495 until his death. He was born in Torrelaguna, in the Kingdom of Castile, and studied at Alcalà de Henares, Salamanca and Rome, where he caught the attention of Pope Sixtus IV. While he was serving Cardinal Mendoza as his Vicar General, Ximénes suddenly gave up his office to become a Franciscan of the Strict Observance in Toledo. His extreme austerity soon attracted crowds of penitents who sought him out as confessor and spiritual advisor, and he fled to a remote monastery. He reluctantly became the personal confessor of Queen Isabella of Spain,[13] who sought his advice on spiritual and political matters. Supported by the Queen, Ximénes began to reform his own Franciscan brothers in Castile in 1491. Soon after the death of his friend Cardinal Mendoza, on 11th January 1495, Ximénes was appointed Archbishop of Toledo and High Chancellor of Castile. Despite his exalted ecclesiastical and political offices, he continued to lead an austere ascetical life. He became virtually the ruler of Castile in 1506 and held the position until King Ferdinand V of Spain, the widower of Isabella, went to assume his regal position there in 1507. The archbishop received the Cardinal's hat that year. Upon the death of King Ferdinand V on 23rd January 1516, Ximénes became the regent of Castile during the minority of King Charles I of Spain.[14] Cardinal Ximénes died on 8th November 1517. In addition to his service to the Church and to Spain, he was a great patron of learning. His leadership formed the background for Spain's ability to supply the Church with extraordinary saints, scholars and leaders during the Catholic Church's Counter-Reformation that followed the Council of Trent.

(e) There were the small but impressive reform movements led by the laity. These movements can be grouped into two: those led by the regular lay believers and those led by the humanists.

The first group approached reform through personal

---

[13] Isabella of Castile (1451-1504), Queen of Spain, was the half-sister of King Henry IV, King of Castile and Leòn. She married her cousin Prince Ferdinand (1452-1516), son of King John II of Aragon, in 1469. She was declared Queen of Castile upon the death of her half-brother in 1474. Ferdinand succeeded his father as King Ferdinand V in 1479. Isabella, however, ruled Castile in her own right as Queen and, upon her death in 1504, she was succeeded by her daughter, Joan the Insane. Isabella was a profoundly religious woman. On the other hand, Ferdinand was a Renaissance prince who constantly sought power and dominions. Under the joint leadership of the couple, Columbus discovered America in 1492, the Moors were expelled from Granada that same year, the Spanish culture was patronized and, through their political shrewdness and marriages of their children, Spain was transformed into a great empire.

[14] King Charles I of Spain, the grandson of Queen Isabella and King Ferdinand of Spain, is better known as Holy Roman Emperor Charles V of Hapsburg.

sanctification, works of charity and daily prayer. Holland saw the establishment of the Brethren of the Common Life. Italy experienced the establishment of the Ursulines in Brescia. On the one hand, the Brethren of the Common Life was an association founded in the fourteenth century with the purpose of promoting a deeper level of Christian commitment. It was founded in Utretch, Holland, by Greet de Groote (1340-1384), who underwent a personal conversion and rejected his luxurious and selfish lifestyle to take up a devout and simple life. He preached throughout Holland against clerical decadence. In the process of his missions, he formed the association, requiring no vows from both clerical and lay followers. He simply asked them to live according to their responsibilities in their respective vocations. His followers put great stress on teaching and offered a first class free education to whomsoever wanted to attend their schools. Following his death in 1384, the Brethren became organized into communities under the leadership of Florentius Radwijns (1350-1400).[15] On the other hand, the Ursulines were founded by St. Angela Merici (1474-1540). While a Franciscan tertiary, she devoted herself to the education of young girls and the care of sick women. While on a pilgrimage to the Holy Land (1524-1525), she became temporarily blind and began to experience spiritual visions. She returned to Brescia, Italy, where the visions continued, and founded there an organization[16] for women in 1535. St. Angela called her organization after her patron St. Ursula, hence the name Ursulines. The organization was made up of virgins who stayed in their own homes while dedicating their lives to Christian education. Pope Gregory XIII (1572-1585), at the instigation of St. Charles Borromeo (1538-1584) in 1572, recognized the charism of the organization and allowed its members to live in community

---

[15] Members of the Brethren of the Common Life included Thomas à Kempis (c. 1380-1471), Pope Adrian VI (1459-1523), and Cardinal Nicholas of Cusa (1401-1464).

[16] At the time of St. Angela Merici, the Catholic Church recognized only cloistered communities for women and did not as yet recognize what came to be known as congregations for women religious. The former are called *nuns* while the latter are called *sisters*.

with simple vows. Thus, the Ursulines became the oldest teaching Congregation of women religious in the history of the Catholic Church. The branch of Ursulines in Paris became strictly cloistered in 1612. Both types of Ursuline communities continue to exist to this day.

The second group of reforming laity consisted of humanists. Their approach rested on their assumption that reform in the Church could be achieved through good example and learning, since learning would increase a person's piety, while knowledge would make one a better Christian. Some of them criticized recklessly the sacred Church institutions and did much to prepare many for the Protestant attack on the Catholic Church. Moreover, many of these humanists rejected Scholasticism. Those humanists who maintained the supremacy of secular values were not much more than pagans. On the other hand, many humanists made some very positive contributions by influencing the renewal of theology that would equip many Catholic Counter-Reformation leaders.

The humanist movement traced its origins to Francesco Petrarch, who was an Italian poet and one of the greatest humanists. He studied law at the University of Montpellier, between 1319 and 1323, and at Bologna, between 1323 and 1325. He became a cleric in Avignon, in 1326, during the Papal Babylonian Captivity. He traveled all over central Europe between 1330 and 1337, visiting scholars, copying manuscripts, and publishing his own poems that dealt with religious and secular themes. He became entangled with the short-lived republican movement in Rome, led by Cola di Rienzo (c. 1313-1354). He subsequently was employed at several political embassies. Throughout his life, Petrarch's religious nature was in constant conflict with his love for pagan culture. Some of his writings were greatly influenced by the great Italian poet and philosopher, Dante Alighieri (1265-1321), particularly by his poem, *The Divine Comedy.*

Many humanists remained faithful to the Church, such as Desiderius Erasmus and St. Thomas More. Desiderius Erasmus (c. 1469-1536) led the Christian Humanists. He was born in Holland

and, as a youth, attended the free school ran by the Brethren of the Common Life in Deventer. He reluctantly became an Augustinian Canon in 1486 and was ordained a priest in 1492. He continued his studies of the classics and the Fathers of the Church at the Universities of Paris and Oxford. While in Oxford, he fell under the influence of John Colet (c. 1466-1519), who helped him develop a deep dislike of Scholasticism and directed him to study the New Testament. Erasmus returned to Paris in 1500, where he immersed himself into the study of Greek. He translated the New Testament from Greek into Latin while he was back in England and before he took up residence in Italy (1506-1509). He returned to England in 1509, taught Greek at Cambridge University, and forged a great friendship with the future Catholic English martyrs, Bishop John Fisher (1469-1535) and Thomas More (1478-1535). He settled down in Basle in 1521, but had to flee the city when the strong wave of Protestantism reached it in 1529. He returned to Basle shortly before his death in 1536. Erasmus was the most renowned scholar of his age. He advocated the study of the Bible and the Fathers of the Church as the foundation of a Catholic critical and historical theology. Although frequently critical of the Catholic Church's institutions and practices, he remained Catholic and rejected the Protestant Reformation till the end his life.

One of Erasmus' greatest friends was St. Thomas More, the former Lord Chancellor of England and a martyr for the Catholic Faith under the English King Henry VIII (1491-1547). Thomas had fallen in love with the classics at an early age. He studied law and was called to the bar in 1501. Having practiced law for three years in London, he entered the English Parliament in 1504. Originally, he had thought he was drawn to the Carthusian life, but discovered that a celibate life was not his calling. He married his first wife, Jane Colt, in 1505, without giving up his devout religious practices. His home in Chelsea became an intellectual center, attracting such minds as John Colet and Erasmus. His brilliant public career began with the ascension of King Henry VIII on the English throne in 1509. He advanced rapidly in the political field and became a renowned writer through the publication of his book, *Utopia*, in 1516. His advancements were not only political in nature, but academic as well.[17] He was very concerned with the Protestant movement in continental Europe. He, along with Bishop John Fisher, helped King Henry VIII, in 1521, to write his book, *Defense of the Seven Sacraments*, against the teachings of Martin Luther. Thomas also wrote treatises dealing with the veneration of saints and images, and on how heretics should be punished. Nevertheless, he never shied away from criticizing abuses in the Catholic Church. His political and personal fortunes radically changed when he opposed King Henry VIII's resolve to divorce his first wife, Queen Catherine of Aragon (1485-1536). Thus, Thomas resigned the office of Lord Chancellor of England in 1532 and retired to his estate. When he refused to take the Oath of Succession[18] in 1534, he was imprisoned in the Tower of London for the next fifteen months. He was beheaded on 6th July 1535. His martyrdom, along with that of his friend, the scholar and theologian St. John Fisher, bishop of Rochester, evoked universal sadness.

(f) Finally, there was also the revival of a misleading popular piety, based on the emotions that were evoked through the popularly growing depiction of a grotesquely suffering Lord and His sorrowful mother. Sometimes, this new devotion developed in such a way that the life-giving sacrifice of the Lord was overshadowed by focusing one's devotion on his sufferings that were depicted so vividly. There was a true risk that dogma and devotion were

---

[17] Thomas More was knighted by King Henry VIII in 1521. He became high steward of Oxford University in 1523, high steward of Cambridge University in 1523, chancellor of the royal Duchy of Lancaster in the same year, and Lord Chancellor of England in 1529, following the political fall of Cardinal Thomas Wolsey (c. 1474-1530).

[18] The Act of Succession decreed that the children of King Henry VIII's second wife, Anne Boleyn (c. 1507- [beheaded] 1536), would succeed Henry, thereby excluding Princess Mary Tudor (1516-1558), daughter of King Henry VIII by his first wife, Queen Catherine of Aragon. As history would have it, Mary Tudor succeeded King Edward VI (1537-1553, king 1547-1553), son of King Henry VIII and his third wife, Jane Seymour (c. 1509-1537), while Princess Elizabeth (1533-1603), daughter of Anne Boleyn, succeeded Queen Mary in 1558.

not aligned. The preaching and writings of St. Vincent Ferrer (c. 1350-1419), St. Bernardine of Siena, and St. John of Capistrano are great examples of how leading Church theologians tried to close their contemporaries' gap between theology and piety. But in places where the gap was not closed, especially in Germany, it began to be taught that sacraments were not necessary for one's spiritual life since an individual's personal prayer and meditation on the Scriptures more than sufficed.

Unfortunately, however, despite some bright lights in the Church reform movement of this era, the general state of the Catholic Church was that of corruption. A general reform of the Church could have succeeded only if the papacy itself led it. This would not take place until the implementation of the decrees of the Council of Trent.

The Protestant Reformation and
The Catholic Church Counter-Reformation

---

68. The Clash between Luther and Rome

We generally associate the Protestant Reformation with Martin Luther. However, Luther's protest against the corruption in Rome was nothing new in the history of the Catholic Church. The Reformation process had begun in the fourteenth century and would last until the seventeenth century. The roots of the Reformation movement can be traced back to the Lollards and the Hussites who attached the hierarchical and legal structure of the Catholic Church. The attack would permeate the entire Reformation movement. It focused most of its criticisms on the Papacy since it was responsible for the entire structure within the Church. Other factors that played a role in the Reformation movement were the rising of nationalism, the diverse kings' attempts to control the Church within their kingdoms, the Papal Babylonian Captivity, the Great Western Schism, the Conciliarist Movement, and the pagan aspects of Renaissance Era. Part of the state of affairs was also due to the gradual negative effects of the Black Death. Finally, there were the ongoing expansion of worldliness at every hierarchical level and unending taxation by Rome.

(a) Martin Luther (1483-1546) is considered the founder of the German Protestant Reformation movement that spread throughout central and northern Europe during his life. He was born in

Eisleben, Saxony,[1] on 10th November 1483, of peasant ancestry. He was educated at Mansfeld, Magdeburg, and Eisenbach before he attended the University of Erfurt, where he graduated with a master's degree in philosophy in 1505. He entered the Augustinian Hermits in Erfurt the following summer, to the great surprise of his family and friends. Luther had stated that he did so to fulfill a vow he had taken while extremely frightened during a thunderstorm. Luther was ordained an Augustinian Hermit priest in 1507. The following year he went to the recently established University of Wittenberg[2] to study theology and to lecture in moral philosophy. He was sent to Rome for one year, beginning in November of 1510, where he was shocked and disillusioned with the worldliness of the Roman clergy. He returned to Erfurt and qualified as a doctor in theology in 1512, whereupon he became the biblical theology professor at Wittenberg University.[3] Shortly thereafter, his teachings began to digress from the traditional Catholic beliefs. His morose personality played a major role in the way he perceived God. His deep anxiety about his personal salvation made him scrupulous. His lack of inner self-appeasement by observing meticulously his religious community's norms and practices made him give up the celebration of Mass and the Divine Office. Some time between 1512 and 1515, he became convinced that the essence of the New Testament was that faith alone, without good works, justified a person before God. This became the trademark of his teaching. He supported his position by referring to some excerpts from the writings of St. Augustine against Pelagianism and from those of some German mystics who spoke of man's nothingness before God. Luther, by 1516, had already denied the role of the Church and the priesthood in a Christian's life since he maintained that one was

---

[1] At the time of Martin Luther, Saxony was an independent principality within the Holy Roman Empire. The princely ruler of Saxony was an Imperial Elector and, hence, wielded a lot of political power.

[2] The University of Wittenberg was founded by Frederick III (1463-1525), Elector of Saxony, in 1502.

[3] Luther held the chair until his death in 1546.

saved by faith alone. He argued that the Church was a cluster of communities with a human and historical origin that lacked divine institution. Such teaching refuted the role of Christ's institution of the papacy and the hierarchy, and the distinction between the ministerial priesthood and the laity.

The theological crisis, which was soon to have pronounced political implications, reached its climax in 1517. At the time, the Dominican preacher Johann Tetzel (c. 1465-1519) was going around Germany preaching and promoting the Indulgence granted by Pope Leo X for the rebuilding of St. Peter's Basilica in Rome.

(b) The Catholic Church's teaching on Indulgences was centuries old. Pope Clement VI had promoted the teaching of Indulgences in 1343 by having officially recognized that Christ and the Saints have left a treasury of merits from which the members of the Church on earth could draw for the remission of the temporal punishment due to their sins. One obtained a share in this treasury by means of an Indulgence, usually granted by a Pope. There were also some conditions for granting of benefits of Indulgences: the recipient's inner disposition to conversion and some good work or monetary donation to some worthy religious cause. The real issue with the Indulgence toward the rebuilding of St. Peter's was the fact that it was generally promoted with no mention of the need for the recipient's personal internal conversion. There was also some free wheeling and dealing among some members of the Roman Curia, the young and vain Archbishop of Mainz and Magdeburg, Cardinal Albert of Hohenzollern (1490-1545), and the banking company of Fugger. Tetzel made the situation more complicated by the fact that he practically told people to "buy" their own way — and that of their deceased loved ones — into heaven! Tetzel had no hesitation to fully commercialize the Indulgence, stating that the bigger the monetary donation, the less time a soul would have to spend in Purgatory. This made some donors reason that the Indulgence had given them some kind of license to sin.

Originally, Luther had no intention to attack the teaching on Indulgences, but to point out the risk of grave misunderstanding given to people by such popular preaching, like that of Tetzel. He wanted to be a faithful Roman Catholic and, initially, had no intention to start any kind of religious revolutionary movement. Thus, Luther objected to such preaching because he found that the way Indulgences were being promoted stood as an obstacle to a person's true repentance and conversion. He argued that Indulgences could remit temporal punishment, but denied that the Pope had any power or control over the merits of Christ and the Saints, or over the souls in Purgatory.

Luther responded to Tetzel by issuing his famous ninety-five theses, in Latin, on 31st May 1517. From that day onward, Tetzel became an avid enemy of Luther and refused to tone down his condemnations for the sake of a possible reconciliation. In less than two weeks, however, Luther's theses were translated into German and his position spread throughout the Imperial German states. While some humanists perceived the situation as an opportune moment to call for Church reform, some secular leaders perceived it as an opportunity to attempt to control Church affairs. Consequently, religious issues overflowed into political life, and a fierce conflict arose throughout Germany.

---

69. Germany in Rebellion

(a) Initially, the Church authorities in Germany hoped to settle the controversy through monastic discipline. Thus, Luther's religious order, the Augustinian Hermits, called an assembly of its German superiors in Heidelberg in 1518.[4] Luther's arguments won over to his side the majority of the friars and the rift became more pronounced. Then, Luther began a series of public university debates in Wittenberg and other cities. The Church's front was led primarily by the German theologian Johann Eck (1486-1543), who had been

---

[4]   Luther was appointed the German regional vicar for the Augustinian Hermits in 1515.

on good terms with Luther until the controversy over Indulgences broke out. In his debate with Eck in 1519,[5] Luther denied papal primacy and the infallibility of General Councils. This led to an investigation by the Roman Curia that ended with the publication of a papal document on 15th June 1520, *Exsurge Domine,*[6] that condemned forty-one theses of Luther's teachings. Luther was given sixty days, from the time of its publication on German soil, to retract his propositions. But Luther felt safe in making his doctrinal denials because he was under the protection of his prince, Elector Frederick III of Saxony, who had originally invited Luther to teach at the Wittenberg University. The doctrinal break with Rome took place in 1520 upon his completion of three writings.[7]

(b) Luther's reaction to Rome's condemnation of his teachings was carried out by burning the papal document in public on 10th December 1520. Since Luther was adamant in his refusal to retract his teachings, Pope Leo X excommunicated him on 3rd January 1521. He was then summoned by Emperor Charles V to appear at the assembly in Worms[8] the following April. Luther's firm refusal to recant brought a second condemnation, this time by the emperor. Luther's prince and protector hid him at Wartburg Castle, where

---

[5] Eck was very instrumental in procuring from Rome the condemnation of Luther's teachings and his eventual excommunication.

[6] The papal document is called a *papal bull*. The Vatican's copy of *Exsurge Domine* is still extant in the Vatican Apostolic Library.

[7] Luther's basic theology was articulated in a trilogy, namely, *On Christian Liberty* (published in 1519), *To the Christian Nobility* and *The Babylonian Captivity of the Church* (both published in 1520). The first document proclaimed the liberation of the Christian by faith and the futility of good works. The second document invited the German princes to carry out Church reform by abolishing tithes to Rome, clerical celibacy, Masses for the dead, pilgrimages, all aspects of religious life, and other Catholic practices and organizations. The third document denied the doctrine of Transubstantiation in the Eucharist and all of the sacraments, except for Baptism and the Eucharist.

[8] The assembly was called the *Diet of Worms*. This assembly was the most famous of a series of Imperial assemblies held in that city. It was at this assembly that Luther, on 18th April 1521 and in the presence of Emperor Charles V and the secular and Church leaders of the Holy Roman Empire, defended his teachings and refused to recant. The assembly formally condemned the Lutheran teachings on 25th May 1521 through the *Edict of Worms*.

he began his translation of the New Testament from Greek into German.[9] Luther, in March 1522, was forced to leave Wartburg to go to Wittenberg to restore peace and quell the popular disorder that had been initiated by some of his extreme followers in that city. Two years later, in 1524, he married the former Cistercian nun, Katharina von Bora (1499-1552), and continued teaching and writing at Wittenberg University. That same year witnessed the *Peasants' Revolt* (1524-1526). Its leaders had based their demands on arguments drawn from Luther's writings. When the revolt turned violent, Luther denounced the peasants and supported the princes in their efforts to restore order. This cost Luther the sympathies of a large section of the German population, apart from the loss of many friends.

The religious and political situation in Germany continued to favor the spread of Luther's teachings and his reforming efforts. Consequently, two Diets were called to meet in Speyer, Germany. The first Diet met in 1526 while Emperor Charles V was busy at war with the Papacy. The Diet decreed that each prince had the authority to order the ecclesiastical affairs and the reform of the local churches within his civil jurisdiction. The second Diet met in response to an appeal made by Pope Clement VII to Emperor Charles V. The Diet met on 21st February 1529. It was controlled by a strong and well organized Catholic contingent that managed to pass legislation to end all toleration of the followers of Luther in Catholic districts. After six princes and fourteen cities made a formal protest to the Imperial Court against the measures, the term "Protestant" began to be used for Luther's supporters.

(c) Luther published his most popular book, *Small Catechism*, in 1529. He presented it in the form of simple questions and answers that dealt with the Ten Commandments, the Apostles' Creed, the Lord's Prayer, baptism and the Lord's Supper. This approach allowed him to present to the laity his evangelical theology in simple

---

[9]   Luther's translation of the New Testament into German became a dominant influence in Protestantism and its language exerted a large influence on the formation of modern German.

language. Although his theology was far from systematic, his work was immensely influential, being inspired by his careful study of the New Testament and selected writings of St. Augustine. Luther taught that God interacted with every person through natural law and through the Gospels. Natural law represented God's demands, while the Gospels represented God's gifts. Every person had some degree of access to natural law through a personal conscience and one's own cultural ethical heritage. Nevertheless, personal sins always distorted an individual's understanding of the law. Although original sin profoundly alienates an individual from God, others and oneself, natural law enables individuals to maintain some sense of order in the world, in society and in one's personal life. Natural law also makes an individual aware of the need for forgiveness and, consequently, leads to Christ. On the other hand, God also interacts with the individual through the Gospels that proclaim God's gift of His Son for the salvation of everyone. According to Luther, man was factually under the complete power of evil and could do nothing but sin. Baptism does not restore one's freedom for the good since God regards a sinful person as righteous because of the merits of Christ and with no need of cooperation from a person. Redemption consists in a person's justification by faith in Christ despite the fact that a person remains sinful. God's activity is all-pervasive.

(d) There were a number of contemporary reasons why the Reformation Movement was able to spread so fast in such a short time. Initially, Luther's Catholic opponents refused to confront him on theological and scriptural grounds. The Catholic German hierarchy took note only of Luther's public refusal of the doctrine of Indulgences, particularly that which was being offered for monetary donations toward the rebuilding of St. Peter's. At the same time, Pope Leo X had no interest in theology and was too preoccupied with Italian politics. The Pope had perceived Luther's rebellion as another priest's passionate opposition and complaint about Church policy. By the time that the Pope took a stance against Luther, the latter's teachings had already received vast recognition by secular princes, some religious, and many lay persons. Most importantly,

Luther had the protection and support of his own prince, Elector Frederick III of Saxony. Papal politics also became an issue in that, in 1518, Rome wanted to procure the Elector's vote against Charles of Hapsburg from being elected Holy Roman Emperor. Hence, the Pope sent Cardinal Cajetan[10] later that year to speak with Luther at Augsburg. The meeting turned out to be disastrous. Luther stuck to his teachings. Once Cardinal Cajetan returned to Rome, Luther's case was put aside. Luther seized this quiet time to promote his views. He engaged himself in public debates with leading Catholic theologians, winning more popular support and coining the phrase "Scripture alone."[11] After Pope Leo X issued his papal bull, *Exsurge Domine*, Luther responded by not only publicly burning the papal bull, but also by issuing three revolutionary documents. While Luther's teachings were spreading like wild fire across Germany, the German prince-bishops failed to clarify Catholic teachings and practices. On the other hand, since Luther's teachings were so widespread, there was a need for a General Council to clarify Church doctrine and practices. The Roman Curia, unfortunately, was radically opposed to this idea.

---

70. Protestantism is Organized

Although Luther's teachings had a wide acceptance in Germany and Pope Leo X had excommunicated him in 1521, there still remained the possibility for reconciliation with the Roman Catholic Church

---

[10] Tommaso De Vio Cajetan (1469-1534) was a prominent Dominican Catholic theologian who served as the General of the Dominican Order from 1508 to 1518. He was created a Cardinal in 1517, and appointed Bishop of Gaeta in 1519. He played a very important role in Church affairs, called for Church reform during the Council Lateran V, helped in the election of Charles of Hapsburg as Holy Roman Emperor in 1519 and, in 1522, contributed to the election of Pope Adrian VI (1522-1523). He was adamantly opposed to the annulment trial of the marriage between King Henry VIII of England and Queen Catherine of Aragon in 1530.

[11] *Sola Scriptura.*

as late as 1530. Time was of essence. The Roman Curia, regretfully, missed many opportunities. Eventually, practicality took over the situation. Decisions had to be made to organize the expanding Protestant communities. It meant the establishment of new church structures. By 1530, most of the Catholic priests who had gone over to the new religion began to marry, and slowly Protestant congregations began to be set up as distinct and in opposition to local Catholic parishes. Ironically, although Luther had emphasized the priesthood of all believers and denied the sacramentality of Holy Orders, the Protestant clergy soon established itself as distinct from the rest of the believers. It set up a clerical hierarchical structure similar to that of the Catholic Church, save any kind of authority resembling that of the papacy.

Emperor Charles V was determined to restore unity in the empire by restoring unity within Western Christendom.[12] But he had been absent from Germany at a very crucial time in the development of the new religion. At the time, he was busy either fighting King Francis I of France (1494-1547)[13] and the Papacy[14] or was in Spain, attending to the needs of his vast Spanish Empire.[15] Moreover, Pope Clement VII failed to procure and to foster any

---

[12] Emperor Charles V used the same rationale that Roman Emperors Constantine the Great and Justinian the Great, and the Holy Roman Emperors Charlemagne and Sigismund had used before him to bring unity within their empires. Charles V tried to restore unity in faith within his two mutually independent Spanish and Holy Roman empires.

[13] Francis I became King of France in 1515. He and Charles I of Spain were the primary candidates for the Imperial Crown in 1519. The electors had chosen Charles I, who assumed the title of Holy Roman Emperor Charles V. Soon thereafter, Francis I began a series of wars in Italy against Charles V. Francis I was captured at Pavia in 1525 and was imprisoned in Spain until 1527. After his ransom and return to France, he continued waging war against Charles until 1529 when the two sovereigns sued for peace. Francis I, having been widowed, took Charles V's sister Eleanor as his second wife later that year. Further inconclusive wars between the two rulers continued between 1536 and 1538, and between 1542 and 1544.

[14] Pope Clement VII, in his anxiety to rid Italy of the imperial armies, joined Francis I of France in the 1527 war against Charles V. The imperial armies sacked Rome that year and held Pope Clement VII prisoner for seven months.

[15] The Spanish Empire ruled by Charles V was distinct from and independent of the Holy Roman Empire that he also governed.

kind of substantial reform within the Church. These circumstances allowed the German Protestants to organize, usually under the leadership of a Protestant secular prince.

---

71. The Peace of Augsburg

The city of Augsburg played a major role in the establishment of Lutheranism in Germany. Emperor Charles V, while there, was presented with the *Confession of Augsburg* on 25th June 1530. The document contained the authoritative Lutheran confession of faith. It was principally the work of Luther's friend, Philip Melanchthon,[16] who published it with the prior approval of Luther. He went the extra mile to use non-offensive language towards the Catholic Church in its wording. The emperor handed over the document to a group of Catholic theologians for their evaluation and response. The response was submitted on 3rd August 1530, and Melanchthon responded by writing his *Apologia for the Confession*. The emperor refused to accept it. A subsequent document, called *The Interim of Augsburg*, was issued eighteen years later at the Diet of Augsburg on 30th June 1548. But the new document did not settle the matter at large. Disunity and unrest continued to pester Germany. Finally, there was the signing of the *Peace of Augsburg* on 25th September 1555. It was imposed on the emperor through a settlement between

---

[16] Philip Melanchthon (1497-1560) was a leading Protestant reformer who, while serving as professor of Greek at the University of Wittenberg, fell under the spell of Luther's teachings. The two men forged a lifelong friendship. Melanchthon's commentaries on Scripture broke new ground in the field. He was a conciliatory man by nature, and this was reflected in his dealings with the leaders of the German Catholic Church and with the Protestant Swiss reformer Ulrich Zwingli (1484-1531). Melanchthon went so far as to sign, in 1537, the *Smalcald Articles*, writing to it an addendum which conceded papal supremacy by human right. On the other hand, he totally rejected Zwingli's teaching on the Eucharist, upholding his faith in the Real Presence, but rejected the Catholic doctrine of Transubstantiation. Melanchthon's approach toward Christianity was more humanistic than most of his contemporary reformers, placing a great emphasis on the role academic studies play in the spiritual life of an individual.

his brother, Ferdinand I,[17] and the German Electors. In essence, the settlement empowered each prince to declare whether the religion within his domain should be Catholic or Lutheran.[18] The peace yielded the phrase, *the religion of the prince is the religion of his subjects.*[19] Thus, the Peace of Augsburg settled the matter of one's faith by territoriality. The system of religious territoriality remained essentially in effect until the Treaty of Westphalia in 1648.

---

72. Interpretation of Sacraments

(a) Ulrich Zwingli (1484-1531) was born in Wildhaus, a small town in the Swiss canton of St. Gall. He was educated at Berne (1496-1498), Vienna (1498-1502) and Basle (1502-1506) before he was ordained a Roman Catholic priest in 1506 and appointed as pastor in Glarus. Being a devoted admirer of Erasmus, he studied in depth Greek and the New Testament. He served as a chaplain to the Swiss mercenaries in the Papal service in 1515. He gave up his pastorate in 1516 and went on pilgrimage to the famous Swiss Shrine of Einsiedeln.[20] There he witnessed many abuses and became determined to reform the Catholic Church. He was elected the People's Preacher at the Old Minster in Zurich on 11th December 1518, a post he held for the rest of his life. He used the office to promote his particular political and religious views. The local citizenry greatly supported him. Though his rupture with Rome was gradual, he is credited with beginning the Swiss Reformation in 1519. He attacked the Roman Catholic doctrine on Purgatory and praying to Saints and, also, called for the abolition of monasteries. He advocated the

---

[17] Ferdinand of Hapsburg (1556-1578) succeeded his brother, Emperor Charles V, in 1556 when Charles V resigned and relegated the German Empire to his brother.

[18] The Calvinist faction of Protestantism was not recognized in the settlement.

[19] *Cuius regio eius religio.*

[20] Einsiedeln was and remains a Swiss Benedictine Abbey and place of pilgrimage in Switzerland. It was founded by St. Benno in 937 and in 1350 became a National Shrine for the Swiss Confederation.

rejection of the Papacy and bishops in 1522. On 29th January 1523 he publicly asserted the Lutheran teaching of "Scripture alone," rejected Papal authority, the Sacrifice of the Mass, praying to Saints, fasting, and clerical celibacy. The city council gave Zwingli its full support by organizing the Minster along his notions and declaring their city's independence of episcopal control. Zwingli had married secretly Anna Meyer in 1522. Then, he made a public event of his marriage to her on 2nd April 1524 at the cathedral. Later that year he taught that the Eucharist was only a symbolic presence in that it was a mere memorial presence of Christ and there was no Real Presence of the Lord in the Eucharist. This view led to an official break with Martin Luther in 1529.[21] Meanwhile, Zwingli's movement had spread to other parts of Switzerland, though it found great resistance in the Cantons of Lucerne, Schwyz, Unterwaden, Uri and Zug. These cantons declared war on the Swiss Protestants in 1531 and launched a sudden attack on Zurich. Zwingli was killed on 11th October 1531 during this war.

(b) John Calvin (1509-1564) was born in Noyon, Picardy, France in 1509. He became a Catholic cleric[22] in 1521, when he obtained the first of several benefices. He studied theology in Paris from 1523 to 1528. He began to question his priestly calling and some tenets of the Catholic Faith during 1527. Following his theological studies and having failed to resolve his interior struggles, he went first to Orlèans and then to Brouges to study law. At Brouges he fell under the influence of Melchior Wolmar and a group of Protestants. He claimed to have had a personal religious experience in 1533 in which he was commissioned to restore the Church to its original purity. He concluded that there is no such thing as apostolic succession for any Catholic bishop, including Popes. Consequently, he severed all ties with Rome. He returned to Noyon in 1534, resigned his benefices, and landed in jail for a very brief period. He fled to Basle in 1535 on the brink of an outbreak of persecution of Protestants by King Francis I in France.

---

[21] Zwingli's view of the Eucharist was also rejected by Philip Melanchthon.
[22] John Calvin was never ordained a Catholic priest.

He published his first version of the *Institutes* in March 1536. The publication was a small book, comprised of six chapters, with the purpose of providing a theological introduction to the Bible and to justify and affirm the Protestant faith.[23] Passing through Geneva the following July, he encountered the Swiss reformer, Guillaume Farel (1489-1565), who persuaded him to stay and help him organize the Reformation there. Calvin was appointed as the preacher and theology professor in the city. He put his heart and soul into his new mission, and soon issued directives that forcefully bound all the inhabitants of Geneva to make a profession of faith approved by the city council. Furthermore, he drew up very strict regulations in regards to one's ability to participate in the Lord's Supper. Calvin attempted to impose the discipline of excommunication in 1538, and refused to conform to the usages at the Protestant Church in Berne. He believed that the key to the success of Protestantism was strict discipline. His failure to control the city led to his and Farel's expulsion from Geneva later that year. Calvin spent the next three years in Strasbourg. There he met and was influenced by Martin Bucer,[24] especially on norms for public worship which later became

---

[23] Calvin revised and expanded the *Institutes* several times, beginning in 1539. The final edition, comprised of eighty chapters, was published in French in 1560. The document is a systematic and clear exposition of Calvin's teachings. Its foundation is God's absolute authority, Scripture alone, man's inability to find pardon and salvation without the working of the free grace from God, and that some people were definitively ordained to go to heaven while the rest were predestined to go to eternal damnation (*predestination*). For Calvin, God was totally hidden since God was absolute "Other," mysterious, transcendent, indiscernible, incomprehensible and unreachable. God revealed Himself in Sacred Scripture through Jesus Christ, His Only Son. Therefore, one gained knowledge of God if one read Sacred Scripture with complete reverence, profound awe, deep faith, and great love. Such a disposition opens one to the Holy Spirit who would open Sacred Scripture to the true believer. It is only because of his total insistence that one's salvation depended entirely on God's absolute gratuitous grace that Calvin had to insist on strict predestination. The document became the textbook of the theology of the Reformation.

[24] Martin Bucer (1491-1551), a German former Dominican priest, was a friend of both Luther and Zwingli. He became the leader of the Reformed Churches in Switzerland after the death of Zwingli in 1531. When his attempts to introduce his brand of Protestantism in Cologne failed, he went to England in 1549, where he lectured at Cambridge University for the rest of his life. Through his influence on Thomas Cranmer, he had a pronounced influence on the *Ordinal* of the Church of England of 1550.

the standard norms for Calvinism. At Strasbourg, Calvin continued to publish his impressive commentaries on the New Testament. He wrote his historic *Epistle to Cardinal Sadoleto* in 1539.[25] The Epistle defended the principles of the Protestant Reformation.

Calvin's supporters in Geneva finally gained the upper hand and invited him back to their city. He returned to Geneva in 1541 and devoted the next fourteen years to establish a local theocracy. He was in complete control of the theocracy from 1555 until his death on 27th May 1564. His crowning achievement was the establishment of the Geneva Academy in 1559. The Academy fully trained all the candidates for Calvinistic ministry.

Calvin was a logical, systematic, and very rigid reformer. His personal bend to be very vindictive and in absolute control of what constituted true Christianity made even his supporters resentful. During his lifetime, his brilliance, his crystal clear theological thinking and writings, his mastery of languages, and his rhetorical finesse made him the most influential person in his brand of Protestantism that was distinct from Lutheranism.[26]

73. The Scandinavian Reformation

(a) The Frankish bishop, St. Anskar,[27] introduced Christianity in Denmark during the ninth century with the help of King Harold. The king had been a recent convert to Christianity from paganism

---

[25] Cardinal Jacopo Sadoleto (1477-1547) was a classical and philosophical scholar who was in charge of the commission for the reform in the Catholic Church and the preparation of a General Council that became known as the Council of Trent.

[26] Lutheranism was preferred in Germany and the Scandinavian countries. Although Lutherans remained in the majority in Germany, there were some German areas that accepted Calvinism, such as the Palatine, Bremen, Anhalt, Hesse and Brandenburg.

[27] St. Anskar (801-865) is called the "Apostle of the North" due to his missionary activities in the Scandinavian countries. He was born near Picardy, educated at the celebrated Benedictine monastery of Corbie, and taught at Corvey, a daughter

while he was a fugitive at the court of the Emperor Louis the Pious. Christianity flourished in Denmark under its Christian convert King Sven I (984-1014), though he had frequent relapses to his old pagan ways but not to its faith. The Christian Faith continued to flourish and became more established under King Canute the Great (1014-1035), who added to his Danish kingdom those of Norway, Sweden and England.[28] Christianity in Denmark was established to the point that the country was given its own hierarchy in 1104. By the late Middle Ages, the Church had become more and more powerful, rich, privileged, and unpopular. Many Danes were deeply disturbed with the ongoing Church scandals throughout Europe. These elements laid the ground for the success of the Protestant Reformation in Denmark. Protestantism took rapid roots in the country between 1520 and 1540.

The Diet of Odense of 1527 declared religious freedom to all believers. This was the beginning of the end of the Catholic influence in Denmark. The country formally adopted a strict version of the Lutheran creed in 1530 and made Lutheranism its state religion. The year 1537 saw the establishment of the Danish Lutheran episcopate and the promulgation of the Danish Lutheran liturgy. All property belonging to the Catholic Church was confiscated and all monasteries were dissolved by 1540.

(b) Sweden began to be evangelized by Christian missionaries since the ninth century, with the arrival of St. Anskar. Olof Skötkonung was the first King of Sweden to be baptized. However, as had happened in Denmark, soon after the death of St. Anskar, Sweden lapsed back to practice paganism. The country, nevertheless, experienced a systematic conversion process in the eleventh

---

house in Westphalia. He was sent as a missionary to Schleswig around 826, and subsequently to Sweden. Emperor Louis the Pious appointed Anskar first bishop of Hamburg in 831. The following year. Pope Gregory IV appointed him papal legate to the Scandinavians. The Swedish mission collapsed after the Vikings destroyed Hamburg in 845. Having been named Archbishop of Bremen in 851, Anskar renewed his missionary efforts in Scandinavia with some success. However, soon after his death, Scandinavia temporarily relapsed into paganism.

[28] Canute the Great ruled over a short-lived northwestern European Empire.

century. It was led by English missionary monks and culminated
in the full Christianization of Sweden by the middle of the twelfth
century. Then, it was time for Sweden to begin its own missionary
work to nearby Finland. Unfortunately, the missionary efforts were
accompanied with military force in that King Eric IX (1150-1160)
forced the Finns to become Christians. Just over two hundred years
later, the Swedish nobles forced their King, Albert of Mecklen-
burg (1364-1389), to renounce his throne in 1389.[29] They, then,
presented the Swedish crown to Margaret I (1353-1412), Queen
Regent of Denmark and Norway. Through the Union of Kalmar,
on 17th June 1397, the three kingdoms once again had one common
sovereign as it had been under King Canute the Great.

The Catholic clergy in Sweden had amassed vast political
power, wealth, property, and privileges by the late Middle Ages.
Then the Church began to face serious problems. The Swedish
national hero Gustavus Vasa (1496-1560) began a war for independence from Denmark in 1521. The war lasted until 1523 when
Gustavus was crowned King of Sweden as Gustavus I Vasa. Having
won the war, he turned his attention to the wealth and privileges of
the local Catholic Church. Gustavus I quickly joined the Protestant
movement. He officially broke off his country's ties with Rome in
1524. The Reformation program in Sweden, however, moved very
slowly since Gustavus I's policy was to adhere to the Lutheran doctrine of justification by faith alone while adopting an ecclesiastical
administration similar to that of the Catholic Church. This policy
led to a brand of Protestantism that was basically nationalistic in
character. Both King John III of Sweden (1568-1592) and King
Sigismund III (1592-1599)[30] tried to reunite Sweden with Rome,

---

[29] He abdicated formally in 1405.

[30] King Sigismund III was already King of Poland when he succeeded King John
III as King of Sweden. The Swedish Parliament declared Sigismund III deposed
in 1599, and proclaimed his uncle, Charles of Söermankland, ruler as Charles
IX. However, King Sigismund was not definitively deposed until 1604. That year
Charles IX assumed the title of "King." He was subsequently crowned in 1607.
Sigismund remained King of Poland until his death in 1632.

while King Charles IX (1599-1607) tried to establish Calvinism in Sweden. All three kings failed in their respective attempts. The Swedes formally adopted the Augsburg Confession in 1593 and committed themselves to a moderate form of Lutheranism, which became the state religion.

(c) The process of the Christianization of Norway began on shaky grounds. Several Norwegian kings unsuccessfully attempted to introduce Christianity into their kingdom during the ninth and tenth centuries. Finally, King Olaf Haraldssön (995-1030), who converted to Christianity while fighting the Danes in England, managed to convert his subjects with the sword. The Church was established adequately enough in Norway to be given its own hierarchy in 1152. The Catholic Church, particularly monastic life, flourished until the reign of King Christian II (1513-1523), a Protestant sympathizer. He had initiated the suppression of monasteries as the seed of the Protestant Reformation began to take roots in the country. Norway ceased to exist as an independent kingdom in 1537.[31] The Danish rulers imposed on Norway a radical form of Lutheranism.

(d) English, Swedish, and Russian missionaries Christianized Finland by the twelfth century. Finland had its own Catholic hierarchy established in 1220 under the Englishman Thomas, Bishop of Räntemäkia. The country managed to produce its own renowned theologians by the end of the fifteenth century. Roman Catholicism, nonetheless, was never a strong feature in Finnish history. Peter Särkilax introduced Lutheranism into his country in 1523. Michael Agricola (1512-1557) led the Protestant Reform movement in the middle of the sixteenth century that took up extreme measures to eradicate the Catholic Church in his country.

---

[31] The country of Norway, after many centuries struggling to regain its independence, was reestablished as a kingdom in 1905 with Prince Carl of Denmark assuming the Norwegian throne as King Håkon VII (1872-1957).

74. The English Reformation

(a) The arrival of Christianity in England has obscure origins. It has been recorded that there were some English bishops present at the First Council of Arles in 314.[32] Christianity suffered a setback with the invasions of the Anglo-Saxon tribes. These tribes became Christianized through the missionary efforts of Celtic monks from Ireland and Scotland and through the mission sent from Rome under the leadership of St. Augustine of Canterbury in 597. The Celtic style Church and the Roman style Church coexisted amidst great tension between them until their liturgical and administrative systems were resolved at the Synod of Whitby in 664. The resolution opted for the Roman system of Church governance and liturgy with one Primatial See in charge of the Church in England. St. Theodore of Tarsus[33] was entrusted with the task of reforming the Church governance in England according to the Roman system. He erected dioceses, unified the Church in England, and established the primatial role of the Archdiocese of Canterbury. St. Theodore became the first of a long list of statesmen-archbishops in the history of England. His tenure as archbishop provided a short-lived Renaissance in Anglo-Saxon Christianity, producing such great churchmen as St. Bede,[34] St. Boniface, and a series of monks, such as Alcuin, who were instrumental in the Carolingian Renaissance.

(b) The Anglo-Saxon Christian civilization experienced a long eclipse due to the ruthless raids and invasions of different

---

[32] The first Council of Arles was summoned by the Roman Emperor Constantine the Great in 314 to deal with the Donatist Schism.

[33] St. Theodore of Tarsus was an Asiatic Greek who was appointed Archbishop of Canterbury by Pope Vitalian.

[34] St. Bede (c. 673-735), Doctor of the Church, is called "the Venerable" and the "Father of English History." He was a Benedictine monk who began his monastic life at Jarrow in the ancient Kingdom of Northumbria, England. He spent his entire life studying Sacred Scripture, teaching, and writing. Even in his lifetime, Bede became legendary as a Sacred Scripture scholar and historian, becoming the primary source of early English history.

parts of England by the Norsemen, particularly the Danes, that had begun back in the ninth century[35] and lingered on to the third part of the eleventh century. The isolation of England from the European continent, in both political and Church matters, began to break down during the reign of King Canute the Great. But England was destined to join mainland Europe instead of remaining a part of the Scandinavian Empire. This event was brought about through the Norman Conquest under King William the Conqueror.[36] With the Norman domination and a string of Archbishops of Canterbury from Normandy and Italy, the Church in England was greatly influenced by papal reforms, particularly those of Pope Gregory VII. The Catholic Church made great strides. It witnessed the reformation of the clergy, the restoration of learning, the building of new cathedrals and abbeys, the reorganization of Church administration, and the introduction of Roman canon law. Henceforth, the Church in England fell under the influence of the Popes. Nonetheless, it was not spared the tensions between kings and bishops, and sovereigns and Popes. The Investiture Controversy led to the martyrdom of St. Thomas Becket. Subsequently, there was the combined victory of the Church and barons over King John (1167-1216) that led to the independence of the Church from royal absolutism and the signing of the *Magna Carta* in 1215. During the long reign of King Henry III (1216-1272), the papacy and the English bishops had a marked ecclesiastical, civil, and political influence on the country. Nevertheless, the Church

---

[35] Alfred the Great (849-899), King of Wessex (871-899), was a temporary stop gap against the Danes. There was a short revival of learning and monasticism during his tutelage.

[36] William I (c. 1028-1087) became Duke of Normandy in 1035 upon the death of his father. William was the illegitimate son of Robert, Duke of Normandy, hence his nickname, William the Bastard. Due to his successful conquest of England in 1066, he was also known as William the Conqueror. William was a relative of the English King, St. Edward the Confessor (1002-1066). William, with the blessing of Pope Alexander II, invaded England in 1066, conquered it, and Normanized it both civilly and ecclesiastically. He ruled Normandy and England with a very firm hand, implemented papal Church reform throughout his domains, presided personally at reforming councils in England and founded some monasteries.

in England was not spared scandals that were similar to those going on in contemporary continental Europe. The aftermath of the failure of the Conciliar Movement and the rapid rise of national self-consciousness saw the signing of concordats between the Papacy and individual rulers. England was no exception to this policy.

(c) The Tudor sovereigns,[37] beginning with Henry VIII, and with the exception of Mary Tudor, found much support among their subjects against the Catholic Church and the Papacy. The laity was highly critical of Church wealth, resentful of the ruthless ways heretics were handled and of the political power that bishops wielded in the Kingdom, bitter on the burdens imposed by Church law, and tired of papal taxation. The majority of the English intelligentsia during the Renaissance Era rejected Scholasticism and scoffed at the Church's decadence. Notwithstanding, there were also some persons who, despite their disappointment and criticism of the abuses going on in the Church at home and overseas, remained faithful Catholics. Numbered among such people were John Colet,[38] Erasmus, St. Thomas More and St. John Fisher.[39]

One can be easily led to believe that the occasion for the English Reformation was begun with King Henry VIII's determina-

---

[37] The House of Tudor ruled England from 1485 till 1603. The sovereigns were: Henry VII (1485-1509); Henry VIII (1509-1547); Edward VI (1547-1553); Mary I (1553-1558); and Elizabeth I (1558-1603). There was no Protestant Movement during the reign of King Henry VII. King Henry VIII rejected it and Queen Mary tried, unsuccessfully, her best to eradicate it from England.

[38] John Colet had studied at the universities of Oxford, Paris, and in Italy. He immersed himself into the study of Greek while in Italy, becoming imbued in the trend of recovering the ancient classical past in the spirit of the Renaissance. His mastery of Greek was a prelude to his study of the New Testament. Back in Oxford, Colet began lecturing on the Pauline Epistles and pleaded for a return to the discipline of the primitive Church. He avidly promoted the education of young men but sharply criticized the upper corrupt Church hierarchy. Colet, still, never challenged the validity of the Church's authoritative teaching. While in Oxford, he became the Dean of St. Paul's in London in 1504 and held that office until his death in 1519.

[39] John Fisher was educated at Cambridge University where, in turn, he left a deep personal mark when he served as one of its prominent professors and chancellors. He was chaplain to Lady Margaret Beauford (1443-1509), mother of King Henry VII, and, subsequently, the confessor of Queen Catherine of Aragon, first wife of King Henry VIII. Fisher was appointed Bishop of Rochester, England, in 1504.

tion to end his marriage with his first wife, Catherine of Aragon.[40] But, the roots for the English Reformation were centuries old. By the time Henry VIII severed England's papal allegiance, a great and long standing dissatisfaction had existed among the English laity regarding the scandalous lifestyle, wealth, power, and abuse of English clerics.

The *Statute of Provisors*, passed in 1306, was the foundation of all subsequent statutes carrying the same name until 1389, and of the *Statutes of Praemunire*, enacted from 1353 till 1393. They were an accumulation of laws that aimed specifically at restricting papal interference in English matters, including the appointment to benefices and bishoprics, appeal to Rome, and taxation by the Holy See. These statutes had gradually prepared the bishops in England not to have recourse to the papal courts. The final blow to the English episcopal loyalty to Rome came from the policy of Cardinal Thomas Wolsey,[41] the Primate of England and Papal Legate. He was

---

During his lifetime he became renowned as a great scholar, theologian, preacher, a saintly bishop, and a promoter of higher education. He avidly opposed the doctrines of Luther and helped King Henry VIII write *The Defense of the Seven Sacraments*. As a result of this writing, Pope Leo X, on 11th October 1521, gave King Henry VIII the papal title of *Defender of the Faith*. As confessor of Queen Catherine, Fisher strongly protested King Henry VIII's plan to divorce his wife. He was the only Roman Catholic bishop in England who openly opposed the king. His opposition led him to be jailed in the Tower of London in 1534. Pope Paul III created Fisher a Cardinal in May 1535 while still a prisoner in the Tower. The papal promotion enraged the king, who had Fisher beheaded on 22nd June 1535. Fisher's writings, especially on the Sacrament of the Eucharist, were widely utilized during the Council of Trent.

[40] King Henry VIII eventually had six wives: (1) Catherine of Aragon (1509-1533); (2) Anne Boleyn (1532-1536); (3) Jane Seymour (1536-1537); (4) Anne of Cleves (1540); (5) Catherine Howard (1540-1542); and (6) Catherine Parr (1534-1538). He divorced two wives (Catherine of Aragon and Anne of Cleves); beheaded two (Anne Boleyn and Catherine Howard); one died in childbirth (Jane Seymour); and one outlived him (Catherine Parr).

[41] Cardinal Thomas Wolsey (ca. 1474-1530) was educated at Oxford University before he was ordained a Catholic priest in 1498. He advanced moderately in his ecclesiastical and civil careers under the patronage of Archbishop Henry Dean of Canterbury. Wolsey became King Henry VII's chaplain around 1507. His advancement took on a rapid pace under King Henry VIII by becoming a privy counselor in 1511, Bishop of Lincoln and Archbishop of York in 1514, Cardinal and Lord Chancellor in 1515. As Cardinal and Chancellor of England, Wolsey

primarily a servant of the state rather than a churchman, managed to eradicate whatever was left of any kind of episcopal loyalty to Rome and transferred that loyalty to the English crown.

When Henry VIII, having cajoled, bullied, charmed, and pleaded with the Pope, failed to procure a declaration of nullity of his marriage to Queen Catherine, he went ahead and secretly married his pregnant mistress, Anne Boleyn.[42] Then he began to take quick steps to sever his ties with Rome. On 15th May 1532, through the Convocation,[43] Henry VIII procured the *Submission of the Clergy* that was embodied in an Act of Parliament in 1534. The submission made the sovereign supreme in all Church matters and acknowledged him as the Supreme Head on earth of the Church in England. He, then, gradually dissolved all English monasteries and abbeys, and allowed the destruction of all shrines. The king did not hesitate to imprison or execute those who did not comply with his royal wishes, whether they were Roman Catholics or belonged to any brand of Protestantism. It was under King Edward VI, Henry VIII's young son, that Protestantism took its first grip of England.

Edward VI was the only legitimate and surviving son of King Henry VIII. His mother was Jane Seymour, Henry's third

---

wielded almost royal power for King Henry VIII practically left all state and Church matters into his hands. His policies fostered royal absolutism in both State and Church affairs. Wolsey also unsuccessfully tried at having himself elected pope in 1521 and 1523. He created many enemies by his arrogance, uncontrolled pride, and ruthless methods of extracting money from the English citizenry to finance an inconclusive war between England and France. He was prepared to do anything to maintain the royal favor. Thus, when King Henry VIII became set on having his marriage to Queen Catherine of Aragon declared null and on marrying Anne Boleyn, Wolsey undertook every effort to please the king. When his plan failed to convince the Pope to allow him to decide the marriage annulment matter, he received the ire of Ann Boleyn and, consequently, the king's displeasure. It was just a matter of a few months before Wolsey gave up all of his political powers and offices (1529) and retired to his archdiocese of York as a broken man. He died in 1530, on his way to London to be tried for high treason.

[42] Since Henry VIII was still married to Catherine of Aragon, his marriage to Anne Boleyn was considered bigamous by both Church and state laws.

[43] The Convocation was the assembly of the English clergy. Such assemblies could be traced back to the time of St. Bede in the eighth century. They became organized under St. Theodore of Tarsus, Archbishop of Canterbury.

wife. Edward succeeded to the English throne at age nine, on 28th January 1547, upon the death of his father. The boy-king was of no political consequence since real power rested first in the hand of his mother's brother, Edward Seymour, First Earl of Hertford, Lord Protector and Duke of Somerset, and later in the hands of John Dudley, Duke of Northumberland.

Edward, a studious youth, was brought up with Protestant ideas and leanings. Consequently, there were many changes in church governance and doctrine during his short reign. These changes took place under the leadership of Thomas Cranmer, archbishop of Canterbury (1532-1556),[44] who leaned heavily toward Calvinism and allowed the State to take complete control over the Church. Cranmer produced the First and Second *Book of Common Prayer* (1549, 1552). He composed the *Forty-Two Articles* and tried to use them as the creed and policy of the Church of England. The English clergy roundly rejected the document, but most of its contents became the working document for the subsequent *Thirty-Nine Articles* in 1563. Cranmer's reformist policy and activity were cut short by the death of the young consumptive King Edward VI on 6th July 1553.

King Edward VI was succeeded by his staunch Catholic half-sister, Mary Tudor.[45] She was the daughter of King Henry VIII and his first wife, Catherine of Aragon. Queen Mary I, with the help of her relative, Cardinal Reginald Pole, did her utmost best to restore Roman Catholicism in England and to undo all the changes that had been introduced by her deceased father and half-brother. She immediately restored the Roman Catholic Mass and papal supremacy. She then launched an avid persecution of Protestants.

---

[44] Although Thomas Cranmer was ordained as the Roman Catholic Archbishop of Canterbury, he was also, in fact, the first Protestant Archbishop of Canterbury. He played a crucial role in overthrowing Papal Supremacy in England, declared as null King Henry VIII's marriage to Queen Catherine in 1533 and the marriage to Queen Anne Boleyn in 1536, and witnessed the marriage and subsequent divorce of Henry VIII with Anne of Cleves.

[45] Mary married her cousin, the powerful King Philip II of Spain, on 25th July 1554. The marriage proved to be disastrous. It was childless, unhappy, and unpopular.

These persecutions and her inability to have children made her very unpopular among her subjects. She died very unhappy on 17th November 1558.

Queen Mary I was succeeded by her half-sister, Elizabeth I, daughter of King Henry VIII and his second wife, Anne Boleyn. It was under her leadership that a distinctive English version of Protestantism became firmly established. The brand of English Protestantism took form through two measures: the Act of Uniformity of 1559, and the *Thirty-Nine Articles* of 1563. The *Second Book of Common Prayer* was re-issued with some changes. It became the established service book of the Church of England. On the other hand, the *Thirty-Nine Articles* were issued as the summary of the Church of England's position in matters regarding the Christian Faith.

Elizabeth I was resolved to handle the religious issues in England through political expediency. She personally lacked any strong religious convictions. She had inherited a kingdom that was essentially strongly attached to the old Catholic Faith and practices, despite the enforced ecclesial structural changes that had been imposed on all English subjects during the reign of King Edward VI. The public's attachment to the practices of the old faith was due mostly to her father's insistence to do away with nothing Catholic, except for Papal Primacy, rather than to Queen Mary I's failed attempt to reestablish Roman Catholicism by force. But, underlying this public sentiment, there was a growing Calvinist undercurrent that was the result of the forced imposition of religious beliefs and practices by Parliament during the reign of King Edward VI. Queen Elizabeth disliked Roman Catholicism because it had declared her illegitimate and she disliked Calvinism because it had no bishops.[46] She, therefore, began to gradually enforce a brand of religion that borrowed from Lutheran Protestantism everything that entailed the absolute supremacy of the sovereign over Church

---

[46] Queen Elizabeth I viewed bishops as an essential group of men who protected the sovereign since the sovereign had appointed them to their ecclesiastical positions.

matters, while maintaining the episcopal organization borrowed from the Roman Catholic Church. The policy of Matthew Parker,[47] her new Archbishop of Canterbury, helped to resolve the chaos that the many changes in Church policy and practice had brought since the reign of her father. Yet, because the Crown had to rely primarily on the support of Protestants, the Church of England and the English government became increasingly reliant on Calvinism. The climax of this State-Church policy was reached when Pope St. Pius V (1566-1572) excommunicated Queen Elizabeth I in 1570 and released her subjects from their allegiance to her. Elizabeth immediately began a systematic persecution of Catholics in England. She had her Catholic cousin, Mary Queen of Scots (1542-1587),[48] beheaded in 1587. This deed was in reaction to the pressure from King Philip II of Spain's threats to invade England and out of fear that Roman Catholics would rally around the Roman Catholic Queen of Scots. The defeat of the Spanish Armada on 8th August 1588 secured Queen Elizabeth's popularity among her subjects. It also established England as a leading Protestant country for centuries to come.

---

[47] Matthew Parker (1504-1575) was educated at the University of Cambridge. Once ordained a Roman Catholic priest, he married, and was able to receive some Church advancement under Kings Henry VIII and Edward VI. Meanwhile, he identified himself with moderate reformers. He was deprived of his clerical benefices under Queen Mary I and lived in obscurity until Queen Elizabeth I chose him as the Archbishop of Canterbury in 1559. His aim as archbishop was to give the English Reformation a moderate course that resulted in severe criticism from those who were loyal to Rome and a great opposition from those who practiced Puritanism.

[48] Mary, Queen of Scots, had been a prisoner in England for nineteen years (1568-1587) before she was beheaded in 1587. Mary was the only legitimate child of James V, King of Scotland, and his second wife, Mary of Guise. Mary became Queen when she was six days old; married Francis, the Dauphin of France in 1558; was Queen Consort of France from 1559 to 1560; married her cousin Henry Stewart, Lord Darnley in 1565; was widowed for a second time in 1567; married James Hepburn, Fourth Earl of Bothwell in 1567. She was forced to abdicate the throne of Scotland in favor of her son King James VI, on 24th July 1567. She was the last Catholic Queen of Scotland.

75. Ecclesiastical and Political Intrigues

Everyone agreed that the Catholic Church was in dire need of reform. Many Church and secular leaders also agreed that there had to be a response from the Roman Church to the spreading Protestant movement. But responding to the situation was not that simple. The events which led to the opening of the Council of Trent were full of theological discussions and political intrigue within the Church itself. Furthermore, the genesis of the Council would not be spared international political intrigue and some personal risk to those who participated in it.

(a) When Luther burnt the papal bull *Exsurge Domine*, he renewed his previous call for a General Council. Pope Leo X issued the bull, *Decet Romanum Pontificem*, excommunicating him. The following 6th March, Emperor Charles V summoned Luther to appear before the Diet of Worms[49] to defend his views. On 18th April, Luther refused to recant and, on the following day, the emperor declared for Rome and demanded that Luther be immediately condemned as a heretic. Then, on 26th May, the emperor signed the Edict of Worms, which formally condemned Luther's teachings and banished him from imperial land. Nonetheless, Luther was given protection by the German Elector, Frederick III, who took him to Wartburg Castle. The emperor did not pursue the matter any further, though in December a more amplified imperial ban was issued against Luther and his followers. It was lifted during February 1522. Soon, Luther embarked on a two year tour of preaching in central Germany. Meanwhile, he responded to English King Henry VIII's *Defense of the Seven Sacraments* by writing a very tactless and abusive response. He also published the translation of the New Testament in German. In the meantime, Pope Leo X had died on 1st December 1521 and the Cardinals, on 9th January 1522, elected a former tutor of Emperor Charles V, the

---

[49] The Diet of Worms was held between 22nd January and 25th April 1521.

Church-reform minded Dutchman Adriaan Florens Boeyens, who took the name of Pope Adrian VI.

(b) The First Imperial Diet of Nuremberg was convened in September 1522 in the presence of the papal legate. Its purpose was the execution of the resolutions of the Edict of Worms against Luther and to decide how to deal with Europe's defense against the fast approaching Ottoman Turks, under their young Sultan, Suleiman the Magnificent. On 6th March 1523, the Diet ordered Luther and his followers to cease publication on religious topics and outlawed preaching that was not in conformity with Catholic doctrine. But the Diet also called for "a free Christian council" on German soil. It was immediately rejected by Rome.

The Second Imperial Diet of Nuremberg saw a new Pope, Clement VII, in Peter's Chair. The Diet was called for the same purpose as the previous one. It demanded a German national council as well as a General Council to settle the religious disputes. Both were expected to be held on German soil. The papal legate immediately rejected the proposal for a national German council due to the politico-religious situation in Germany, but there was no absolute objection to calling a General Council. Emperor Charles V also rejected the proposal of a German national council, but proposed the imperial city of Trent as the possible site for a General Council. There followed a political falling out between the emperor and the Pope, and there was no talk about any kind of council until August of 1526, by which time Saxony and Hesse had become, for all practical purposes, Protestant. In the meantime, Luther continued his preaching, teaching, and writing. He married the former Cistercian nun, Katharina von Bora on 13th June 1525. German peasants took to arms against their Catholic rulers on a number of occasions, including the Peasants' Revolt (1524-1526), but, in the end, Luther sided with the secular authorities.

(c) The First Imperial Diet of Speyer took place during August of 1526. The Diet legalized the Protestant reforms, suspended the decisions of the Edict of Worms, and conceded power to local rulers to decide how much reform should be enacted within their respective territories. By this time, Luther had already fathered a number of children, was celebrating Mass in German, and continued on with his writings. Between the First and Second Imperial Diet of Speyer,[50] Luther continued preaching, publishing, and also evaluated the Protestant clergy. At this last Diet, the papal legate informed its members that the Pope was ready to help the Germans in their struggle against the Ottoman Turks, urged restoration of peace among Christian rulers, and declared the Pope's intention to call a General Council. It was due to the walking out at this Diet by the German princes supporting Luther that they started being called "Protestants."

Luther published his *Small Catechism* in March of 1529. This was followed with the publication of the *Large Catechism* on 4th May of the same year. He also met with Zwingli on 1st October, with the unsuccessful intention of uniting all Protestants.

(d) Emperor Charles V and Pope Clement VII met in Bologna at the beginning of 1530. Peace was established between them, and the Pope crowned him Holy Roman Emperor.[51] The Pope gave into the emperor's unrelenting wish of calling a Council, if it became necessary. The issue of convening a Council was also discussed at the Diet of Augsburg that was assembled on 8th April 1530, with the purpose of settling the religious question and to make plans as to how to resist the menacing Ottoman Turks. It was during this Diet that, on 25th June, the *Augsburg Confession* was presented to the emperor. Melanchthon was its principal author. The Confession was a basic statement on Protestant teachings. But the emperor rejected the Confession, closed the Diet on 19th November, and ordered the restoration of the Catholic Faith by the following April of 1531, pending the convening of a General Council within a year. In reaction, eleven imperial cities and eight Protestant princes formed

---

[50] The Second Imperial Diet of Speyer was held from 21st February through 22nd April 1529.

[51] Emperor Charles V was the last Holy Roman Emperor to receive a papal coronation.

the Schmalkaldic League on 29th March 1531, which demanded that they hold on to all Church property they had already seized and refused to defend Germany against the Ottoman Turks unless complete freedom was granted. Thus, the emperor was forced to convene the Third Imperial Diet of Nuremberg in 1532. It established peace in that the emperor, fearing a Turkish invasion, granted the demands of the Schmalkaldic League.

---

76. The Eve of the Opening of the Council of Trent

(a) Cardinal Alessandro Farnese had strongly favored the calling of a General Council. During the Conclave that followed the death of Pope Clement VII, he openly urged to put aside the unnerving memories of the Conciliarist Movement, and to realize that the Protestant Reform was rapidly expanding not only at the level of the laity but also among civil rulers. He was elected Pope on 13th October 1534, and took the name of Pope Paul III. As the newly elected Pope, and despite his worldly private lifestyle,[52] he spoke of the need to call a Council. But the majority of the Cardinals stood in opposition to the idea. Nonetheless, the Pope sent nuncios to the diverse major courts of Europe, to feel out the proposal. All secular rulers objected to Rome as being the site for the assembly. The German Protestant rulers, supported by Kings Francis I of France and Henry VIII of England, rejected the proposed Council.

The emperor met with the Pope in Rome at the beginning of 1536 and both agreed on the convening of a General Council. Thus, on 2nd June 1536, Pope Paul III issued a papal bull through which he called the convocation of a General Council to be held at

---

[52] Cardinal Farnese was one of the few Popes to have fathered children before his election. His first appointment of Cardinals took place on 18th December 1534, which created as Cardinals his grandsons Alessandro Farnese and Ascanio Sforza, aged fourteen and sixteen years respectively.

Mantua on 23rd May 1537. The German Protestant rulers, though they had demanded a Council back in 1530, refused the invitation. The greatest obstructionists, however, were King Francis I of France and Federico II Gonzaga (1500-1540), Duke of Mantua. The former, being at war with the emperor, stated that the French bishops would not be able to leave their country. On the other hand, Gonzaga stated that he was unable to accept the papal conditions made on his city for the duration of the Council. The opening of the Council was consequently put off until 1st November of that year, and it was later decided to postpone it until 1st May 1538, and be held in Vicenza. When the Pope and the French king met at Nice in 1538, they agreed to defer the opening of the General Council until Easter of 1539. Soon thereafter the emperor wanted another postponement. Due to the failure of the negotiations between the emperor and the French king, the Council was put off indefinitely on 21st May 1539. In the meantime, despite Protestant opposition to the convening of a General Council, Luther wrote the *Schmalkaldic Articles* in preparation for it.

(b) The Pope and the emperor met again in Lucca during September of 1541. The Pope, who by now was determined to convene a General Council, brought up the issue once more. The emperor consented to convening the Council at Vicenza, but the Doge of Venice would not agree. Thus the emperor once again proposed Trent, while the papal legate suggested Mantua. The impasse was broken when the representatives of both the emperor and the King of France met with the Pope and the Cardinals in Rome and it was determined that the Council would be held in Trent. On 22nd May 1542, Pope Paul III issued a papal bull, convoking an Ecumenical Council to be opened in Trent on the following 1st November. The Protestants reacted violently to the news, and King Francis I refused permission for the papal bull to be published in his kingdom.

The conduct of Emperor Charles V and King Francis I once again delayed the opening of the Council. There also was another falling out between the emperor and the Pope because the latter remained neutral in the escalating threats of war between the two sovereigns. War broke out between Germany and France. It ended with the Peace of Crespy on 17th September 1544, and with another reconciliation between the emperor and the Pope. On the other hand, the French king withdrew his objections to the convocation of an Ecumenical Council.

77. The Council of Trent Is Convened

Pope Paul III, on 19th November 1544, issued the papal Bull, *Laetare Hierusalem*, convoking a General Council to meet at Trent on 15th March 1545. The following February of 1545, he appointed Cardinals Giovanni del Monte,[53] Marcello Cervini,[54] and Reginald Pole as the papal legates to preside at the Council. Since only a few bishops were present at Trent in March, the opening date had to be deferred once again. The emperor, however, desired a speedy commencement. Thus, the 13th December 1545 was selected as the date of the first formal session of the Council. Finally, on that day, Cardinal del Monte, as the first president of the General Council, celebrated the Mass of the Holy Spirit in the choir of the cathedral of Trent. The papal Bulls of convocation and appointment of the Council legates were read. Cardinal del Monte declared the Ecumenical Council opened, and established 7th January 1546 as the date of the second session.

The Council of Trent was a major first step in the Counter-Reformation undertaken by the Catholic Church. It was the 19th Ecumenical Council. It was convened in what might be viewed as three phases, between 13th December 1545 and 4th December

---

[53] Cardinal Giovanni del Monte would succeed Pope Paul III as Pope Julius III. He was elected on 7th February 1550 and died on 23rd March 1555.

[54] Cardinal Marcello Cervini was elected Pope to succeed Pope Julius III. He was elected Pope on 10th April 1555, taking the name of Pope Marcellus II. He died on 1st May 1555.

1563,[55] in the city of Trent.[56] It is considered one of the most important Councils in the history of the Roman Catholic Church, clearly specifying current Catholic doctrines on salvation, the sacraments, and the biblical canon. The Council standardized the Mass throughout the Church, largely by abolishing local variations. This became known as the *Tridentine Mass* from the city's Latin name Tridentum. The Council also commissioned the first Catholic catechism, the Roman Catechism.

On adjourning, the Council Fathers asked Pope Pius IV to ratify all the Council's decrees and definitions passed during the pontificates of Pope Paul III and Pope Julius III. The Pope, on 26th January 1564, in the papal Bull, *Benedictus Deus*, confirmed all of the conciliar decrees and definitions.

The decrees of the Ecumenical Council were accepted and promulgated in Italy, Portugal, Poland, and by the Catholic princes of Germany. King Philip II of Spain accepted them for Spain, the Netherlands and Sicily, but with the proviso that provisions which infringed on his royal prerogative were excluded. The King of France officially recognized only the doctrinal parts. There was no attempt made to introduce them in England, then being ruled by Queen Elizabeth I. Pope Pius IV asked Mary, Queen of Scots, to publish them in Scotland, but she dared not do so in the face of John Knox (c. 1510-1572) and the Reformation.

The Counter-Reformation had begun in the Roman Catholic Church. The decrees of the Ecumenical Council of Trent would have far reaching positive effects for centuries to come.

---

[55] The first phase, 13th December 1545 to 17th September 1549, was under Pope Paul III. The second phase, from 1st May 1551 to 28th April 1552, was under Pope Julius III. The third and final phase, from 18th January 1562 to 4th December 1563, was under Pope Pius IV.

[56] The Council, due to an outbreak of the plague, was temporarily transferred to Bologna on 12th March 1547, though the Council members faithful to Emperor Charles V remained at Trent. Pope Paul III suspended the Council the following 17th September.

Appendix I: Apostolic Succession of the Bishops of Rome[1]

The following list will indicate that there are pontificates whose exact dates are imprecise.

St. Peter the Apostle (c. 60-64 or 67)

St. Linus (68-79)

St. Anacletus - *also known as Cletus* (80-92)

St. Clement I - *also known as Clement of Rome* (92-99 or 68-76)

St. Evaristus (96 or 99-108)

St. Alexander I (108 or 109 or 116-119)

St. Sixtus I - *also known as Xystus* (117 or 119-126 or 128)

St. Telesphorus (127 or 128-137 or 138)

St. Hyginus (136-142 or 149)

St. Pius I (142 or 146-157 or 161)

St. Anicetus (150 or 153-157 or 168)

St. Soter (162 or 168-170 or 177)

St. Eleutherius (171 or 177-185 or 193)

St. Victor I (186 or 189-197 or 201)

St. Zephyrinus (198-217 or 218)

St. Calixtus I (217-222)

> *St. Hippolytus - antipope (217-235) died c. 236*

---

[1] The list is based on the *Annuario Pontificio*, 2007 and *The Book of Pontiffs* (*Liber Pontificalis*): *The ancient biographies of the first ninety Roman bishops to AD 715*. Translated with an introduction by Raymond Davis. Liverpool: Liverpool University Press, 1989. When known, the Pope's baptism name is in parentheses.

St. Urban I (222-230)

St. Pontian (21 Jul 230 - 28 Sept 235)

St. Anterus (21 Nov 235 - 3 Jan 236)

St. Fabian (236 - 20 Jan 250)

St. Cornelius (6 or 13 Mar 251 - Jun 253)
   Novatian - antipope (251)

St. Lucius I (Jun or Jul 253 - 5 Mar 254)

St. Stephen I (12 Mar 254 - 2 Aug 257)

St. Sixtus II (30 Aug 257 - 6 Aug 258)

St. Dionysius (22 Jul 259 - 26 Dec 268)

St. Felix I (5 Jan 269 - 30 Dec 274)

St. Eutychianus (4 Jan 275 - 7 Dec 283)

St. Gaius - *also known as Caius* (17 Dec 283 - 22 Apr 296)

St. Marcellinus (30 Jun 296 - 25 Oct 304)

St. Marcellus I (306 or 307 or 308 - 16 Jan 308 or 309 or 310)

St. Eusebius (18 Apr 309 - 17 Aug 309 or 310)

St. Miltiades - *also known as Melchiades* (2 Jul 311 - 10 Jan 314)

St. Sylvester I (31 Jan 314 - 31 Dec 335)

St. Mark (18 Jan - 7 Oct 336)

St. Julius I (6 Feb 337 - 12 Apr 352)

Liberius (17 May 352 - 24 Sept 366)
   Felix II - antipope (355 - 22 Nov 358)

St. Damasus I (1 Oct 366 - 11 Dec 384)
   Ursinus - antipope (24 Nov 366 - 367) died 385

St. Siricius (15 or 22 Dec 384 - 26 Nov 399)

St. Anastasius I (27 Nov 399 - 19 Dec 401)

St. Innocent I (22 Dec 401 -12 Mar 417)

St. Zosimus (18 Mar 417 - 26 Dec 418)

St. Boniface I (28 or 29 Dec 418 - 4 Sept 422)[2]

---

[2]   In July 420, Emperor Honorius decreed that if two candidates were elected Pope, the government would only recognize the one elected unanimously. This was the first ever imperial interference in papal elections.

Eulalius - antipope (27 or 29 Dec 418 - 3 Apr 419) died in 423

St. Celestine I (10 Sept 422 - 27 Jul 432)

St. Sixtus III (31 Jul 432 - 19 Aug 440)

St. Leo I "the Great" (29 Sept 440 - 10 Nov 461)

St. Hillary (19 Nov 461 - 29 Feb 468)

St. Simplicius (3 Mar 468 -10 Mar 483)[3]

St. Felix III (II) (13 Mar 483 - 25 Feb or 1 Mar 492)

St. Gelasius I (1 Mar 492 - 21 Nov 496)

Anastasius II (24 Nov 496 - 19 Nov 498)

St. Symmachus (22 Nov 498 - 19 Jul 514)[4]

     Laurence - antipope (22 Nov 498 - 499 or 502 or 506)

St. Hormisadas (20 Jul 514 - 6 Aug 523)

St. John I (13 Aug 523 - 18 May 526)

St. Felix IV (III) (12 Jul 526 - 20 or 22 Sept 530)

Boniface II (20 or 22 Sept 530 - 17 Oct 532)

     Dioscorus - antipope (20 or 22 Sept 530 - 14 Oct 530)

John II (Mercurio: 31 Dec 532 or 2 Jan 533 - 8 May 535)[5]

St. Agapetus I (13 May 535 - 22 Apr 536)

St. Silverius (8 Jun 536 - abdicated and died in same month of Mar 537)

Vigilius (29 Mar 537 - 7 Jun 555; became legitimate after St. Silverius abdicated)[6]

Pelagius I (16 Apr 556 - 4 Mar 561)

---

[3] Pope Simplicius, in 483, asked Odoacer, Herulian king of Italy (476-493), to intervene should disorders arise during the next vacancy of the Holy See. Odoacer immediately issued a law prohibiting the election of the Pope without his authorization or that of the prefect of the pretorium exercised in his name.

[4] In the disputed election of 22nd November 498, between Pope Symmachus and antipope Laurence, both factions for the chair of St. Peter appealed to Theodoric, Ostrogothic king of Italy (493-526), who assigned Symmachus as the rightful Pope.

[5] John II was the first Pope to change his name.

[6] After defeating the Ostrogoths in 552, the Byzantine emperors claimed for themselves the right of *placet* in the papal elections. Gregory III, in 731, was the last pope to request the imperial *placet*.

John III (17 Jul 561 - 13 Jul 574)

Benedict I (2 Jun 575 - 30 Jul 579)

Pelagius II (26 Nov 579 - 7 Feb 590)

St. Gregory I "the Great" (3 Sept 590 - 12 Mar 604)

Sabinian (13 Sept 604 - 22 Feb 606)

Boniface III (19 Feb - 10 Nov 607)

St. Boniface IV (25 Aug 608 - 8 May 615)

St. Adeodatus I - *also known as Deusdeit* (19 Oct 615 - 8 Nov 618)

Boniface V (23 Dec 619 - 23 Oct 625)

Honorius I (27 Oct 625 - 12 Oct 638)

Severinus (elected in Oct 638; reigned 28 May - 2 Aug 640)

John IV (elected in Aug 640; reigned 24 Dec 640 - 12 Oct 642)

Theodore I (elected on 12 Oct 642; reigned 24 Nov 642-14 May 649)

St. Martin I (5 Jul 649 - 16 Sept 655)[7]

St. Eugenius I (10 Aug 654 - 2 Jun 657)

St. Vitalian (30 Jul 657 - 27 Jan 672)

St. Adeodatus (11 Apr 672 - 16 Jun 676)

Donus (2 Nov 676 - 11 Apr 678)

St. Agatho (27 Jun 678 - 10 Jan 681)

St. Leo II (elected in Jan 681; reigned 17 Aug 682 - 3 Jul 683)

St. Benedict II (elected in 683; reigned 26 Jun 684 - 8 May 685)[8]

John V (23 Jul 685 - 2 Aug 686)

Conon (23 Oct 686 - 21 Sept 687)[9]

Theodorus - antipope (687)

Paschal - antipope (687)

St. Sergius I (15 Dec 687 - 7 Sept 701)

---

[7] Martin I did not seek imperial confirmation of his election as Pope.

[8] This pope obtained from Emperor Constantine Pogonatus (668-685) the abrogation of the imperial *placet*. The emperor agreed that in future papal elections should be ratified by the exarch in Italy (at Ravenna) not by Constantinople, thereby enabling the Pope-elect to assume office with the minimum delay.

[9] During the short reign of Pope Conon, Byzantine Emperor Justinian Rhinotmetus (685-695) reclaimed the right of imperial *placet* for a papal election.

John VI (30 Oct 701 - 11 Jan 705)

John VII (1 Mar 705 - 18 Oct 707)

Sisinius (15 Jan 708 - 4 Feb 708)

Constantine (25 Mar 708 - 9 Apr 715)

St. Gregory II (19 May 715 - 11 Feb 731)

St. Gregory III (18 Mar 731 - 28 Nov 741)[10]

St. Zachary (3 Dec 741 - 15 Mar 752)

Stephen II (III) (26 Mar 752 - 26 Apr 757)[11]

Paul I (elected in Apr 757; reigned 29 May 757 - 28 Jun 767)

    Constantine II – antipope (5 Jul 767 - 30 Jul 768)

    Philip – antipope (31 Jul 768)

Stephen III (IV) (7 Aug 768 - 24 Jan 772)

Adrian I (9 Feb 772 - 25 Dec 795)[12]

St. Leo III (27 Dec 795 - 12 Jun 816)

Stephen IV (V)(22 Jun 816 - 24 Jan 817)

St. Paschal I (25 Jan 817 - Feb or May 824)

Eugenius II (Feb or May 824 - Aug 827)

Valentine (Aug - Sept 827)

Gregory IV (elected in Sept 827; reigned 29 Mar 828 - 25 Jan 844)

    John - antipope (25 Jan 844)

Sergius II (25 Jan 844 - 27 Jan 847)

St. Leo IV (elected in Jan 847; reigned 10 Apr 847 - 17 Jul 855)

Benedict III (elected in Jul 855; reigned 29 Sept 855 - 17 Apr 858)

    Anastasius "the Librarian" - antipope (21-24 Sept 855) died in 879

St. Nicholas I (24 Apr 858 - 13 Nov 867)

Adrian II (14 Dec 867 - Nov or Dec 872)

---

[10] The last Pope to seek approval from the Byzantine Emperor of the papal election.

[11] Stephen II was Pope-elect on 22nd March 752. He died a couple of days later and before he was consecrated. Consequently, he is not listed in the *Liber Pontificalis*.

[12] A spurious document stated that Adrian I acknowledged that Charlemagne and his successors were to confirm the election of the new Pope.

John VIII (14 Dec 872 - 16 Dec 882)

Marinus I (Dec 882 - 15 May 884)[13]

St. Adrian III (17 May 884 - Aug or Sept 885)

Stephen V (VI) (Sept 885 - 14 Sept 891)

Formosus (6 Oct 891 - 4 Apr 896)

Boniface VI (11 - 26 Apr 896)

Stephen VI (VII) (May or Jun 896 - Jul or Aug 897)

Romanus (Jul or Aug - Nov 897)

Theodore II (Dec 897 - Dec 897 or Jan 898)

John IX (Dec 897 or Jan 898 - 1 May 900)

Benedict IV (1 May 900 - Jul 903)

Leo V (Jul - Sept 903)

    Christopher - antipope (Sept 903 - Jan 904)

Sergius III (29 Jan 904 - 14 Apr 911)

Anastasius III (Jun or Sept 911 - Jun or Aug or Oct 913)

Lando (Jul or Nov 913 - Mar 914)

John X (Mar or Apr 914 - May or Jun 928)

Leo VI (May or Jun 928 - Dec 928 or Jan 929)

Stephen VII (VIII) (Jan 929 - Feb 931)

John XI (Mar 931 - Jan 936)

Leo VII (Jan 936 - 13 Jul 939)

Stephen VIII (IX)(14 Jul 939 - Oct 942)

Marinus II (elected on 30 Oct 942; reigned Nov 942 - May 946)

Agapetus II (10 May 946 - Dec 955)

John XII (Octavian of the Counts of Tusculum; 16 Dec 955 -
    14 May 964)[14]

---

[13] Pope Marinus I decreed that in the future the Holy Roman Emperor's *placet* would be necessary for the consecration of a new Pope. This decree was renewed by Adrian III.

[14] Invalidly deposed by a local council of Rome on 4th December 963. The identity of the legitimate Pope at this time is confusing in that Leo VIII, his successor, was elected on the same day.

Leo VIII (elected on 4 Dec 963; reigned 6 Dec 963 - Mar 965)[15]

Benedict V (May 964 - 4 Jul 964 or 965) died in 966[16]

John XIII (1 Oct 965 - 6 Sept 972)

Benedict VI (elected in Dec 992; reigned 19 Jan 973 - Jul 974)

   Boniface VII - antipope (Franco Ferrucci, first time: Jun 974 - Jul 974)

Benedict VII (Oct 974 - 10 Jul 983)

John XIV (Peter Campanora: Nov or Dec 983 - 20 Aug 984)

   Boniface VII - antipope (Franco Ferrucci, second time: Aug 984 - 20 Jul 985)

John XV (Aug 985 - Mar 996)

Gregory V (Bruno, Duke of Carinthia: 3 May 996 - Feb or Mar 999)

   John XVI - antipope (John Filagato: Feb or Mar 997 - May 998) died in 1013

Sylvester II (Gerbert d'Aurillac: 2 Apr 999 - 12 May 1003)

John XVII (Siccone: 16 May - 6 Nov 1003)

John XVIII (Giovanni Fasano: 25 Dec 1003 - Jun or Jul 1009)

Sergius IV (Pietro Bucca Porci: 31 Jul 1009 - 12 May 1012)

Benedict VIII (Theophylactus II, Count of Tusculum: 18 May 1012 - 9 Apr 1024)

   Gregory - antipope (May to Dec 1012)

John XIX (Romano, Count of Tusculum: 19 Apr 1024 - 1032)

---

[15] The pontificate of Leo VIII is somewhat confusing. He is regarded as an antipope from 4th December 963 to 14th May 964, and as a valid Pope from 14th May 964 to March 965. He had been invalidly elected pope, at the insistence of Emperor Otto I, by a Roman synod which invalidly deposed Pope John XII, who was still alive, in December 963. When John XII regained control of Rome, he called a synod which deposed Leo VIII in March 964. Then John XII died suddenly the following 14th May. The situation becomes more confusing since the people of Rome elected Benedict V as the new Pope. Emperor Otto, however, imposed Leo VIII. Another local Roman synod deposed Benedict on 23rd June 964, but it seems that Benedict accepted the deposition and abdicated as Pope. He was then taken to Germany where he died in 966.

[16] Holy Roman Emperor Otto I, in July 964, extracted from the citizens of Rome a promise not to elect a Pope without imperial approval. Benedict, after being deposed, willing abdicated the papacy on 23rd June 964.

Benedict IX (Theophylactus III, Count of Tusculum: first time, Aug or Sept 1032 - Nov 1044) deposed

Sylvester III (Giovanni, Bishop of Sabina: 13 or 20 Jan 1044 - Mar 1045) deposed

Benedict IX (Theophylactus III, Count of Tusculum: second time, 10 Mar - 1 May 1045) abdicated

Gregory VI (Giovanni Graziano: 1 May 1045 - 20 Dec 1046) abdicated on 20 Dec 1046; died in 1048

Clement II (Suitgero, Lord of Morsleben and Hornburg: 24 Dec 1046 - 9 Oct 1047)[17]

Benedict IX (Theophylactus III, Count of Tusculum: third time, Oct 1047 - Jul 1048) deposed for the last time; died in either 1055 or 1056.

Damasus II (Poppo: 17 Jul - 9 Aug 1048)

St. Leo IX (Bruno, Count of Egisheim-Dagsburg: elected 2 Feb 1049; reigned 12 Feb 1049 - 19 Apr 1054)

Victor II (Gebhard, Count of Dollnstein-Hirschberg: 13 Apr 1055 - 28 Jul 1057)

Stephen IX (X) (Federick, Duke of Lorraine: elected 2 Aug 1057; reigned 3 Aug 1057 - 29 Mar 1058)

Benedict X - antipope (John Mincius: 5 Apr 1058 - Jan 1059) died c. 1073 or 1080

Nicholas II (Gérard de Bourgogne: elect in Dec 1058; reigned 24 Jan 1059 - 27 Jul 1061)[18]

Alexander II (Anselmo da Baggio: elected 30 Sept 1061; reigned 1 Oct 1061 - 21 Apr 1073)

Honorius II - antipope (Peter Cadalus: 28 Oct 1061 - 31 May 1064) died in 1071 or 1072

---

[17] Clement II, during his very brief pontificate, renewed in favor of Henry III (1046-1056) the privilege of the Holy Roman Emperor to confirm the election of a new Pope.

[18] Nicholas II, on 12th or 13th April 1059, issued the decree, *In Nomine Domini* which, among other things, stated that it was not necessary to seek Imperial confirmation of the election of the new Pope.

St. Gregory VII (Hildebrand of Soana: elected 22 Apr 1073; reigned 30 Jun 1073 - 25 May 1085)[19]

Clement III - antipope (Guiberto of Ravenna: appointed on 25 Jun 1080; reigned 23 Mar 1084 - 8 Sept 1100)

Bl. Victor III (Desiderius: elected 24 May 1086; reigned 9 May 1087 - 16 Sept 1087)

Bl. Urban II (Odo of Lagery: 12 Mar 1088 - 29 Jul 1099)

Paschal II (Raniero of Bieda: elected 13 Aug 1099; reigned 14 Aug 1099 - 21 Jan 1118)

Theodoric - antipope (Theodoric, Bishop of Albano: 1100, deposed Jan 1101) died 1102

Albert - antipope (Albert or Adalbert, Bishop of Santa Rufina: 1101)

Sylvester IV - antipope (Maginulfo, archpriest of S. Angelo in Pescheria: 18 Nov 1105 - 12 or 13 Apr 1111)

Gelasius II (Giovanni Caetani: elected 24 Jan 1118; reigned 10 Mar 1118 - 28 Jan 1119)

Gregory VIII - antipope (Maurizio Burdino: 10 Mar 1118 - 22 Apr 1121) died in 1137

Calixtus II (Guy de Bourgogne: elected 2 Feb 1119; reigned 9 Feb 1119 - 13 or 14 Dec 1124)

Honorius II (Lamberto Scannabecchi: elected 15 Dec 1124; reigned 21 Dec 1124 - 13 or 14 Feb 1130)

Celestine II - antipope (Teobaldo Boccapecci or Boccapeconai: December 15 or 16, 1124 to 1125 or 1126) abdicated

Innocent II (Gregorio Papareschi: elected 14 Feb 1130; reigned 23 Feb 1130 - 24 Sept 1143)

Anacletus II - antipope (Pietro Pierleone: elected 14 Feb 1130; reigned 23 Feb - 25 Jan 1138)

Victor IV - antipope (Gregorio Conti: Mar - 29 May 1138)

Celestine II (Guido of Castello: elected 26 Sept 1143; reigned 3 Oct 1143 - 8 Mar 1144)

Lucius II (Gerardo Caccianemici dell'Orso: 12 Mar 1144 - 15 Feb 1145)

---

[19] The last Pope to seek Imperial confirmation of his election as Pope.

Bl. Eugenius III (Bernardo Paganelli: elected 15 Feb 1145; reigned
    18 Feb 1145 - 8 Jul 1153)

Anastasius IV (Corrado of Suburra: elected 8 Jul 1153; reigned
    12 Jul 1153 - 3 Dec 1154)

Adrian IV (Nicholas Breakspeare: elected 4 Dec 1154; reigned
    5 Dec 1154 - 1 Sept 1159)

Alexander III (Rolando or Orlando Bandinelli: elected 7 Sept
    1159; reigned 20 Sept 1159 - 30 Aug 1181)

Victor IV - antipope (Ottaviano de Monticello, of the Counts of Tus-
culum: elected 7 Sept 1159; reigned 10 Oct 1159 - 20 Apr 1164)

Paschal III - antipope (Guido di Crema: elected 22 Apr 1164;
reigned 26 Apr 1164 - 20 Sept 1168)

Calixtus III - antipope (János de Struma: Sept 1168, submitted to
Pope Alexander III on 29 Aug 1178) died before 1184

Innocent III - antipope (Lando di Sezza: 29 Sept 1179 - Jan 1180)

Lucius III (Ubaldo Alluncingoli: elected 1 Sept 1181; reigned
    6 Sept 1181 - 25 Nov 1185)

Urban III (Uberto Grivelli: elected 25 Nov 1185; reigned
    1 Dec 1185 - 20 Oct 1187)

Gregory VIII (Alberto de Morra: elected 21 Oct 1187; reigned
    25 Oct - 17 Dec 1187)

Clement III (Paolo Scolari: elected 19 Dec 1187; reigned
    20 Dec 1187 - 25(?) Mar 1191)

Celestine III (Giacinto Bobone Orsini: elected 10 Apr 1191:
    reigned 14 Apr 1191 - 8 Jan 1198)

Innocent III (Lotario dei Conti di Segni: elected 8 Jan 1198;
    reigned 22 Feb 1198 - 16 Jul 1216)

Honorius III (Cencio Savelli: elected 18 Jul 1216; reigned
    24 Jul 1216 - 18 Mar 1227)

Bl. Gregory IX (Ugolino dei conti di Segni: elected 19 Mar 1227;
    reigned 22 Mar 1227 - 22 Aug 1241)

Celestine IV (Goffredo da Castiglione: elected 25 Oct 1241;
    reigned 28 Oct - 10 Nov 1241)

Innocent IV (Sinobaldo Fieschi: elected 25 Jun 1243; reigned
    28 Jun 1243 - 7 Dec 1254)

Alexander IV (Rinaldo dei Signori di Ienne: elected 12 Dec 1254; reigned 20 Dec 1254 - 25 May 1261)

Urban IV (Jacques Pantaléon: elected 29 Aug 1261; reigned 4 Sept 1261 - 2 Oct 1264)

Clement IV (Gui Fulques or Fulquois, or Guy le Gros: elected 5 Feb 1265; reigned 22 Feb 1265 - 29 Nov 1268)

Bl. Gregory X (Tedaldo Visconti: elected 1 Sept 1271; reigned 27 Mar 1272 - 10 Jan 1276)

Bl. Innocent V (Peter of Tarentaise: elected 21 Jan 1276; reigned 22 Feb - 22 Jun 1276)

Adrian V (Ottobono Fieschi: 11 Jul - 18 Aug 1276)

John XXI (Pedro Julião or Pietro di Giuliano or Pietro Ispano, or Pedro Hispano: elected 16 Sept 1276; reigned 20 Sept 1276 - 20 May 1277)[20]

Nicholas III (Giovanni Gaetano Orsini: elected 25 Nov 1277; reigned 26 Dec 1277 - 22 Aug 1280)

Martin IV (Simon Monpitie de Brie or de Brion: elected 22 Feb 1281; reigned 23 Mar 1281- 28 Mar 1285)[21]

Honorius IV (Giacomo Savelli: elected 2 Apr 1285; reigned 20 May 1285 - 3 Apr 1287)

Nicholas IV (Girolamo Masci d'Ascoli: 15 Feb 1288 - 4 Apr 1292)

St. Celestine V (Pietro da Morrone: elected 5 Jul 1294; reigned 29 Aug - 13 Dec 1294) abdicated; died on 19 May 1296

Boniface VIII (Benedetto Caetani: elected 24 Dec 1294; reigned 23 Jan 1295 - 11 Oct 1303)

Bl. Benedict XI (Niccolò Boccasini de Treviso: elected 22 Oct 1303; reigned 27 Oct 1303 - 7 Jul 1304)

Clement V (Raymond Bertrand de Got: elected 5 Jun 1305; reigned 5 Jun 1305 - 14 Apr 1314)

John XXII (Jacques Duèse: elected 7 Aug 1316; reigned 5 Sept 1316 - 4 Dec 1334)

---

[20] There is no Pope with the name of John XX.

[21] Due to the confusion of the names Marinus and Martinus, there is no Pope called Martin II or Martin III.

Nicholas V - antipope (Pietro Rainalducci: elected 12 May 1328; reigned 25 Aug 1328 - 25 Aug 1330) abdicated, died 16 Oct 1333

Benedict XII (Jacques Fournier: elected 20 Dec 1334; reigned 8 Jan 1335 - 25 Apr 1342)

Clement VI (Pierre Roger: elected 7 May 1342; reigned 19 May 1342 - 6 Dec 1352)

Innocent VI (Etienne Aubert: elected 18 Dec 1252; reigned 30 Dec 1352 – 12 Sept 1362)

Bl. Urban V (Guillaume de Grimond: elected 16 Oct 1362; reigned 6 Nov 1362 - 19 May 1370)

Gregory XI (Pierre Roger de Beaufort: elected 30 Dec 1370; reigned 3 Jan 1371 - 27 Mar 1378)

Roman Line – Canonical Popes

Urban VI (Bartolomeo Prignano: elected 8 Apr 1378; reigned 18 Apr 1378 - 15 Oct 1389)

Boniface IX (Pietro Tomacelli: elected 2 Nov 1389; reigned 9 Nov 1389 - 1 Oct 1404)

Innocent VII (Cosmo Migliorati: elected 17 Oct 1404; reigned 11 Nov 1404 - 6 Nov 1406)

Gregory XII (Angelo Corrier: elected 30 Nov 1406; reigned 19 Dec 1406 - 4 Jul 1415) abdicated; died 18 Oct 1417

Avignon Line - Antipopes

Clement VII - antipope (Robert of Geneva: elected 20 Sept 1378; reigned 31 Oct 1378 -16 Sept 1394)

Benedict XIII - antipope (Pedro Martinez de Luna: elected 28 Sept 1394; reigned 11 Oct 1394 - deposed by council of Pisa 5 Jun 1409; further deposed by Council of Constance on 26 Jul 1417, but continued as antipope until his death on 23 May 1423)

Clement VIII - antipope (Gil Sánchez Muñoz: 10 Jun 1423 - 23 Jul 1429) died 28 Dec 1447

Benedict XIV - antipope (Bernardo Garnier: 12 Nov 1425 - 1430)

Pisan Line - antipopes

Alexander V - antipope (Pietro Filargis: elected 26 Jun 1409; reigned 7 Jul 1409 - 3 May 1410)

John XXIII - antipope (Baldassare Cossa: elected 17 May 1410; reigned 25 May 1410, but deposed by the Council of Constance on 29 May 1415) died 27 Dec 1419

Roman Line (continued)

Martin V (Oddone Colonna: elected 11 Nov 1417; reigned 21 Nov 1417 - 20 Feb 1431)

Eugene IV (Gabriele Condulmer: elected 3 Mar 1431; reigned 11 Mar 1431 - 23 Feb 1447)

Felix V - antipope (Amadeus VIII of Savoy: elected 5 Nov 1439;   reigned 24 Jul 1440 - 7 Apr 1449) abdicated; died 7 Jan 1451

Nicholas V (Tommaso Parentucelli: elected 6 Mar 1447; reigned 19 Mar 1447 - 24 Mar 1455)

Calixtus III (Alonso Borja: elected 8 Apr 1455; reigned 20 Apr 1455 - 6 Aug 1458)

Pius II (Aeneas Silvius Piccolomini: elected 19 Aug 1458; reigned 3 Sept 1458 - 14 Aug 1464)

Paul II (Pietro Barbo: elected 30 Aug 1464; reigned 16 Sept 1464 - 26 Jul 1471)

Sixtus IV (Francesco della Rovere: elected 19 Aug 1471; reigned 25 Aug 1471 - 12 Aug 1484)

Innocent VIII (Giovanni Battista Cibo: elected 29 Aug 1484; reigned 12 Sept 1484 - 25 Jul 1492)

Alexander VI (Rodrigo de Borja: elected 11 Aug 1492; reigned 26 Aug 1492 - 18 Aug 1503)

Pius III (Francesco Todeschini-Piccolomini: elected 22 Sept 1503; reigned 8 - 18 Oct 1503)

Julius II (Giuliano della Rovere: elected 1 Nov 1503; reigned 26 Nov 1503 – 21 Feb 1513)

Leo X (Giovanni de' Medici: elected 11 Mar 1513; reigned 19 Mar 1513 – 1 Dec 1521)

Adrian VI (Adriaan Florensz: elected 9 Jan 1521; reigned
    31 Aug 1522 - 14 Sept 1523)

Clement VII (Giulio de' Medici: elected 19 Nov 1523; reigned
    26 Nov 1523 - 25 Sept 1534)

Paul III (Alessandro Farnese: elected 13 Oct 1534; reigned
    3 Nov 1534 - 10 Nov 1549)

Julius III (Giovanni Maria Ciocchi del Monte: elected 7 Feb 1550;
    reigned 22 Feb 1550 - 23 Mar 1555)

Marcellus II (Marcello Cervini: elected 9 Apr 1555; reigned
    10 Apr - 1 May 1555)[22]

Paul IV (Gian Pietro Carafa: elected 23 May 1555; reigned
    26 May 1555 - 18 Aug 1559)

Pius IV (Giovan Angelo Medici: elected 26 Dec 1559; reigned 6
    Jan 1560 - 9 Dec 1565)

---

[22] This Pope kept his baptism name upon his papal election.

Appendix II: Doctors of the Church

Following is the list of Doctors of the Church who lived up to the end of the Middle Ages, starting with their name(s), the Pope who proclaimed them and the date on which this occurred:

* Ambrose, Jerome, Augustine and Pope Gregory the Great declared by Pope Boniface VIII on 20th September 1295.
* Thomas Aquinas declared by Pope St. Pius V on 11th April 1567.
* Athanasius, Basil, Gregory of Nazianzus and John Chrysostom declared by Pope St. Pius V in 1568.
* Bonaventure declared by Pope Sixtus V on 14th March 1588.
* Anselm of Canterbury declared by Pope Clement XI on 3rd February 1720.
* Isidore of Seville declared by Pope Innocent XIII on 25th April 1722.
* Peter Chrysologus declared by Pope Benedict XIII on 10th February 1729.
* Pope Leo the Great declared by Pope Benedict XIV on 5th October 1754.
* Peter Damian declared by Pope Leo XII on 27th September 1828.
* Bernard of Clairvaux declared by Pope Pius VIII on 20th August 1830.
* Hilary of Poitiers declared by Pope Blessed Pius IX on 3rd May 1851.
* Cyril of Alexandria and Cyril of Jerusalem declared by Pope Leo XIII on 28th July 1882.

* John Damascene declared by Pope Leo XIII on 9th August 1890.
* Bede the Venerable declared by Pope Leo XIII on 13th November 1899.
* Ephrem of Syria declared by Pope Benedict XV on 5th October 1920.
* Albert the Great declared by Pope Pius XI on 16th December 1931.
* Anthony of Padua declared by Pope Pius XII on 16th January 1946.

Appendix III: Patriarchs of Constantinople

The Church of Constantinople claims the Apostle St. Andrew as its founder. It was originally governed by bishops, then archbishops and finally by Patriarchs. The following list covers the same time period as the one listing the Popes in Appendix I. It is the official list recognized by the Orthodox Patriarchate of Constantinople.

(a) Apostolic Succession for the Byzantine Church

St. Andrew the Apostle (founder)

Bishops of Byzantium:

Stachys the Apostle (38-54)
Onesimus (54-68)
Polycarp I (69-89)
Plutarch (89-105)
Sedecion (105-114)
Diogenes (114-129)
Eleutherius (129-136)
Felix (136-141)
Polycarp II (141-144)
Athenodorus (144-148)
Euzois (148-154)
Laurence (154-166)
Alypius (166-169)
Pertinax (169-187)

Olympianus (187-198)
Mark I (198-211)
Philadelphus (211-217)
Cyriacus I (217-230)
Castinus (230-237)
Eugenius I (237-242)
Titus (242-272)
Dometius (272-284)
Rufinus I (284-293)
Probus (293-306)
Metrophanes (306-314)
Alexander (314-337)

Archbishops of Constantinople:

Paul I (337-339)
Eusebius of Nicomedia (339-341)
 Paul I (341-342) - restored for the first time
Macedonius I (342-346)
 Paul I (346-351) - restored for the second time
Macedonius I (351-360) - restored
Eudoxius of Antioch (360-370)
Evagrius (370 or 379)
Demophilus (370-380)
Gregory I Nazianzus, the Theologian (379-381)
[Maximus (380) rival]
Nectarius (381-397)
John Chrysostom (398-404)
Arsacius of Tarsus (404-405)
Atticus (406-425)
Sisinnius I (426-427)
Nestorius (428-431)
Maximian (431-434)
Proclus (434-446)
Flavian (446-449)
Anatolius (449-458) - *became Patriarch of Constantinople in 451*

Patriarchs of Constantinople:

Gennadius I (458-471)
Acacius (472-489)
Fravitas (489)
Euphemius (489-495)
Macedonius II (495-511)
Timothy I (511-518)
John II the Cappadocian (518-520)
Epiphanius (520-535)
Anthimus I (535-536)
Menas (536-552)
Eutychius (552-565)
John III Scholasticus (565-577)
   Eutychius (577-582) - restored
John IV Nesteutes (582-595)
Cyriacus (596-606)
Thomas I (607-610)
Sergius I (610-638)
Pyrrhus I (638-641)
Paul II (641-653)
   Pyrrhus I (654) - restored
Peter (654-666)
Thomas II (667-669)
John V (669-675)
Constantine I (675-677)
Theodore I (677-679)
George I (679-686)
   * *Theodore I (686-687) restored*
Paul III (687-693)
Callinicus I (693-705)
Cyrus (706-711)
John VI (712-714)
Germanus I (715-730)
Anastasius (730-754)
Constantine II (754-766)

Nicetas I (766-780)
Paul IV (780-784)
Tarasius (784-806)
Nicephorus I (806-815)
Theodotus I Kassiteras (815-821)
Antony I Kassiteras (821-836)
John VII Grammatikos (836-842)
Methodius I (842-846)
Ignatius I (846-858)
Photius I (858-867)
   Ignatius I (867-877) - restored
   Photius I (877-886) - restored
Stephen I (886-893)
Antony II Kauleas (893-901)
Nicholas I Mystikos (901-907)
Euthymius I Synkellos (907-912)
   Nicholas I Mystikos (912-925) - restored
Stephen II of Amasea (925-928)
Tryphon (928-931)
Theophylactus (931-956)
Polyeuctus (956-970)
Basil I Scamandrenus (970-974)
Antony III the Studite (974-980)
Nicholas II Chrysoberges (984-995)
Sisinnius II (996-999)
Sergius II (999-1019)
Ephstathius (1020-1025)
Alexius I the Studite (1025-1043)
Michael I Cerularius (1043-1059)
Constantine III Lichoudis (1059-1063)
John VIII Xiphilinos (1063-1075)
Kosmas I of Jerusalem (1075-1081)
Eustathius Garidas (1081-1084)
Nicholas III Grammaticus (1084-1111)
John IX Ieromnemon (1111-1134)

Leo Styppis (1134-1143)
Michael II the Kourkouas (1143-1146)
Kosmas II Atticus (1146-1147)
Nicholas IV Mouzalon (1147-1151)
Theodotos II (1151-1153)
Neophytos I (1153)
Constantine IV Chliarenos (1154-1156)
Luke Chrysobergis (1156-1169)
Michael III of Anchialus (1170-1177)
Chariton Eugeniotis (1177-1178)
Theodosius II Vorradiotis (1179-1183)
Basil II Kamateros (1183-1186)
Niketas II Mountanis (1187-1189)
Leontius Theotokitis (1189-1190)
Theodosius III or Disitheus (1190-1191)
George II Xiphilinos (1191-1198)
John X Kamateros (1198-1206)
Michael IV Autoreianos (1207-1213)
Theodore II Eirenikos (1213-1215)
Maximos II (1215)
Manuel I Charitopoulos (1215-1222)
Germanos II (1222-1240)
Methodius II (1240)
Manuel II (1244-1255)
Arsenios Autoreianos (1255-1260)
Nikephorus II (1260-1261)
   Arsenius Autoreianus (1261-1267) - restored
Germanos III (1267)
Joseph I Galesiotes (1267-1275)
John XI Vekkos (1275-1282)
   Joseph I Galesiotes (1282-1283) - restored
Gregory II Cyprius (1283-1289)
Athanasius I (1289-1293)
John XII (1294-1304)
   Athanasius I (1304-1310) - restored

Niphon I (1310-1315)
John XIII Glykys (1315-1320)
Gerasimus I (1320-1321)
Jesaias (1323-1334)
John XIV Kalekas (1334-1347)
Isidore I (1347-1350)
Callistus I (1350-1354)
Philotheus Kokkinos (1354-1355)
   Callistus I (1355-1363) - restored
   Philotheus Kokkinos (1364-1376) - restored
Makarios (1376-1379)
Neilos (1380-1388)
Antonius IV (1389-1390)
   Makarios (1390-1391) - restored
   Antonius IV (1391-1397) - restored
Kallistos II Xanthopoulos (1397)
Matthew I (1397-1410)
Euthymios II (1410-1416)
Joseph II (1416-1439)
Metrophanes II (1440-1443)
Gregory III Mammas (1443-1450)
Athanasius II (1450-1453)
Gennadios II the Scholar (1454-1456)
Isidore II (1456-1462)
   Gennadios II (1462) - restored
Sophronios I (1463-1464)
   Gennadios II (1464) - restored
Joasaph I (1465-1466)
Mark II (1466)
Symeon I (1466)
Dionysios I (1467-1471)
   Symeon I (1471-1475) - restored
Raphael I (1475-1476)
Maximos III (1476-1481)
   Symeon I (1482-1486) - restored

Niphon II (1486-1488)
  Dionysios I (1488-1490) - restored
Maximos IV (1491-1497)
  Niphon II (1497-1498) - restored
Joachim I (1498-1502)
  Niphon II (1502) - restored
Pachomios I (1503-1504)
  Joachim I (1504) - restored
  Pachomios I (1504-1513) - restored
Theoliptos I (1513-1522)
Jeremias I (1522-1545)
Joannicios I (1526)
Dionysios II (1546-1556)
Joasaph II (1556-1565)

(b) Latin Patriarchs of Constantinople[1]

Latin Patriarchs:

Thomas Morosoni (1204-1211)
Sede Vacante (1211-1215)
Gervase (1215-1219)
Sede Vacante (1219-1221)
Matthew (1221-1226)
John Halgrin (1226)
Simon (1227-1233)
Sede Vacante (1233-1234)
Nicholas de Castro Arquato (1234-1251)
Sede Vacante (1251-1253)
Pantaleon Giustiani (1253-1286)

---

[1] The title was abolished by Pope Paul VI in 1965.

Titular Latin Patriarchs:

Peter Correr (1286-1302)
Leonard Faliero (1302 - c. 1305)
Nicholas, Archbishop of Thebes (1308 - c. 1331)
Cardinalis (1332-1335)
Gozio Battaglia (1335-1339)
Roland de Ast (1339)
Henry de Ast, Bishop of Negroponte (1339-1345)
Stephen de Pinu (1346)
William (1346-1361, *was administrator* 1361-1364)
St. Peter Thomas, Archbishop of Crete (1364-1366)
Paul, Archbishop of Thebes (1366-1370)
Hugolin Malabranca (1371 - c. 1375)
James d'Itri, Archbishop of Otranto (1376-1378)
William, Bishop of Urbino (1379)
Paul (1379-?)
Angelo Correr (1390-1405)
Louis, Archbishop of Mitylene (1405-?)
Cardinal Antonio Correr (*administrator*, 1408)
Alphonese, Archbishop of Seville (1408-?)
Francis Lando, Patriarch of Grado (?-1409)
John Contarini (1409-?)
John de La Rochetaillee (1412-1423)
   *John Contarini (1424-?) – resumed title
Gregory Mamme (1451-1459)
Cardinal Bessarion (1459-1472)
Peter Riario (1472-1474)
Jerome Lanod, Archbishop of Crete (1474-1493/6)
Cardinal John Michael (1497-1503)
Cardinal Juan Borja (1503-1503)
Cardinal Francis de Lorris (1503-1506)
Tamás Bakócz (1507-1521)

The names of the titular Latin Patriarchs are unknown from 1521
to 1594.